TOWARD A BETTER AMERICA

Books by Howard D. Samuel:

CONGRESS AT WORK, with *Stephen K. Bailey*

GOVERNMENT IN ACTION, with *Stephen K. Bailey*
and *Sidney Baldwin*

/\./\./\./\./\

TOWARD A BETTER AMERICA

Edited and with an Introduction by

Howard D. Samuel

THE MACMILLAN COMPANY, NEW YORK

COLLIER-MACMILLAN LTD., LONDON

Acknowledgment is gratefully given to the following publishers and authors (or their representatives) for permissions granted to reprint articles, speeches and chapters from their books or newspapers.

Ashmore, Harry S., for address "Dilemma in Race Relations," in 1957 to the Anti-Defamation League.

Blassingame, Lurton, agent for Ira Harkey, for "Confusing Times, Dangerous Times," "You May Be Next," and "Push 'em Back, W-A-A-Y Back!", Copyright © 1963 by Ira Harkey. Editorials from the Pascagoula Mississippi *Chronicle*, 1962.

Block, Herbert L., for the cartoons "Don't Mind Me—Just Go Right on Talking," "Fire," "Help! I'm Being Followed," "Always Happy to Take the Word of a Lady," "I Don't Need You to Protect Me, Junior" and "Say, What Ever Happened to Freedom From Fear?" from *The Herblock Book*. Boston: Beacon Press, 1952.

Cahn, Mrs. Lenore, for "Can the Supreme Court Defend Civil Liberties?", a lecture given by Edmond Cahn in 1956 at The New School for Social Research.

CBS News for "American Week" with Eric Sevareid, correspondent, and Ernest Leiser, producer, program of July 4, 1954.

Chase, Stuart, for "Will Communism Conquer the World?—A Balance Sheet," which first appeared in *The Progressive* in 1962.

Commager, Henry Steele, for "How Not to Be a World Power" from his testimony in 1967 before the Senate Foreign Relations Committee on the War in Vietnam.

Cousins, Norman, for "We Need Not Lose Asia," a summary of his remarks at a conference on Eastern studies in 1956 at the University of Rochester.

Emmerich, J. O., for "When Terrorism Wins People Are Enslaved" and "Law Tests to Be Made in McComb Wednesday," editorials from *The Enterprise Journal* (McComb, Mississippi), 1964.

Evjue, William T., for "The Weapon of Fear," address at the 1952 Hillman Prize Award luncheon.

Contents

Part Two: Civil Liberties

Part Three: Public Welfare

Part Four: Foreign Affairs

Acknowledgments

THE WORK OF compiling this volume could not have been done without the support and encouragement of the general officers of the Amalgamated Clothing Workers of America: Jacob S. Potofsky, President; Frank Rosenblum, Secretary-Treasurer; and Hyman Blumberg, Executive Vice President; and of the adviser to the union and general counsel of the Foundation, Maxwell Brandwen.

In addition, the editor wishes to express his appreciation to Jane Mushabac, who assists in conducting the work of the Foundation, for the many hours of sometimes tedious, sometimes complex work involved in making this volume whole.

H. D. S.

Introduction

HOWARD D. SAMUEL

THE ORIGINS OF this volume can be found in the flood of immigrants coming to the United States at the turn of the century. Escaping from hunger and repression in half a dozen lands of Europe, they looked to "golden America" for a new life and found instead a land of sweatshops and slums.

The sweatshops were particularly characteristic of the needle trades, and in the men's clothing industry specifically, the chaos of cutthroat competition had driven working conditions to subhuman levels. Working hours, in season, ranged from 56 to 72 hours, six days a week, for take-home pay as low as $2.50 and $3.00 a week. Out of season there was nothing. Workers had no paid holidays or vacations or health insurance, and when they grew old or ill they were fired. Their wives and children brought work home for the needed income. Lacking job security of any kind, they also had little hope; the existing union had proved itself unable to improve their situation.

Although the immigrants fought to organize themselves, most of the early revolts were crushed. It was not until 1914, after years of struggle and some modest victories in Chicago and New York, that the immigrants amassed enough strength to form a new union. As their president they chose a twenty-seven-year-old clothing cutter from the Ukraine named Sidney Hillman.

Hillman had already made a name for himself in the early strike at Hart Schaffner & Marx in Chicago. In the three decades he served as president of the Amalgamated, his leadership was distinguished by a wide-ranging idealism and a desire to correct injustice wherever it existed—as well as by a pragmatic and realistic approach to solving problems, one step at a time. He not only won the affection of his union members, but the trust of the employers he dealt with and in time the respect of the nation's highest leaders.

The formation of the new union was the signal for wide-ranging organizational effort. In city after city, workers came together, struck or were locked out, won their first contracts, were beaten back, had to strike again, and finally formed permanent organizations. Within two decades the Amalgamated had won contracts for more than 150,000 members—almost the entire men's clothing industry in the United States and Canada—and during the New Deal upsurge the union branched out into the shirt industry (where child labor and sweatshop conditions in the 1930s rivaled the city slums of 30 years before) and allied industries, such as laundry, cleaning and dyeing, retail apparel clerks. It also ventured far from the original city slums into new areas, the deep South, the rural Midwest, the Southwest and even Puerto Rico. Today the Amalgamated has 385,000 members, in 41 states and four provinces of Canada.

There were some notable elements in the union's growth. Hillman and his associates sought to achieve stability and improvement through a rule of law; they worked to end the chaos and violence that had characterized earlier industrial relationships. One of the nation's first provisions for arbitration of grievances had been established in the union's earliest contract, and arbitration received much of its subsequent development in the experiences of the clothing industry. Later, in order to moderate the effects of competition—especially between regions—on working conditions, the Amalgamated pioneered in developing a pattern of industry-wide bargaining. Substantial advances were made for the clothing workers, but by and large they were made peacefully. There has not been a major strike for 40 years.

Its growth is only a small part of the union's story. Hillman and his associates conceived of the union as a vehicle not only for winning improvements in the members' working conditions but in their living conditions as well. Soon after the first flush of organization had brought a measure of decency and security to the clothing workers on the job, the union's leaders turned to other areas. In order to ameliorate the curse of joblessness in what was then a seasonal industry, in 1923 the organization formed the nation's first unemployment insurance fund. Lacking adequate low-cost housing, particularly in New York, the clothing workers formed a cooperative and by 1926 were building their own apartment projects. Victimized by the absence of banks that were interested in meeting the needs of workers, the Amalgamated started its own labor banks.

These were not fly-by-night ventures. The unemployment insurance fund, its original purpose being taken over by the Social Security Act, was converted into a health and retirement program, utilizing a unique self-operated insurance company to reduce costs and maximize benefits. By 1967 it had paid out $535 million to Amalgamated's members. The first apartment projects were steadily augmented until now there are more than 5,000 ACWA-sponsored units housing almost 20,000 people. The Amalgamated Bank in New York has enlarged its assets to $160 million and still offers the lowest cost loan and checking service in the city.

Hillman and his associates, knowing that one trade union's strength reinforces the strength of others, made the Amalgamated a pillar of the Americán labor movement. In 1919, as the union was just emerging from its earliest insecurity, it contributed the astonishing sum of $100,000 to the striking steelworkers. In the 1930s the ACWA was a founding union of the Congress of Industrial Relations and helped a number of new unions—particularly the textile workers—get their first footholds.

The Amalgamated, under Hillman's leadership, also awakened union members to their obligation to educate themselves and participate in the political life of the nation. It became apparent that on the one hand many of the workers' goals could only be won through government legislation or administrative action, while on the other hand accomplishments already won through collective bargaining could be taken away by government. President Roosevelt's years saw the first widespread Amalgamated political activity in a major campaign, and by 1940 Hillman was giving leadership to the entire CIO in its campaign efforts.

By the end of the 1930s Hillman had become one of the major leaders of the nation's growing labor movement and was appointed by President Roosevelt to serve as co-director of the National Defense Advisory Commission, the federal agency charged with preparing the nation's defenses before World War II. In 1944 Hillman became even more widely known for his activity in the Presidential election, in which the CIO's Political Action Committee played an important part. After the war Hillman was extending his concern to the international labor scene when his career was cut short by his premature death, at age fifty-nine, in 1946.[1]

Within a few months of his death, members of his union and of other unions, as well as employers in the men's apparel industry, had contributed a million dollars toward a Foundation to bear Hillman's name. Hillman had been a man of unusual breadth of vision; his interests ranged from new ways of achieving industrial peace and improving workers' living conditions to the advancement of labor's participation in our democratic society and the government's support of the general welfare. Because his activities encompassed so many fields, it was felt that only through a continuing Foundation program could his record of service to the public welfare be honored and advanced. This has been the goal of the Sidney Hillman Foundation.

Since it had limited resources, the Foundation determined to channel its efforts into several fields appropriate to its goals. Thus although a number of grants have been made for such broad purposes as medical research and scholarships for deserving college students, much of its support has gone into three programs: the Sidney Hillman Prize Awards, the Sidney Hillman Reprint Series and the Sidney Hillman Lectureship program. The pieces in this volume are taken from these programs.

Inaugurated in 1950, the Prize Awards were intended to recognize a sense of social responsibility and the courage to deal with important issues, however controversial, as well as talent and skill. Since the program's inauguration a total of 82 awards of

[1] In 1952 Doubleday & Co. (New York) published a definitive biography, *Sidney Hillman, Statesman of American Labor*, by Matthew Josephson.

$500 each have been given to writers of newspaper and magazine articles and books and to writers and producers of radio and television programs.

The Reprint program, started in 1954, was designed to provide to high schools and colleges, without cost, the texts of outstanding speeches and articles that were not easily available. Through 1967 the Foundation had produced 31 reprints, of which close to three million have been used by more than 20,000 teachers.

Through its lectureship program which began in 1949 the Foundation has made it possible for several hundred distinguished academicians, public servants, authors and other leaders to spend a day or more on a college campus, exchanging views with students and faculty and usually speaking before a public audience involving the neighboring community. The Foundation's purpose is not only to expose the campus to fresh thinking on current problems but also to use the lectureship occasion to strengthen the bonds between campus and community.

The selections which comprise this volume represent only a fraction of the total number of prize-award materials, lectureships and reprints available. They were chosen on the basis of their continued cogency, as landmark statements of the period or as typical of a significant point of view. It is hoped that in reflecting American thinking at its most enlightened and forward-looking they will elicit the spirit of the age at its best. It is hoped, too, that they further the broad-ranging goals of Sidney Hillman, which he himself expressed a few weeks before his death:

We want a better America, an America that will give its citizens, first of all a higher and higher standard of living so that no child will cry for food in the midst of plenty. We want to have an America where the inventions of science will be at the disposal of every American family, not merely for the few who can afford them. An America that will have no sense of insecurity and which will make it possible for all groups, regardless of race, creed or color to live in friendship, to be real neighbors; an America that will carry its great mission of helping other countries to help themselves.

PART ONE

Civil Rights

/\/\/\/\/\/\

Perhaps the most memorable achievement of the postwar years was the civil rights revolution, signaled most notably by the U.S. Supreme Court school desegregation decision of 1954. Three years earlier, Carl T. Rowan, a youthful Negro reporter for the Minneapolis *Tribune,* made a return trip to the land of his birth. His report, a vignette of the South poised unknowingly on the edge of a revolution, concludes with a startling prophecy. Similarly prophetic was the experience of a Negro father named Brown, who aroused the animal instincts of his neighborhood when he sought to move his family into a Chicago housing project. His aspirations, recorded on the scene by Eric Sevareid, are echoed more fiercely today from a hundred urban stages.

The Supreme Court decision opened a new era, and the Dykeman-Stokely chapter catches the South facing the whirlwind—defiant, blind, troubled, hopeful. Harry Ashmore, one of the great commentators of his time and place, summed up the Southern dilemma in 1957, just as his region plunged into a period of violence and bitterness. But if Little Rock and Mississippi are ugly landmarks in our history, some citizens stood firm—as the editorial excerpts demonstrate.

In the South, by 1960, the civil rights forces were capturing the initiative, and it was reported in glowing terms by Edward P. Morgan and memorialized movingly by a native but most untypical Southerner, the late Lillian Smith. At the same time, in the North, the causes of discord were described in scholarly terms in Davis McEntire's study of segregation, and discussed in searching terms by Dr. Kenneth B. Clark, master analyst of the ghetto. The period covered by this volume closes with a summing up by Roy Wilkins, one of the architects of the revolution, who painted an ominous picture of the period ahead.

How Far from Slavery?
Southern Negroes Get
Recreation in Segregated Style

CARL T. ROWAN

McMinnville, Tenn.—I am scribbling these words as I sit in a dumpy little cafe which townspeople call "The Slobbery Rock."

That name aptly describes this shaky old structure which sits on a rocky ledge just two blocks from the heart of downtown.

A jukebox blares out a blues tune. High school youngsters of 13, 15, 17, and one drunken woman, at least 55, drag across the sawdust-strewn dance floor. The air is thick with smoke, heavy with the mingled odors of laborers and schoolgirl perfumes.

Here gather 99 per cent of McMinnville's Negro youth, out for their week-end entertainment.

As I sit at a grimy table, covered with a wrinkled oilcloth, I watch bootleggers, gamblers and harlots ply their trades. But I know I have not come slumming. This was MY club 10 years ago.

From 1938 through 1942, week-end after week-end, I was here or in the adjoining pool hall. My mother still may not know that at 14 I was the "colored Willie Hoppe" of our town.

When I was a youth, Negro youngsters had two choices for

In 1951 Carl T. Rowan won a Hillman Prize Award for his series, "How Far from Slavery?", which he wrote as a reporter for the Minneapolis *Tribune*. This article is the third in the series.

4

away-from-home entertainment. They went to one of two segregated movies, where they sat in a balcony not even provided with a rest room, then they went to "The Rock." Or they went to one of these movies, and then home.

It takes no sociologist to guess which course they chose.

McMinnville did have one other small Negro cafe. It was too small for dancing, usually closed very early.

There was a skating rink in McMinnville—barred to Negroes.

There was a tax-supported swimming pool—barred to Negroes.

I remember when I would swim in the Barren Forks river with buddies—Buford Hunter, Franklin Woodley, Paul Officer, all good swimmers.

Often, after a heavy rain, the river was muddy. You could squeeze a handful of water and watch the red residue settle between the fingers as the water oozed out.

Still, we swam, for it was a recreation gift from nature.

We would swim a half-mile upstream from our rendezvous and tread water under a bridge carrying the highway to Camp Forest. There on the shore was the city swimming pool where whites frolicked in blue, chlorinated water.

We swam nearby, sometimes for hours, masking our resentment in wisecracks.

Woodley might look longingly at the pool's blue water and murmur, "Where there's life, there's hope."

Hunter would cease splashing the murky water and add, "Yeah, where there's a tree, there's a rope."

Then we would file up the weedy bank to the highway and climb the steel rails of the bridge. We would stand on tiptoes, flexing our muscles, peering at the water some 75 feet below.

Then a white swimmer would see us. Perhaps a girl, then a boy, then another girl would run toward the bridge to see the "daring" divers.

When we had lured the girls from the pool (we knew the boys would follow), we would "peel off" like fighter planes and knife into the water below.

Each would emerge with the same proud observation: "Not a soul seems interested in that pretty pool with the clear blue water. Must be that awful chlorine that stings the eye."

Then we would splatter downstream, having rationalized away any bitterness at a discrimination in recreational opportunity.

McMinnville has changed very little. "The Slobbery Rock" is still "the place to go." There is one new place, Harvey's Bar B-Q stand. Harvey's is clean and the food is delicious but the Negro community threatens to boycott it.

Harvey's, owned by Harvey Faulkner, a Negro, is segregated.

Negro youngsters complain that, when they ask for straws in their soft drinks, they are told none are available. In the other side of Harvey's, however, whites sip through straws.

"Worst insult of all," said a Negro teacher, "are the signs put up in the colored side: 'NO DRINKING, NO CURSING, NO MATCHING.' " Faulkner had put no such signs up in the white side.

I asked Faulkner why he put up a Jim Crow place.

"I've got to live," he said. "White folks represent nearly half my trade."

But Harvey Faulkner had set no precedent. Negro McMinnville had done that in many ways.

Had not Bernard high school, my alma mater, set aside the first two rows annually for white guests who came to see our closing-of-school play?

Had not the Church of Christ reserved many of the front seats for whites who came to its tent revival?

As I stood in Harvey's, thinking of the concessions he, I and others had made to Jim Crow, I remembered two incidents that gave me my first knowledge of the south's double standard of life.

When I was about 7 my teacher tried to teach us the manners of a gentleman: "He removes his hat in the house, especially in the presence of ladies . . ."

One day I puzzled my mother by asking, "Are there only colored gentlemen?" Then I explained that white salesmen and patent medicine men seldom removed their hats in our house whereas my father always took his off at the house of Mr. John Davis (a white man).

My mother tried to explain that whites were not yet willing to consider colored females ladies, just women.

It was a few years later, however, that I got to know the meaning of words like "inferior," "darky," "nigger" and "discrimination."

The Negro school was located where a group of homebound white children had to pass it daily on leaving school. They met homebound Negro school children and, due to friction aroused over racial epithets, fighting broke out over use of the sidewalks.

White parents apparently complained to the school superintendent, who called the Negro principal. Soon I stood before our principal with several schoolmates.

"This fighting must stop," the principal said. "If the whites want the sidewalk, get off. Walk in the street."

With those words—words I dislike to remember—peace came to McMinnville. Peace remains with McMinnville in the sense that no one fights over sidewalks.

McMinnville is what her Negro citizens call a "good southern town."

They mean that for a quarter-century there have been no lynchings, no race riots. Policemen do not "pick on" Negro neighborhoods. There are no cross burnings, no people shouting in the streets that all Negroes must be shipped to Africa.

But peace stays with McMinnville today because "no Negro in his right mind" would show up at the city swimming pool with trunks and the intention of swimming.

Nor does any Negro go to the tax-supported public library and ask for a book to sit down and read. If Negro pupils want books, their teachers must go to the library and bring them OUT to the pupils.

Until two injured Negroes died in the basement, none "in his right mind" would seek a bed in the city clinic.

Shortly after the clinic was built, one of my schoolmates was taken there for an emergency appendectomy. A few hours later, the operation performed, an ambulance delivered her at her home.

"I didn't know you could come home after getting your APPENDIX out," exclaimed one Negro woman.

"In her case it was come home or spend the night outdoors," her neighbor explained. "They have 'no accommodations for colored' at our city clinic."

Recently, after the basement deaths, a Negro veteran with an ill wife stormed angrily into the clinic. Now Negroes get a bed in a corner on the first floor.

White McMinnville will resent my telling these things. Strangely, so will Negro McMinnville. They defend this town, even as I have defended it before derisive northerners.

"I hear Negroes have to take off their hats and say 'Yassuh' to a white mule in Tennessee," an Oberlin college classmate once teased me.

"The south isn't really so bad," I countered, knowing I was lying. I felt then, as Negroes who now defend the south must feel, that to admit to being oppressed and downtrodden was to admit docility and weakness on my part.

As I sit in this honky-tonk, literally watching good girls and boys become bad, I am not so sure that is untrue. I remember the words of a World War II shipmate, Lt. Abady of Richmond, Va., who spoke after hearing the sidewalk story.

"Perhaps you have been too docile," he said. "Perhaps you have been too willing for too long to get off the sidewalk and walk in the street."

Race Riots at Trumbull Park

ERIC SEVAREID

WHEN I LEAVE Trumbull Park, only part of me leaves. Actually I'm still out there, worrying about my wife, worrying about my daughters. I can't work, I can't think, I can't do anything—I can't even eat, wondering if the mob has gotten to them as they promised to do—if they've hurt my pregnant wife or my little daughters, if they've bombed them out yet. I can't wait to get home so that I can see that they're all right—and worry about leaving the next day and worry again about them being all right. This goes on and on and the mob promises and carries out on their promises to some extent—I just wonder if they're carrying out their promise to get rid of my family—my daughters and my wife.

These rioters in Trumbull Park here are not really bad people. Oh yes, they throw rocks and they curse and they would kill me, I think, but they've been made bad—they've been made bad by people who profit from their throwing rocks, who profit, who would profit if I threw rocks at them. So I won't throw rocks at them—I shall never throw rocks at them. They want them to hate me and they want me to hate them but I shan't. I won't play that game. When I see a little girl walk up in the middle of this mob, white as the snow and dirty, and her hair just as dirty as she is and smile and say "hi" and smile at me as though she were on my side, I can't hate 'em because I know that that's the way they really are.

Eric Sevareid's July 4th "American Week" CBS television program on the racial conflict at Trumbull Park Housing Development in Chicago won him a 1954 Hillman Prize Award. This excerpt is the statement of the Negro father, Frank Brown, whose effort to move into the development prompted the riots.

My mother told, or asked me rather, when I called her up one day almost in tears because a kid had thrown a rock at my wife, and she said "Well, why are you staying out there? Why don't you come home to Mama? I've still got a place for you."

I said, "No Mom, I'm going to stay out here—I'm going to stay out here because this is where I belong." *This* is the frontiers that the Westerners once traipsed across (BOMB), and they were asked by the Easterners, why are you going out there? *My* reason for staying out here is because I feel I have a duty to stay out here—a duty to every Negro in the world, a duty to every white person in the world who believes in democracy, not to let them down by showing that the mob can win by scaring you with the bomb that just went off. Not to let the people down who are working in the factories and who read the paper every day and say, "Is he staying, did he move, did he move?" I'm not moving. I'll never leave here. I won't let you down. They will have to carry me out of here. And by the way my wife has told me that they will have to carry her. And little Debby, my daughter, says "me too" and Sherry doesn't say me too, but they'll have to carry her. We'll never walk out of here in retreat.

You Have Heard Their Voices

WILMA DYKEMAN and
JAMES STOKELY

HE IS A tall, white-haired doctor of divinity. His high, unwrinkled forehead, keen eyes behind steel-rimmed glasses, and rigid collar encasing his thin, wrinkled neck, all seem in harmony. In fact, as he sits austerely on the antique sofa of the parsonage drawing room, he appears to be almost a portrait of reality rather than reality itself. Born in England, he has a peculiarly Southern background, having lived in many parts of the region from Kentucky to Miami and been married to a Carolinian, one of whose ancestors was a signer of the famous Mecklenburg Declaration. In many corners of the South you may encounter ladies and gentlemen still fighting the Civil War, but there are only a handful who deplore the Revolution. The doctor is one of them:

"I'm concerned about all this agitation and unrest stirring in our beloved Southland today." His talk is as courtly as his manner, with no sloppiness around the edges. "I am disturbed by the Supreme Court which has reached beyond the bounds of propriety and needlessly interfered in state and personal affairs. I look back at the beginning of this century and recall the peace and harmony which seemed to exist then, and I wonder where this dissatisfaction today is leading us. It was a shame that matters could not

A 1957 Hillman Prize Award was given to Wilma Dykeman and James Stokely, two Southern writers, for their book *Neither Black Nor White* (New York: Holt, Rinehart and Winston, Inc., 1957), an assessment of the South as it faced the consequences of the 1954 Supreme Court decision. Chapter 3 gives a sampling of Southern attitudes.

have been settled more amicably back in the 1860s, and the War averted, with all its bloodshed and bitterness reaching down into the present day. The whole world seems so unsettled and unhappy. I have often thought what a pity it was that the English-speaking peoples could not have stuck together back in the troubled times of the 1770s. If only more reasonable counsel might have prevailed then and that War been averted and the colonies remained a part of the Empire, who knows that the whole world could not have been united in a Christian spirit today?"

The veteran newspaper reporter tamps down the tobacco in his pipe slowly and firmly. "Well, this matter of prejudice, it's a long study. If we live long enough, we'll all encounter it someday. I know something about it firsthand because I was born and brought up in Laurel, Mississippi, and my folks were Catholics! When I was in Boston and New York years ago, studying journalism, writing a little, I couldn't get over the prejudice there against the Jews. That was something new to me. And I discovered that that prejudice seemed to work from the top down, while our Negro prejudice down here seems to work strongest from below up. I believe that this is true because prejudice always seems to be greater wherever the economic threat is greatest. Down South the blue-collar whites and the Negroes are in closest competition; those are the only jobs Negroes can hold—and the economic fear is great. Up North there is a great deal of wealth centered in Jewish hands, in banking, clothing, entertainment, many fields, and it's at this economic level that the fear and competition enter there.

"Something happened here in the city this afternoon that I haven't quite gotten over yet. We have a neighborhood here where a Negro housing unit is on one block and whites live on the next block. A white woman on this street accused a Negro boy in the neighborhood of throwing his arms around her. The police went out there, drove into the Negro family's yard—they've got a nice house, brick, fifteen to twenty thousand dollars, nicely furnished—and sent a couple of kids playing nearby to get this boy. When he came, they took him down to a local station, didn't tell his mother or father they were taking him. Down there three or four of the policemen held him an hour or two, hit him over the head so hard with a flashlight that they broke it, hit him around the thighs with their night sticks, poked him in the sides with their elbows, making him entertain them, dance around singing, 'I'm a nigger, I'm a nigger. I'm a black-skinned nigger, I'll be a nigger till I die.' I did a little research on the boy, found out he's fifteen years old, a good student at school, goes to Sunday School and sings in the church choir, never arrested before for anything. He says the only thing he can think of that made the woman accuse him of such a thing was when he was delivering papers a couple of days ago, a car nearly hit his bike and he swerved it over to the sidewalk and one of the handle bars did touch some woman, maybe this woman, but he swears that was all. Anyway, he's still in jail; and no matter what he did, he doesn't have to be entertaining the police force. Actually, I think the boy's father has gotten to the heart of the matter: he says maybe this white woman was jealous because the Negroes in this neighborhood, and particularly his family, live better than some of the white families. They work out at one of the new plants that is integrated, get good pay, buy a nice home and car, and the whites don't like it."

More than two thousand listeners have gathered in a little suburban community to hear the prominent political speaker from the nearby city. He sums up the history of the Negro race by asserting that no civilization of any importance has been developed by other than white men. "The nigra occupied Africa for at least ten thousand years without realizing any of the continent's economic potential until the white man arrived. The nigra had remained content throughout that period to sleep all day, frolic all night, file his teeth, eat his fellow tribesmen and sell his brother into slavery."

The Negro insurance man is obviously prosperous and even more obviously eager to talk with any white person who will share concern in mutual problems. "We had a case about public beach segregation here in the courts recently. And the lawyer on the other side said to me one day, 'Aren't you fellows trying to rush this thing? You've got the white man down with this Supreme Court school decision, now you're trying to start on the parks. It's like stomping in his face. That made me sort of mad. I said, 'Let's look at a little history. Let's be factual. In 1863, Lincoln signed the Emancipation Proclamation. It's nearly a hundred years later. Is that rushing? Look, the Constitution of the United States was written by all white men, didn't have a single Negro signer. The Federal Court in South Carolina and the other states in the 1954 lawsuit were all white men. The nine men on the Supreme Court of the United States are all white, not a single Negro. We're just trying to get the white people to keep their own laws. We've not made any new ones or broken any old ones!' "

In the green quiet village in southside Virginia, a filling-station operator changes tires for you. Big, friendly in a gruff, gross way, he talks and puffs as he works. "This school situation's in a bad twist. You can't trust anybody any more. Your vote don't mean nothing. Might as well stay home and watch the ball game on TV. We ain't got no privileges any more. Everything's done for the nigger. There ain't a lawyer or a judge that wouldn't sell his grandmother for a dime cash. White folks ain't got a chance.

"I tell you, you can't trust a nigger. I've worked 'em and I know. A nigger's ignorant and filthy and sassy and as full of disease as a dog is fleas. I don't want 'em around. If I had my way, and the way of most folks I know, they'd be back in Africa tomorrow. That's the way I feel about it. Maybe I oughtn't to, but I can't help it. We could just have another Civil War over this thing, looks like that's what we're coming to. I tell you, it's serious. It might come to more than they bargained for up there. I don't know nobody who's civilized who's for mixing the races. The law says so, and they've got the money. They also get the votes when they need 'em. A poor man ain't got a chance, that's about what it boils down to."

At the sleepy Sunday-morning town in Florida, you talk with the awkward, overgrown seventeen-year-old who looks you in the eye across the gas pumps. "Whatever they do in the schools down here won't bother me. I'd as soon they brought the nigras in. They're just people like anybody else. They've got to live like everybody else. There aren't many right here in town but several out in the county. I grew up about a hundred miles from here and there were a lot more around there. I had some good nigra friends there, played with them. And you go into the service, you're with them, everybody all the same. We might as well be getting used to it."

The woman's voice in Clay, Kentucky, was very loud as she

called, "We don't believe in mob violence, but this is one question, if they want to push it, we'll be waitin' for 'em."

The university professor is very tired and very troubled. The green lawn in front of his house is unusually well trimmed and neat, and the desk in his little study where you talk is also neat and uncluttered. "The most disappointing feature of the last few years in the South has been, to me, the failure of our leadership. Those who should be making themselves felt are simply not doing so." He offers you a cigarette and looks around the room slowly, at his typewriter, shelves of books and the window between the shelves. "The difficulty of trying to be a true moderate in the South today is almost insurmountable. If you speak, you're often a traitor to one side and no good to the other. I think most of the Southerners probably belong to this group, certainly a large number, but they are not vocal. I've never minded standing up and being counted in a cause if it will do some good. I have never seen any reason just to be counted."

The mountain man with the round, open face and blue eyes full of suspicion talks with you earnestly: "I tell you, it's the hardest thing in the world to live a Christian life. I want to treat the nigger right, and I know I ought to, but there's just something about it all that worries me. You know there's something in the blood that's agin mixing. We can talk about it all we want to— justice, equality, all that sort of thing, talking—but when we come right down to it, that's what it's all about: a nigger a-marrying your sister or your daughter."

The elderly Negro man sits in his office and looks at you shrewdly. You know that, during a long lifetime of being known as a "fighter" and a "trouble shooter," he has had to make many such evaluations of white people. After a while, he chuckles and tells you a story. "About four weeks ago I went to town just north of here to make a talk. I had a little time before my appointment, and so I went into a restaurant I knew to get a cup of coffee. It's a bootleg joint, too, and there were three white men in there. It was Sunday morning, about eleven thirty. When I came in the Negro waiter repeated my name out good and loud a couple of times and after I sat down in one of the booths, one of the white men came over to me. 'I read something you said a while back on intermarriage. I don't believe I agree with what you advocate.' 'I'm not advocating anything,' I said. 'I was asked if I believed in intermarriage and I said yes. If I was asked if I believe in sunshine, I'd say yes. I know the sun's shining. That's a fact. I know my grandfather was a white man. There's nothing you can do about it, nothing I can do about it. Maybe neither one of us like it, but two human beings are mixed in me. And there are about two million you can identify who are white and Negro. And then there are about three million more you can't identify, unless they tell you. So that's an eternal verity, like the sun shining.' Well, the man went and got another drink and came back: 'But I'm a Southerner.' I said, 'Southerner's met Southerner then. Where you from?' 'Georgia.' 'Well, I'm from Virginia, and when's Georgia been more Southern than Virginia?' He got another drink, came back and leaned on my table: 'God Himself is against intermarriage.' 'Maybe so,' I said. 'You read the twelfth book of Numbers. Moses married an Ethiopian woman. Anyway, I'm sitting here looking at you, part white and part black, just like the sun is shining. The sun's a fact and I'm a fact.' "

The young Floridian, native of Georgia with both the University of Georgia and the University of Chicago in his schizophrenic educational background, mulls over a leisurely Saturday-morning omelet. His Bermuda shorts and plaid shirt are casual, as befits home life in Florida with two small children, but there is nothing casual about his conversation when he says, "One of the things that makes me maddest about this whole segregation-integration issue is that people seem to assume you aren't a Southerner if you're not wild for segregation. In everything else I think of myself as a true Southerner, born, reared, mostly educated in the South— but there are people who act like I'm somehow not Southern because I'm for integration. This is especially irritating in Northerners, who seem to expect all Southerners to be exactly alike, and think there's something wrong when they're not.

"We're just like people everywhere. Some of us change. I was brought up in the old South tradition, didn't change till I went to college, began to grow up, things gradually seeped in. I got a

scholarship at college that required my research to be done in the
field of race relations. I wasn't particularly interested in the field,
but I was interested in the scholarship. So I went into the Negro
community hat in hand, so to speak. And I found out when I went
to call on Negro doctors and ministers and businessmen that I had
to wait in their offices until they could see me. It was at their
convenience. And I began to talk with them, and for the first time I
came to know Negro people as people, and then as equal. After a
while I did some special studies on domestic help, and I was
shocked to discover what they earned. In my town, in Georgia, in
1940, the average cash wage for household help was two dollars
and fifty cents a week. There were two families in town who paid
as high as ten dollars. I guess I've been interested in segregation
ever since."

As you walk down the street in Richmond, the air is fragrant
with the biting sweetness of the smell of tobacco everywhere. The
gentleman who walks with you, in his broad Panama hat, is as
much a part of the past and present of Virginia as that tobacco. He
puts his thoughts into words easily and well: "People are talking a
great deal about the South. Just what is the South? Did you ever
stop to consider how many different Souths there are? What makes
it stand apart as a region then? Geography and climate didn't
make the South. We vary from a rainfall of eighty-five inches in
some parts to less than fifteen inches a year in others. Virginia and
Texas are no more alike geographically than Virginia and the
steppes of Asia. I'd say there were four things that have made the
South.

"First, an indigenous people. We're nearly all North European.
Take the Scotch-Irish. I'm interested in that because it's my background. My ancestors landed at the middle ports, up in Pennsylvania, spread out into the interior, down into Virginia.

"Second, practically all of us in the South are identical as to
faith and religious beliefs. We're almost wholly Protestant.

"Third, we're rural. We're still all essentially people of the soil
or only one generation removed.

"But fourth, and most important, and what really made the
South, was the presence of this completely unassimilable people. If
there had been a belt between Virginia and Montana, and Negroes

had been there the way they've been down here—you'd have the same attitudes. That's always the way, no matter where you are, in South Africa or anywhere else. The white people are going to insist on complete segregation from the black people. The white people down here now are perfectly calm about this. They know some way is going to be found to educate the white children if the schools close. But what about the Negro children? Who's going to see about them?"

The troubled young man looks out of the car window at the rich Delta acres rolling along the miles. "We pulled all this down on ourselves. I sure inherited a lapful of problems and I'd just sorta like to see some of them solved. This business of buck-passing has gone on long enough. Grandpa didn't do anything; Pa didn't do anything; but I'd like to think my kid might live in a little peace. Somebody's got to get started owning up to trouble and facing it sometime, and I reckon it might as well be me."

The Dilemma in Race Relations

HARRY S. ASHMORE

THE DICTIONARY DEFINES dilemma thus: "An argument presenting an antagonist with two or more alternatives, but equally conclusive against him, whichever he chooses." And it offers this secondary definition: "A situation involving choice between equally unsatisfactory alternatives."

To some degree every American has felt the thrust of the horns. In a philosophical sense, the problem of accommodating our Negro minority has always been, as Gunnar Myrdal termed it, an American dilemma. Now, in the wake of the great redistribution of the Negro population in a single generation, every major American community must face it in practical terms.

The horns are sharpest, however, for the South—still the home of the majority of American Negroes, and the only region whose social structure has been largely shaped by their presence.

To the South the "unsatisfactory alternatives" appear to have been clearly drawn by the steady development of a public policy which now forbids legal segregation in any activity prescribed by law or sustained by public funds. Most Southerners see them thus: To comply with the new requirements of the Supreme Court at the cost of severe dislocation of the existing social order; or to defy the national government at the cost of disrupting the judicial process, calling down the moral condemnation of non-Southerners, incur-

---

In 1957 Harry S. Ashmore, editor of the Arkansas *Gazette,* addressed a forum sponsored by the Anti-Defamation League. This address was used in the Hillman Reprint Series. A year earlier Ashmore had won a Hillman Prize Award for his editorials in the Arkansas *Gazette.*

ring political penalties, and handicapping the late-blooming economic development of the region.

You may say that the Southern view is vastly oversimplified—and you will be right. You may argue that this estimate of the alternatives before the region is emotional rather than rational—and again you will be correct. It remains, however, the prevailing view, and therefore the reality with which any consideration of the dilemma in race relations must begin.

The issue *is* emotional—on both sides. This was so when the debate was couched in terms of human slavery; it is not less so now that we argue over second-class citizenship.

In the march of generations the condition of the American Negro has been steadily improved—in recent years by his own efforts, and earlier by the assistance of sympathetic whites. He has been the principal figure in a great moral crusade that has run through all our history, a crusade that had its roots in that part of the nation where, until recent years, the Negro did not live. But he has also received sympathy and support in his long struggle from those who have always been his neighbors—the Southern whites.

Ironically, it is in part these advances—economic and political —that complicate the American Negro's existence today. His sights are higher, his demands are greater, and his patience has grown thin. But his forward progress has not yet significantly altered the basic attitude of the American white. The late Howard Odum, the great student of the Southern region, once undertook what he called a sort of hidden poll of the great mass of Southern folk and found at the heart of the Southern credo this central theme: "The Negro is a Negro and nothing more." And Odum added in his last formal advice to his people: "It was of the utmost importance that Southerners face the plain assumption that they did not appraise the Negro as the same sort of human being they themselves are."

This, then, is the first truth in the dilemma of race relations.

But there is another of equal importance—the fact that in its over-all implications the Southern white attitude toward the Negro is not substantially different from the prevailing American white attitude. Southerners translated their viewpoint into the legal barriers of segregation, which are now being systematically struck down by judicial interpretation. Non-Southerners did not, in most cases, but, faced with a rising tide of Negro immigration, they have erected extralegal barriers that have attained the same end. With only rare exceptions Negroes everywhere in the United States live in segregated communities; the lines in Chicago, for example, are if anything more sharply drawn than they are in Atlanta.

The tradition in the South is different. The practice, however, is not now significantly different from that which prevails in all the great cities where Negroes have arrived in late years to take their place in the ghettos vacated by earlier generations of immigrants. So it is with the prevailing white attitude toward this "visible minority." The dilemma, then, may be reduced to this summary statement which applies with equal force in every community where Negroes have congregated in considerable number: The American white is not yet ready to accept the Negro as his equal, and the American Negro is no longer willing to accept anything less.

These are the polar attitudes, and there is a great range between them among the members of both races. Yet they are the attitudes that have colored the current conflict—the attitudes to which the advocates on either side give angry voice. The Southern political leadership, as was demonstrated by the recent Manifesto, remains formally committed to working out a pattern of race relations within the old "separate but equal" concept, despite its rejection by the Supreme Court. The new, militant Negro leadership as a matter of principle opposes segregation in any form—legal or extralegal, voluntary or enforced—as a mark of inferiority.

The immediate conflict centers now in the sensitive area of public education, but its implications go far beyond the classroom. We are, in fact, called upon by the new public policy to re-order our society in many important ways. Put another way, we are called upon to make changes in the patterns of our everyday life that the great majority of white Americans are reluctant to undertake.

Does this mean the evolving pattern of desegregation by law is bound to fail? I do not think so; on the basis of all the evidence I think rather that it is bound to succeed. Powerful forces are working to preserve segregation, but in every significant test for the last twenty years the forces working against segregation have proved stronger.

It is not unusual to find the declared public policy in conflict with the public attitude in this area. It has always been so. Public policy forbade the mistreatment of bondsmen in the era of slavery, but did not effectively protect them; the Plessy doctrine called for equal public facilities in the days when separation was legal, but discrimination prevailed. Bringing practice into conformity with policy is one of the ultimate tests of democracy, which must protect the declared rights of the minority while it is bound by the will of the majority.

These polar attitudes I have described do not preclude compromise—they demand it. The white citizens of Louisville have accepted the principle of integration in their public schools and have begun the transition on a limited scale; I expect Dr. Omer Carmichael, the Superintendent of Public Schools, would agree that the most forceful leadership could not have persuaded them to undertake integration on a wholesale basis. The attitude of the white citizens of Louisville has not changed; they still do not regard the Negro as their equal. But, under the pressure of the law and the prodding of a few wise men, they have accepted the necessity of granting him a greater measure of equality of opportunity.

This, I think, is the essential distinction. Frequently we are trapped by the catch-phrases that have had long currency in this great debate—the terms that carry with them emotional overtones of the old moral argument. Equality of person is not a fact of American life and never has been. Equality of opportunity is the goal. The concept is negative rather than positive; what we seek to guarantee our children is not a certain place in society, but a clear field on which no child will be especially handicapped by his race or religion.

This, surely was the concept embodied in the Supreme Court decision in public school cases. Yet it has been obscured by two false notions widely and stubbornly held—one on each side of the central controversy.

One is the belief that any association between whites and Negroes beyond that of master and servant inevitably leads to intermingling of the races.

The other is the belief that any separation of the races is inherently discriminatory and therefore morally wrong.

Even cursory reading of the record should dispel both notions.

The only widespread intermingling of the races occurred in the days of the Negro's enforced degradation; it has declined almost to the vanishing point with the general social improvement of the minority race.

So it is with the notion that segregation has always been discriminatory. In historical perspective the separate-but-equal doctrine may be seen as a necessary bridge in the transition from slavery to citizenship. If it denied the Negro certain rights granted to whites, it also guaranteed him certain privileges and immunities at a time he was not equipped to compete on equal footing with his white neighbors. The gross abuses and the calculated exploitation that were cloaked by legal segregation are an essential part of the record. They were and are indefensible—and because of this they provided the cutting-edge that has removed the legal underpinning of segregation. But noblesse oblige was part of the system, too— the recognized obligation of the strong to protect the weak—and this, too, is disappearing in the transition that is now well under way.

Both these deeply-held ideas will survive for the foreseeable future. They will provide the rallying point for those who, in Ralph McGill's phrase, are now engaged in guerrilla fighting among the ruins of the old segregated society. They will continue for some years to shape political decisions and social customs. Yet already an increasing number of Southerners are groping for new accommodations—not because the old attitudes are necessarily changing, but because they are beginning to understand that the shifting racial pattern is only part of the great change that is sweeping over the region—and by no means the most important part.

Legal segregation was only one of the three peculiar institutions that set the Southern region apart through most of its history. The other two were the one-crop agrarian economy—made possible by the slave, and necessary by his emancipation—and the one-party political system, brought into being as a means of disfranchising the freedmen. All three of these institutions are so closely interrelated as to be virtually one, and none can survive the others. Thus the Southern leaders who are working, with marked success, to industrialize the region are undermining the system of segregation many of them so passionately defend.

The pattern of change is not even, nor is it likely to be. I have myself here come perilously close to being trapped by one of the oversimplifications I have been deploring. There is not one South, but many souths—each significantly different in the racial composition of its population and in its tradition. Segregation in education is already a dead letter in more than half the states that required it prior to the Supreme Court decision in the public school cases. The border states are well along in the transition, and now the process is beginning on a limited scale in a few of the upper Southern cities—with Louisville the most notable among those that could be considered primarily Southern in character. This trend will continue, I believe, in the upland counties of the Southern states proper—the counties where the Negro population is sparse and the practice of segregation has never been buttressed by unyielding social sanction. In the Deep South there is not yet any perceptible break in the solid front—and indeed the immediate result of every popular test in the recent election may be taken to indicate that none is in prospect.

Yet a closer look at the general scene shows signs of significant change everywhere. First of all, the physical violence which many hotspurs predicted and many sober Southerners feared has not developed except in isolated cases. The most extreme actions of the new Citizens Councils fall far short of the outright reign of terror undertaken by the Ku Klux Klan a generation ago. There have been shocking examples of denial of such basic civil rights as the franchise, yet even in the Deep South the participation of Negroes in the recent election was the greatest in history. It was, in fact, so great that most observers give the Negro voters credit for cracking the solid Democratic front in such states as Louisiana and Tennessee. Here, then, is new and important political leverage being employed by Negroes in their own right.

In the meantime the great out-migration of Negroes from the South continues, literally changing the complexion of the region year by year. Every Southern city has grown steadily whiter in recent years—while every major non-Southern city has witnessed a sharp and continuing increase in the proportion of its Negro population. If I had to cite the single most significant fact in American race relations today I would say that it is the fact that the city of Chicago today contains more Negroes than the entire Confederate state of Arkansas—and that this vast change has taken place in a single generation that saw millions of Negroes not only change their place of residence but their way of life, exchanging the values of their agrarian background for those of an urban people.

Inside the South and out of it, the Negro has come by a long and tortuous road to the point reached before him by previous generations of immigrants. He is set apart as were the Jews, the Poles, and the Irish before him—huddled into the worst housing, assigned to the most menial jobs, beset by his own inferior background. He is still in his time of horizontal migration, from farm to city, and from south to north. But his vertical migration is beginning, and it will accelerate; he too will break out of his ghettos and gain greater acceptance as his improved opportunities enable him to earn it.

In many ways his problems are special. The walls of prejudice are perhaps harder to scale than those that confronted any of the other minorities who found their place in this conglomerate nation of ours. But time is working on his side, and the law—and the moral force which has made him a burden on every white American's conscience throughout our national history.

The dilemma is real. The horns are sharp. But its resolution is at least as certain as the survival of the democratic concept in a nation which has never attained its goal—but has never considered abandoning it.

NEWSPAPER EDITORIALS

During a period when Southern opposition to integration was frequently expressed in terms of violence and repression, a few Southern editors persisted in their efforts to bring reason and understanding to their communities.

For a number of years the Sidney Hillman Foundation recognized the courage of these editors through its Prize Awards. Among them were: Andrew M. Secrest of the Cheraw, South Carolina *Chronicle*, (1957); Ralph McGill, publisher of the Atlanta *Constitution*, (1958); Sylvan Meyer of the *Daily Times*, Gainesville, Georgia (1960); Ira Harkey of the Pascagoula, Mississippi, *Chronicle* (1962); and Jay Oliver Emmerich of the McComb, Mississippi, *Enterprise-Journal* (1964).

These samples, some excerpted, of their work convey a sense of the problems they faced and the atmosphere in which they worked.

Civil Liberty
and the Supreme Court

A. M. SECREST

The Cheraw *Chronicle*, South Carolina, June 27, 1957

BEFORE WE SUCCUMB to the popular pastime these days of attacking the rulings and the motivation of the U.S. Supreme Court, we should make sure that we understand exactly what it has ruled, and not just what the headlines, or some disgruntled newspaper columnists, SAY it has ruled. Sometimes there's a big difference between the two.

Criticism of the Court is nothing new. Twenty years ago it was the liberals and New Dealers who assaulted the Court. They said that it represented the forces of reaction, that the "nine old men" stood in the way of social progress, that the justices were blocking the will and intent of Congress and thereby usurping the proper function of the legislative branch of government.

President Roosevelt then revealed his Court packing plan, which would increase the number of judges he could appoint, so that he could get onto the bench liberal thinkers who would go along with his domestic programs of economic recovery. Thanks to Congress, among them some of our finest Southern leaders, the President's ill-conceived scheme failed.

Today the criticism of the Court has been renewed, and is growing, but for entirely different reasons. Now the Court's critics say that its decisions are too radical, that the justices are too social-minded and too far ahead of the will of Congress or of the people. Although Roosevelt's scheme did not pass Congress, he still was able to pack the Court because of the fortuitous death or retirement of the older judges.

Roosevelt appointees were in the liberal vein, as were those of Truman (to a lesser extent) and of Eisenhower (to a greater extent). Now we hear that the present Court has substituted psychology and sociology for the law, that it has, thereby, replaced judicial decision with legislative fiat, and that it has, consequently, usurped the powers and prerogatives of the Congress.

We believe that there is some justification for alarm when the Supreme Court splits five-four on many decisions and when it overturns its own rulings from one year to the next. That way leads to legal confusion and chaos on a broad scale.

However, the present Court has made some very important and, from our point of view at least, some necessary rulings during the past few weeks to safeguard civil liberties of all Americans. If these rulings, while making it somewhat more difficult to prosecute a few subversives, strengthen the rights and liberties of 170 million Americans against abuses of Big Government, then we believe it's a profitable exchange.

For there can be no real doubt that during the hey-day of the McCarthy era, Congressional Committees did abuse their investigative powers and in the process, many innocent victims were wronged. The investigative powers of Congress are limited to legitimate legislative purposes, and when that purpose is exceeded, the Court has a duty to call a halt.

One of the Court justices recently said that High Tribunal decisions are becoming more and more "like a one-way train reservation, good for today only." The danger of such judicial flippancy and whimsicality could be exceeded only by too stern and rigid adherence to the principle of "stare decisis"—a legal term which means that a judicial question has been decided and should be allowed to rest.

If justices were never to depart from principle of "stare decisis," then judicial errors (and we shall always have errors whenever the human mind and heart are involved) could never be corrected by subsequent courts. The only thing worse than error is the failure to correct it when the error becomes apparent. Judicial decisions should always be subject to review and correction in the light of new evidence and more complete information.

It is incorrect to state that the Supreme Court always substitutes "psychology and sociology" for law. Who would deny the justices the right to apply the lessons of these important subjects to their cases? How else could they hope to make a reasonable interpretation of the law? Is it to be disputed that the advantages of a liberal education are just as important in applying and interpreting the law as they are in the formulation or the execution of the law?

The Supreme Court is one of three equal branches of our governmental system. It has been a vital and integral part of our republic since the days of its infancy. During the period following the Civil War the Supreme Court stood between the South and a vengeful and bloodthirsty Congress. It has historically stood for the protection of the citizen's civil liberties. We cannot strait-jacket the Court without endangering our constitutional system of government. Careless and unrestrained criticism of the Court, in a spirit of momentary antagonism occasioned by a series of decisions with which we may personally disagree, can lead to dangerous consequences.

A Church, A School . . .

RALPH McGILL

Atlanta *Constitution*, October 13, 1958

DYNAMITE IN GREAT quantity Sunday ripped a beautiful Temple of worship in Atlanta. It followed hard on the heels of a like destruction of a handsome high school at Clinton, Tenn.

The same rabid, mad-dog minds were, without question, behind both. They also are the source of previous bombings in Florida, Alabama and South Carolina. The school house and the church are the targets of diseased, hate-filled minds.

Let us face the facts.

This is a harvest. It is the crop of things sown.

It is the harvest of defiance of courts and the encouragement of citizens to defy law on the part of many Southern politicians. It will be the acme of irony, for example, if any one of four or five Southern governors deplore this bombing. It will be grimly humorous if certain state attorneys general issue statements of regret. And it will be quite a job for some editors, columnists and commentators, who have been saying that our courts have no jurisdiction and that the people should refuse to accept their authority now to deplore.

It is not possible to preach lawlessness and restrict it.

To be sure, none said go bomb a Jewish temple or a school.

But let it be understood that when leadership in high places in any degree fails to support constituted authority, it opens the gates to all those who wish to take law into their hands.

There will be, to be sure, the customary act of the careful drawing aside of skirts on the part of those in high places.

31

"How awful," they will exclaim. "How terrible. Something must be done."

But the record stands. The extremists of the citizens' councils, the political leaders who in terms violent and inflammatory have repudiated their oaths and stood against due process of law, have helped unloose this flood of hate and bombing.

This, too, is a harvest of those so-called Christian ministers who have chosen to preach hate instead of compassion. Let them now find pious words and raise their hands in deploring the bombing of a synagogue.

You do not preach and encourage hatred for the Negro and hope to restrict it to that field. It is an old, old story. It is one repeated over and over again in history. When the wolves of hate are loosed on one people, then no one is safe.

Hate and lawlessness by those who lead release the yellow rats and encourage the crazed and neurotic who print and distribute the hate pamphlets, who shrieked that Franklin Roosevelt was a Jew, who denounce the Supreme Court as being Communist and controlled by Jewish influences.

This series of bombings is the harvest, too, of something else.

One of those connected with the bombing telephoned a news service early Sunday morning to say the job would be done. It was to be committed, he said, by the Confederate Underground.

The Confederacy and the men who led it are revered by millions. Its leaders returned to the Union and urged that the future be committed to building a stronger America. This was particularly true of Gen. Robert E. Lee. Time after time he urged his students at Washington University to forget the War Between the States and to help build a greater and stronger union.

But for too many years now we have seen the Confederate flag and the emotions of that great war become the property of men not fit to tie the shoes of those who fought for it. Some of these have been merely childish and immature. Others have perverted and commercialized the flag by making the Stars and Bars, and the Confederacy itself, a symbol of hate and bombings.

For a long time now it has been needful for all Americans to stand up and be counted on the side of law and the due process of law—even when to do so goes against personal beliefs and emotions. It is late. But there is yet time.

What's the Issue?

SYLVAN MEYER

Daily Times, Gainesville, Georgia, March 14, 1960

MOST GEORGIANS DO not comprehend the issues. The issue is not segregation vs. integration in the schools. The issue is not whether the Supreme Court was right in its decision; the Supreme Court is always right simply because there is no one who can be any righter than it is.

The issue involved is individual freedom against statutory discrimination. Government is blind to color, religion and groups. It cannot write laws on the state level treating some people differently from other people. This is the issue.

To resolve this issue, Georgia must find some way to cease discriminating against Negro students in class assignments. It's as simple as that.

Confusing Times, Dangerous Times

IRA HARKEY

Pascagoula *Chronicle*, Mississippi, September 19, 1962

A PALL OF contradiction covers our state as if every one of us had developed schizophrenia.

The newspapers and politicians who hailed Gov. Barnett's address call upon citizens not to resort to violence. "Do they really mean it?" is the question, for these same papers and people have long been advocates of a "fight to the finish" and now they may see just what it is they have raised up. How can we defy the law "to the finish" without resorting to violence?

Then there is the call upon the United States of America not to send marshals into our state to enforce the law. How can we make such a demand without appearing devoid of all sense? Does the burglar announce to the police that he will not observe anti-burgling statutes because they violate his way of life and then expect the police to issue him an exemption?

Gov. Barnett knows full well how laws are enforced when the lawless are defiant. He himself has sent troops into counties to search out a bottle of whiskey here, to shatter a crap table there. Federal marshals enforce the law except in rebellions which are tended to by troops. How do we think that the United States will enforce the law now? By sending in the Peace Corps? Postmen? Soil conservationists? When orders are ignored, force is applied. Gov. Barnett knows that.

A Sunday editorial in a state capital paper is titled "Future

Economic Growth Hinges on State Income Conditioners," as if there will be any growth but of hate, any conditioners but strife, any state income but grief in the turmoil of anarchy we are approaching.

At a lunch meeting Monday at beautiful Longfellow House in Pascagoula a group of local leaders heard a talk by a Mississippi State University official. He spoke on plans the university has for its educational program in Jackson County—as if there will be any education after Ole Miss has been padlocked or burned down or whatever it is Gov. Barnett has planned for it.

Meanwhile, the first Mississippian to decline Gov. Barnett's invitation to go to jail is Judge Sidney Mize of Gulfport. The day after the governor's speech, Mize issued an order directing Ole Miss to admit James Meredith without delay. Mize followed instructions of the federal circuit court of appeals rather than Gov. Barnett's call to suicide.

In a madhouse's din, Mississippi waits. God help Mississippi.

You May Be Next

IRA HARKEY

Pascagoula *Chronicle*, Mississippi, October 19, 1962

A TERRORIST GROUP has been organized in your county. Its first targets are this newspaper and any white persons designated by the group's "action committee" as "nigger-lovers."

The group has been given a quasi-official status because it was sponsored by the chief law enforcement officer of your county.

It will attack the *Chronicle* initially by "putting pressure" on its advertisers. Only a few of its members are people of any moral or economic standing in the community. The rest can apply pressure only through threats, intimidations and, ultimately, destruction. Among its members are a dozen men whose lives have been dedicated to participation in violence.

Ten days ago the *Chronicle* called upon the decent element in our county to announce publicly that it wants law and order and to insist that our officials maintain law and order. We received an immediate response to that appeal—a bullet fired through our front door that night, blasting a two-foot section from the plate glass.

Now this.

If the responsible leaders of our community—its company presidents, club and fraternal heads and Christian churchmen—do not recognize the evil nature of this threat, do not organize immediately—tonight—and notify our sheriff in no uncertain terms that he is leading our county and himself to disaster, they can say goodbye right now to their investments and their hopes and dreams for their future and that of their children.

We are under no illusion that anybody here cares what happens to Ira Harkey. But think long on this: what happens to him can happen to you. You may be next.

Anti-learning demagogues:

Push 'em Back, W-a-a-y Back!

IRA HARKEY

Pascagoula *Chronicle*, Mississippi, January 10, 1963

INDUSTRY USED TO move south to take advantage of untapped natural resources, temperate climate, competition-free markets. But most of all it moved south to dip into our large pool of cheap labor.

To these attractions later was added a ladling of socialistic sauce. Communities began building plants for industry, thus assuming industry's greatest investment burden. Such programs as Mississippi's "Balance Agriculture with Industry" project lured many a concern away from its New England home.

Those days, while not gone completely, have passed high noon and are waning on toward sunset. Clodhopper labor no longer is desirable, no longer is even useful. Industry more and more is automated and the people pushing the buttons are skilled technicians, engineers, scientists with advanced college degrees.

Because of this, industry now is moving to states and communities where intellectual resources are available. "Modern technological developments require the most advanced intellectual skills for their conception and progress. Without such skills, industry of today cannot compete or even begin. Thus, the concentration of modern industry in close proximity to the high scientific skills in graduate schools is not surprising."

The words in quotation marks are from a recent edition of Tulane University's "Dimension Education," a feature published

38

on the *Chronicle*'s editorial page every Monday. This one was titled "Education: key to industry" and it discussed the "obvious" relationship between high-level industry and high-level educational institutions.

We bring it up again in order to point out that this stage in the technological advance of US society is not the time for Mississippi to allow politicos to cripple its educational institutions. Our campuses must be posted off-limits to demagogues of all echelons, or the furnaces will grow cold all over Mississippi.

When Terrorism Wins People Are Enslaved

J. O. EMMERICH

Enterprise-Journal, McComb, Mississippi, November 9, 1964

SOMEONE FIRED A shot through one of the front plate glass windows of the *Enterprise-Journal*. The bullet was recovered by the police inside of the building.

If efforts of this kind are purposed to frighten our people they can serve no good purpose.

If efforts of this kind are committed in the spirit of vandalism then it is a symptom of the deterioration of law and order.

Isaiah of scriptural writ, said, "Come now and let us reason together."

First: The *Enterprise-Journal* has appealed editorially to our people to take a responsible view of the problems which beset us.

Surely no solid citizen would argue that we should advocate irresponsible action.

A community moves ahead when it possesses responsible officials, responsible businessmen, responsible ministers, responsible citizens in general.

Terrorism is not the responsible way to meet our problems.

Second: The *Enterprise-Journal* firmly believes that our problems will be responsibly met and solved. We have faith in our people. Others may despair for McComb's future. But our faith in the eventual solution of the problems which beset us is firm. But this faith stems from the belief that our people will turn to responsible action.

Third: Life is conflict and adjustment. Every age has been tested by conflicts and has been confronted with the task of making responsible adjustments to these conflicts.

Who are we of this generation in McComb to think that we should be an exception to this rule of history? We are not history's fair-haired child. We have our conflicts and our leadership must measure up to the challenge of finding a solution and applying it.

Fourth: We must recognize that our emotions can deceive us. This is not an idle statement. Emotions can deceive good men even to the point of creating a sense of patriotic ardor while pursuing a course which is damaging to the community they want to help.

Fifth: There is nothing more American than our Bill of Rights —freedom of the press, freedom of speech, freedom of assembly, freedom of worship and other concepts so essential to our cherished American liberties.

In keeping with these American concepts we should not resent earnest expressions of editorial opinion. Freedom of the press was not written into the United States Constitution as a personal prerogative of editors. It was conceived as a means of providing all Americans with freedom of information.

Editorial opinions stand or fall, win or lose, triumph or fail in keeping with their relationship of truth and logic.

Responsible journalism is not something to try to curb with intimidation. It is an American asset, an essential ingredient of individual and political freedom.

Sixth: The world's unfortunate people are not the Americans who have the freedom to read editorial comment. Our people are free because our problems are subjected to editorial analysis. It is because the American people have freedom of information. The world's unfortunate people are the crushed, enslaved citizens living in countries where editors cannot be articulate—the people of Cuba, Spain, Yugoslavia, Red China, East Germany, the Soviet Union. These people are enslaved because ideas cannot be debated. Their enslavement is the result of applied terrorism.

A citizen from Little Rock said recently, "We, in Little Rock, know how to sympathize with the people of McComb. We were besieged with problems very much like your own. We were afraid and frustrated. But with time, our people joined together, took a responsible view of the entire situation. Today we can say that none of the great fears which then disturbed us ever developed. This, I believe, will happen in McComb."

The *Enterprise-Journal* believes that this is a sound, responsible and positive approach to problems of our people in McComb.

Law Tests to Be Made in McComb Wednesday

J. O. EMMERICH

Enterprise-Journal, McComb, Mississippi, November 17, 1964

TOMORROW REPRESENTATIVES OF the NAACP are scheduled to be in McComb. Their purpose will be to test some of the civil rights law.

They would fail miserably should they attempt to test alleged laws which had not been passed by the House of Representatives, the U. S. Senate and subsequently signed by the President of the United States.

It is reasonable to believe that they will succeed ultimately if the laws to be tested have the validity of Congress and the signature of the President behind them.

Southern senators staged an historic filibuster to prevent the passage of these laws. The filibuster was a long, arduous debate. But the filibuster failed. Southern Congressmen and Southern senators were out-voted.

Actually, the effort scheduled for Wednesday is not really a test of the laws. It is a test of our recognition of the validity of laws enacted by Congress.

We repeat the choices available to our people when these tests are made Wednesday.

The operators of motels, cafes, drug stores and organizations, have three choices: (1) To obey the law, (2) to defy the law and risk court trials with potential jail sentences, or (3) to go out of business.

The police department has two choices: (1) To provide police protection to all people concerned, or (2) To ignore the request for police protection and risk potential martial law with federal troops in charge.

The patrons of these businesses have two choices: (1) To recognize the limited choices available to operators of these businesses, or (2) to boycott them and force them out of business, thus depriving the community of the business houses affected and causing the owners to suffer severe monetary losses.

The public has two choices: (1) To panic and riot and further damage the image, the economics and the serenity of the people of the McComb area, or (2) to recognize that laws must be upheld and respected.

The City of McComb has two official choices: (1) To meet the situation responsibly and attain a new sense of stability and serenity as proved possible by the history of other Southern cities, or (2) to ignore the successful patterns of Southern cities and bog deeper in chaos and retrogression.

All of us should earnestly study the limited choices available to all concerned—the limited choices of the operators of the business establishments involved, the choices of the patrons of these business houses, the choices of the police department, and the choices of the public. There is no need of everyone being excited or aroused. Emotionalism can serve to hurt our own people and will accomplish nothing.

This is not an unblazed trail. When Mayor Allen Thompson of Jackson was met with a request to provide police protection to those who complied with the law, he responded with a positive and unequivocal "Yes." His decision furthered the cause of ending widespread violence in our capital city. The City of McComb would do well to ponder Mayor Thompson's decision. Wednesday will be just another day if we, the people, will simply respond responsibly.

Social and Economic Consequences of Residential Segregation

DAVIS McENTIRE

IN CONSIDERING THE consequences of residential segregation, a fundamental distinction must be drawn between voluntary and imposed segregation. The voluntary congregation of people who seek each other's society is an exercise of freedom; if it carries disadvantages, those concerned may choose whether to pay the price of living with the group. Economic-class segregation is also a different matter because individuals may escape it by improving their economic condition. But segregation that is enforced upon a group is a deprivation of freedom—a deprivation especially onerous when its basis is the unalterable fact of race or ancestry. An eminent authority has defined personal liberty as "the power of locomotion, of changing situation, or removing one's person to whatsoever places one's own inclination may direct, without imprisonment or restraint, unless by due course of law."[1] This is the

Davis McEntire, professor of social welfare at the University of California, received a 1960 Hillman Prize Award for *Residence and Race* (Berkeley: University of California Press, 1960), the last volume in a series edited by McEntire, sponsored by the Commission on Race and Housing, and financed through a grant by the Fund for the Republic. These excerpts are taken from Chapters 5 and 20.

[1] Blackstone Commentaries 134, quoted in dissenting opinion of Justice Harlan, *Plessy* v. *Ferguson*, 163 U. S. 537 (1896).

45

freedom abridged by compulsory residential segregation. Because it is basic to the enjoyment of many other liberties and opportunities, its restriction has far-reaching consequences which touch virtually every aspect of life of the segregated group and of the relations between them and the dominant majority.[2]

As previously described, residence restrictions are applied with varying intensity against different groups, and the subject groups vary in their response to restrictions. The Negro is everywhere the most severely limited, and also, because of his history, he has fewer cultural defenses against discrimination than the Oriental groups or Jews. Hence, the Negro suffers most from the consequences described here, which are felt in reduced measure by other groups.

As Charles S. Johnson has remarked, "racial segregation in residential areas provides the basic structure for other forms of institutional segregation."[3] A group segregated in residence is necessarily segregated in schools, recreation, and other facilities organized on an area basis. Discriminatory in itself, residential segregation permits and stimulates other forms of discrimination. When a minority group is physically isolated, differential treatment follows almost as a matter of course. In the South, although legal segregation is justified as separate-but-equal, the separate facilities provided for Negroes are rarely if ever equal. The inequality of Negro schools is notorious, but as Myrdal observes, "Virtually the whole range of other publicly administered facilities—such as hospitals, libraries, parks, and similar recreational facilities—are much poorer for Negroes than they are for whites. . . . Water provision, sewage and garbage removal, street cleaning, street lighting, street paving, police protection and everything else is neglected or withheld while vice is often allowed."[4]

In the North and West, public facilities for Negro neighborhoods are more neglected than deliberately withheld. Often where Negroes have inherited the oldest districts, the school buildings

[2] In the preparation of this article, I have made extensive use of an unpublished research memorandum prepared for the Commission on Race and Housing by Jitsuichi Masuoka and Preston Valien of Fisk University, "Social Consequences of Racial Residential Segregation."

[3] Charles S. Johnson, *Patterns of Negro Segregation* (New York: Harper & Brothers, 1943), p. 8.

[4] Gunnar Myrdal, *An American Dilemma: The Negro Problem and Modern Democracy* (New York, Harper & Brothers, 1944), pp. 335, 643.

and other public institutions are old and worn out. In these heavily built-up and congested areas, parks and playgrounds are few.[5]

Mexican-Americans in the Southwest, although suffering less discrimination than Negroes, usually receive even fewer public facilities in their neighborhoods. On the West Side of San Antonio, one of the largest Mexican communities in the country, a recent study reports "many examples of what are called 'corrals,' in which up to twenty or thirty families share one pit privy and a single cold-water tap. There are great numbers of shacks on rutted, wholly unimproved streets, without inside plumbing or running water."[6] These conditions are widespread and probably more aggravated in the smaller towns and rural districts than in the larger cities. Throughout the Southwest, great numbers of poor Mexican-Americans live in all-Mexican shack towns, often called camps, that are wholly lacking in paved streets or modern sewerage facilities and are subject to flooding in wet weather. Conditions in these Mexican slums are a serious health menace.[7]

Law enforcement is usually less strict in minority neighborhoods than elsewhere. Often zoning and building laws are not enforced, leaving residents unprotected against conversions and land uses destructive of residential quality. Vice and petty crime that would not be tolerated in good neighborhoods often flourish in the Negro districts.

Against public neglect the residents of a neighborhood have ordinarily two remedies. They can move away or they can act, singly or together, to make demands upon the public authorities— demands enforceable by political process. Well-kept neighborhoods usually have some kind of defensive organization such as a property owners' association, or if not, the residents can be counted on to organize informally to repel a threat or obtain a benefit. Such organization is essential, for a high standard of public

---

[5] Charles Abrams, *Forbidden Neighbors: A Study of Prejudice in Housing* (New York: Harper & Brothers, 1955), pp. 74-75; James Ford, *Slums and Housing,* I, p. 436; T. J. Woofter, Jr., *Negro Problems in Cities,* p. 281; Arnold and Caroline Rose, *America Divided* (New York: Alfred A. Knopf, 1948), pp. 160-161.

[6] Jack E. Dodson, "Minority Group Housing in Two Texas Cities, in Glazer and McEntire, (eds.), *Studies in Housing and Minority Groups."*

[7] John H. Burma, *Spanish-Speaking Groups in the United States* (Durham: Duke University Press, 1954), pp. 88-92. See also Pauline R. Kibbe, *Latin Americans in Texas* (Albuquerque: University of New Mexico Press, 1946), pp. 130-132 *et passim.*

services and strict enforcement of protective laws is seldom conferred upon a neighborhood by external benevolence; generally it is achieved by the watchful insistence of neighborhood residents.

Neither remedy is fully available to the members of segregated minority groups. They are not free to move away from undesirable conditions. Organized action for neighborhood defense presupposes a degree of economic strength, cultural development, and political experience not yet achieved by most Negroes, Puerto Ricans, or Mexican-Americans. In much of the South, moreover, the disfranchisement of Negroes renders them powerless to influence public officials or to protect themselves against governmental discrimination.

Where Negroes vote and have developed leadership and some political strength, as in Atlanta, they have been able to gain municipal recognition of their housing needs and racially neutral law enforcement, even under segregation.[8] In some Mexican-American communities of California, organization and political participation have brought paved streets and other public improvements in long-neglected neighborhoods.[9] On the whole, however, organized effort for neighborhood defense and improvement is little developed in minority communities.

The supply of housing available to segregated groups is determined primarily not by their demand expressed in the market but by the interplay of forces determining their segregation pattern. Minority individuals gain access to a wider range of possibilities only as the housing supply designated for the group as a whole expands. Regulated by factors other than market demand, additions to the minority housing supply may be too little or too much in relation to the group's demand for housing at any given time. Too little means scarcity; too much raises the familiar threat of falling property values.

[8] Robert A. Thompson, Hylan Lewis, and Davis McEntire, "Atlanta and Birmingham: A Comparative Study in Negro Housing," in Glazer and McEntire, (eds.), *Studies in Housing and Minority Groups.*

[9] California Federation for Civic Unity, *Get Out if You Can, the Saga of Sal si Puedes,* an account by Fred W. Ross of an American Friends Service Committee project among Mexican-Americans in a northern California Community (San Francisco, 1953). Harry Lawton, "Casa Blanca—Tangible Example of Civic Pride at Work," *Riverside Press-Enterprise,* August 18, 1956.

The housing for which minority homeseekers are permitted to compete is not only a small but on the whole a very inferior part of the total housing supply. Thus restricted, nonwhites receive poorer housing than do whites, even when they pay the same rents or purchase prices. The differential is very wide in the South, but it exists throughout the country and through the whole range of rents. There are great numbers of nonwhite families who can afford only cheap housing; yet the dwellings they receive are poorer than need be on the basis of rent alone.

Disadvantage in obtaining mortgage credit is another consequence for minority home buyers of the inferior areas in which they live. In old and run-down districts, many mortgage-lending institutions will not lend at all. Mortgage credit, when available in these areas, is customarily extended in smaller amounts (relative to values) and for shorter repayment periods than loans in preferred residential areas. In these practices, mortgage lenders are discriminating against high-risk areas and not necessarily against a racial group, but the group is nonetheless disadvantaged. Direct racial discrimination occurs when lenders refuse mortgage credit to a nonwhite trying to buy a house in a white area. Where nonwhites have been able to gain access to good quality residence areas, their disadvantage in obtaining mortgage loans tends to disappear.[10]

The most favorable terms of mortgage credit, made possible by government insurance or guarantee, have been available chiefly on new development housing in suburban locations. Because nonwhites are rarely permitted to buy into new developments (except those intended for minority occupancy), they have less than equal opportunity to share in the benefits of government mortgage insurance.

Minority families are often obliged to occupy housing ill-suited to their particular needs or to family use generally. Common in many areas which have passed from white to nonwhite or (in New York City) to Puerto Rican occupancy are large, old houses built for the conditions of an earlier day and for a higher-income group

[10] See also Chester Rapkin and William G. Grigsby, *The Demand for Housing in Racially Mixed Areas. A Study of the Nature of Neighborhood Change.* (Special Research Report to the Commission on Race and Housing and the Philadelphia Redevelopment Authority, prepared in the Institute for Urban Studies, University of Pennsylvania. Berkeley and Los Angeles: University of California Press, 1960.)

than the present occupants. Often they present a rather stately and graceful appearance. But even if structurally sound, these old houses were obsolescent in the white market before the minority group arrived, and many have reached the stage of heavy maintenance costs. The new occupants can make use of these old-style houses only by sharing them among several families or individuals, although they were never designed or equipped for multifamily occupancy. Structural alterations and additional facilities needed to create livable smaller units are sometimes provided, but often the space sharing is accomplished by makeshift arrangements, placing many families in quarters without proper cooking or sanitary facilities. One type of conversion, frequent in New York and some other large cities, is the rooming house where entire families will occupy a single room without private plumbing.

Lack of space is probably the deficiency of minority-group housing most harmful in its impact on family living. Adequate space is generally recognized as an indispensable requisite of good housing, whether the buildings be new or old, well or poorly equipped. A good family life is hardly possible unless there is space for carrying on and separating different activities, and for individual privacy. To maintain cleanliness and order is extremely difficult in cramped quarters used by too many people for too many purposes. The constant association of household members, unrelieved by opportunity for privacy, is apt to generate more tension than affection. There is evidence that crowding may be damaging to mental health and to the personality formation of children.[11] Persons with concern for family life, when they are in the market for a house, try to pay particular attention to factors of design, facilities, and location which promote happy family relations.[12] But most Negro or

[11] American Public Health Association, Committee on the Hygiene of Housing, *Basic Principles of Healthful Housing* (New York: 1939, reprinted, 1954), p. 16; F. Stuart Chapin, "The Psychology of Housing," (*Social Forces*, Vol. 30, Oct., 1951), quoting J. S. Plant, psychiatrist, and other authorities; Chapin, "Some Housing Factors Related to Mental Hygiene," *American Journal of Public Health*, Vol. 41, July, 1951).

[12] Glenn H. Beyer, Thomas W. Mackesey, and James E. Montgomery, *Houses Are for People: A Study of Home Buyer Motivations* (Research Publication No. 3, Housing Research Center, Cornell University, 1955). See also Svend Riemer, *American Journal of Sociology*, XLVI (May, 1941), 865-872, and *American Sociological Review*, 8(3):272-278 (June, 1943) and 12(2):155-159 (April, 1947).

Puerto Rican families have little opportunity for these choices.

Considerable family disorganization has long been characteristic of the lower socioeconomic class of Negroes, a legacy of slavery and the frequent inability of Negro men to discharge the economic responsibilities of husband and father. A larger proportion of Negro youth, consequently, grows up deprived of the profoundly important training and personality-forming influences which only a functioning family can supply.

The housing conditions of the majority of Negroes have been an additional heavy handicap to the development of stable families. The crowded, deficient, disordered dwelling can scarcely be a home in the warm, emotional meaning of the term. As E. Franklin Frazier remarks:

> Even those Negro families which are disposed to gather for meals are very often denied this opportunity because of the absence of space or facilities. . . . For a large proportion of Negro families in the city, the house is not a home but a place to cook and eat as individuals and sleep at night. When the weather permits it is generally a place from which one escapes. This is true of adults as well as children. This fact probably explains why so many Negroes congregate on the streets of Negro neighborhoods. So far as the children are concerned, the house becomes a veritable prison for them.[13]

Compulsory segregation is a powerful stimulant to racial prejudice. In the first place, to concentrate the members of a racial group increases their visibility and causes their distinctive characteristics to stand out more prominently.[14] Persons of Irish or of Italian descent, for example, although they possess certain group characteristics, are seldom recognizable in the ordinary public mingling of people. But if one goes into an Irish or Italian neighborhood, he becomes immediately conscious of a distinct group. It is the same with nonwhites. An occasional dark face in the crowd will be hardly noticed, but a large number of different appearing people, all in one place, has an immediate impact. It is obvious that the tendency to think of Negroes (or Jews, or others) as all alike,

[13] E. Franklin Frazier, *The Negro in the United States*, rev. ed. (New York: Macmillan, 1957), pp. 635-636.

[14] Morton Deutsch and Mary Evans Collins, *Interracial Housing: A Psychological Evaluation of a Social Experiment* (Minneapolis: University of Minnesota Press, 1951), p. 141.

disregarding individual differences (prejudice), must be enormously strengthened by segregation.

Imposed segregation connotes not merely difference but inferiority of the segregated group. When individuals or groups are excluded from a neighborhood, the inescapable implication is that they are considered not fit to live there. Since the character of neighborhoods carries corresponding implications about the character and worth of the residents, the minority groups are further stigmatized by the obvious inferiority of their residence areas. Compulsory segregation is, therefore, an unceasing public announcement of the separateness and inferior status of the minority groups. In his famous dissent from the separate-but-equal decision of *Plessy* v. *Ferguson,* Justice Harlan asked:

> What can more certainly arouse race hate, what more certainly create and perpetuate a feeling of distrust between these races, than state enactments which, in fact, proceed on the ground that colored citizens are so inferior and degraded that they cannot be allowed to sit in public coaches occupied by white citizens? . . . The thin disguise of "equal" accommodations . . . will not mislead anyone, nor atone for the wrong this day done.[15]

Segregation minimizes personal contacts which would lead members of majority and minority groups to perceive each other as individuals. Most contacts between whites and Negroes, for example, are formal or casual and marked by a wide status difference between the parties, as in employer-employee relations. Rarely do whites have opportunity to know Negroes as individual personalities or to share experiences with them, but they see them only in the mass, not as persons but as Negroes.[16] Most whites acquire their attitudes toward minority groups not from actual contacts with members of these groups but from contact with prevailing attitudes toward them.[17] And these received attitudes tend to be self-perpetuating, since whites have few experiences which might challenge them.

Lack of communication across racial lines leads to misunder-

---

[15] *Plessy* v. *Ferguson,* 163 U. S. 537 (1896).

[16] Deutsch and Collins, *Interracial Housing . . . ,* pp. 5, 142.

[17] Daniel M. Wilner, Rosabelle Price Walkley, and Stuart W. Cook, *Human Relations in Interracial Housing: A Study of the Contact Hypothesis* (Minneapolis: University of Minnesota Press, 1955), p. 5 and authorities cited.

standing and mistrust between the racial groups. A revealing instance is described in a report from Fisk University. A Negro property owner applied to the Nashville zoning board for a waiver to construct a hotel in a racially mixed residential area. Two groups of homeowners, one white and one Negro, appeared before the board. The spokesman for the white group bitterly attacked the Negro group, presuming that it had come to support the waiver request of the Negro property owner. When the spokesman for the Negro group also opposed the waiver, the whites stared in amazement. After the hearing, they surrounded the Negroes as though the latter were men from Mars. In the absence of communication, the whites had no conception of Negroes as homeowners like themselves.[18]

Under segregation, competition among individuals tends to be transformed into conflict between groups. Minority homeseekers appearing outside the segregated areas are generally regarded not as people looking for homes, who may be good, bad, or indifferent, but as invaders, to be repelled if possible or escaped if need be. The terms commonly used to describe the replacement of majority by minority group—threat, infiltration, invasion, panic, flight, and the like—are indicative of the conflict inherent in the situation.

By inhibiting the participation of the minority groups in the activities of the community, residential segregation limits their experience and their opportunities, as well as their incentives, to learn. Because of past deprivation, most Negroes, Puerto Ricans, and Mexican-Americans are at present poorly prepared to compete on equal terms with the white majority. In education and occupational skills they lag far behind the general standard. They are retarded in knowledge of the values, standards, and accepted ways of behaving characteristic of the dominant group. In these respects they resemble many immigrant groups of the past. The immigrants or their children climbed the socioeconomic ladder as they shed their foreign ways and adopted the dominant American values and behavior. If the present minority groups are to achieve equality with the rest of the population, they, too, must draw abreast of their fellow Americans in preparation for work and general cultural development.

To do this is essentially a learning process. The importance of

[18] Masuoka Jitsuichi and Preston Valien, "Social Consequences of Racial Residential Segregation," (Dept. of Social Sciences, Fisk University).

education needs no emphasis. It has always been, in the United States, a major avenue of social and economic advancement. In the modern world of technology and paper work, a good basic education plus specialized training are prerequisite to a constantly widening range of occupations and opportunities. Formal schooling, however, is only part of education in the broad sense of preparation for life. In the total education of a person, the family plays a vital role, and another great part comes from associations and experiences in the community.

The young person growing up in the isolation of a segregated community has few contacts and few experiences that would teach him the ways of the larger world. He is not wholly isolated, of course, and may readily learn to desire the common goals of money, good cars, good clothes, and the like, but he is less apt to learn the ways of pursuing these goals and the whole complex of values surrounding them. If he attends a segregated school, he will miss the stimulus and broadening influence of association with others of different backgrounds. The school itself is unable to perform its educational function fully when all or most of the students come from a depressed minority group. It is almost a truism among educators that effective schooling requires the coöperation of school, family, and community. When the community is a minority group lacking traditions of education and many of the families are weak and disorganized, the school can scarcely achieve a high standard. The students, coming from similar backgrounds of deprivation, cannot learn from each other, but can only reinforce each other in common ignorance. Many students fail to develop appreciation of the value of education and drop out of school. It has been calculated that if the education of Negro males were brought up to the level of white males, the number of Negro college graduates each year would be more than tripled and the number of high school graduates each year would be nearly tripled as compared with performance in 1950.[19]

In being set apart and treated as inferior, minority children may themselves develop feelings of inferiority and hopelessness.[20] The

[19] Eli Ginzberg, *The Negro Potential* (New York: Columbia University Press, 1956), p. 52.

[20] Esther Milner, "Some Hypotheses Concerning the Influence of Segregation on Negro Personality Development," *Psychiatry*, Vol. 16 (1953), 291-297.

Supreme Court saw this as one of the evils of compulsory school segregation. Speaking for a unanimous Court, Chief Justice Warren said: "To separate them [Negro pupils] from others of similar age and qualification solely because of their race generates a feeling of inferiority as to their status in the community that may affect their hearts and minds in a way unlikely ever to be undone."[21]

Frazier observes that in the segregated community inferior standards of excellence are set up.[22] Lacking the stimulus of competition in the larger world, many Negro youths fail to develop aspirations or incentives to achievement. All of this, together with the objective data of education and occupations, reveal the dimensions of the cultural lag affecting Negroes and some other groups. The gap is not likely to close rapidly until Negroes are brought into more frequent contact with the white population in learning situations.

To the Negro and Oriental middle classes, segregation is an immediate and direct blockage of opportunity. These sections of the minority populations have largely overcome the cultural handicaps characteristic of their ethnic groups; they share the behavior and values of the white middle class, but the expected rewards are in great part withheld.

Deprivation of housing opportunity is probably felt more keenly by the advanced members of minority groups than by the lower classes. The middle class, including the minority middle class, seeks not just housing but neighborhoods. For families at this level, good housing means, in addition to an adequate dwelling unit, those qualities of quiet, order, cleanliness, good facilities, and social prestige usually associated with a desirable neighborhood. Hence, for a middle-class family to be refused entry to a neighborhood of its choice is a serious deprivation not compensated for by the availability of housing elsewhere. Moreover, at higher levels of income and cost, housing requirements become increasingly individualized. The low-income homeseeker must perforce be content with little; he is fortunate to obtain a "minimum adequate" dwell-

[21] *Brown* v. *Board of Education of Topeka,* 347 U. S. 483 (1954).

[22] E. Franklin Frazier, *Negro Youth at the Crossways: Their Personality Development in the Middle States* (Washington, D.C.: American Council on Education, 1914), p. 290. See also Ginzberg, *The Negro Potential,* p. 115.

ing. But the family who can afford a higher-priced home and whose housing values are well developed typically brings a particular set of preferences and requirements into the market. It may want a specific location, a certain style of architecture, a certain amount of space, or a particular complement of facilities. It may place a high or low value on prestige factors. Probably not many families achieve their dream house completely. Minority families have less chance of doing so than others, and they must make more compromises because the search must be conducted in a limited part of the housing market.

The social isolation which segregation entails has direct, limiting impact on the minority middle class. In business and the professions, opportunities depend closely upon associations and participation in community groups. The person who wishes to rise in business or in a profession must know the "right" people, take part in the organized life of his business group, and live in a suitable neighborhood. This behavior is or would be appropriate to the minority middle classes. Their natural links are with others of similar business and professional interests much more than with the racial groups into which they were born. But segregation cuts them off from otherwise normal associations and in so doing obstructs the customary channels of advancement.

Enforced segregation has damaging consequences not only for the segregated groups but for the general community as well. One broad result, already touched upon, is the stimulation of racial prejudice and antagonism. In a society composed of diverse racial, ethnic, and religious groups there is an undoubted public interest in maintaining harmonious relations among the various groups. Segregation is sometimes defended on the grounds of keeping peace between potentially antagonistic groups, but it is far more likely to have the opposite effect and hence is contrary to the public interest in interracial tolerance.

Another consequence for the community is the hampering of slum clearance and housing improvement programs. To relocate and rehouse populations of slum dwellers is a difficult problem at best. The difficulties are vastly increased when those who must be relocated consist in great part, as they do, of groups whose housing alternatives are limited by racial discrimination. Access to a sufficient quantity and variety of housing resources is a basic condition of effective relocation. But in fact, for the large majority of dis-placed families, urban renewal authorities are obliged to limit their relocation efforts to that part of the housing market which is open to minority groups. Also, unless the supply of housing available to minorities in any community increases more rapidly than popula-tion, relocation will tend to increase congestion in areas that already have too many people. When this occurs, and there is evi-dence that it has happened, the reduction of slums in urban re-newal project areas may be offset by the worsening of housing conditions in relocation areas. The ability of urban renewal pro-grams, therefore, to achieve their purpose of housing and commu-nity betterment is dependent upon an adequate supply of housing available to minority groups.

The largest cost of segregation to the nation is the waste of human resources which results from the retarded development of the segregated groups. The interest of the community and nation in the development of their individual members is recognized by all. It is expressed in many ways, above all in the large expenditures of public funds for education at all levels and in laws making school attendance compulsory. Any condition which prevents individuals from achieving the potential of which they are capable harms the national interest. Because racial discrimination and segregation hamper the development of many millions of people, the nation is militarily weaker, economically less productive, and culturally poorer than it would be were the disadvantaged minority groups contributing equally with the rest of the population.

Still another part of the cost of racial discrimination to the nation is the damage that it does to the prestige of the United States abroad. It tends to cast doubt on the sincerity of American advocacy of freedom and equality and so impairs the moral leader-ship of the United States in the world. Among Asian and African peoples, almost all of whom are nonwhite, racialism is associated with the hated colonial system. It is difficult to persuade these new nations that the United States really considers them as equals when people of like racial stock are subordinated within the United States.

The racial problem in the United States is publicized throughout the world. It places in the hands of the country's enemies an easy and constantly exploited propaganda weapon. Charges of mistreatment of racial groups in the United States, however distorted, are difficult to counter because of the element of fact which they contain.

But although racial discrimination is an international liability, the fact that the United States is a racially mixed nation is potentially an important asset in its relations with Asia and Africa. The value of this asset can be realized when white and nonwhite citizens stand on an equal footing as members of the American community.

Conditions and Prospects for Housing Desegregation

It is appropriate to conclude the present study with a brief summary of research findings that bear directly on methods for bringing about changes in the race relations of housing in the direction of equal opportunity. Knowledge of this kind is, of course, especially valuable to the numerous organizations dedicated to racial equality, and to legislative bodies and public officials responsible for public policy in the area. The findings summarized below are by no means the original contribution of the present study, although this research has affirmed them in various particulars. They are the product of many sociological and psychological investigations, not limited to the specific problems of housing or race relations. Some of the most significant contributions have come from basic research in human behavior without reference to practical application. Sources have been cited throughout the present work and will not be repeated here.

1. Action aiming to reduce discrimination is more promising if focused directly on controlling discriminatory conduct, rather than attempting to change attitudes of prejudice. Attitudes are important in discrimination, but they are not the cause either of discriminatory or nondiscriminatory behavior.

2. The most effective means of changing behavior as well as attitudes is through introducing a change in the situation in which decisions are made and attitudes formed. A change in the basis of expectations concerning the outcome of a racial situation (*e.g.,* in an interracial neighborhood, the emergence of dynamic leadership or the inauguration of an urban-renewal program) will have more effect on behavior than any amount of exhortation or dissemination of information. It is doubtful whether attitudes can be signifi-

cantly modified merely by educational means without changes in the surrounding conditions.

Another highly important type of situational change is the creation of counter pressures against the social forces which impel people to discriminatory action. In situations that are full of pressures to discriminate (within the real estate business, for example, or in an all-white suburban neighborhood) even the most tolerant individuals can scarcely follow their inclinations unless supported by counter pressures. It is unrealistic to treat discriminatory behavior as ignorant or irrational, requiring only a proper assessment of the facts for its correction. In many circumstances, discriminatory conduct may be entirely rational—certainly it is often the course of least resistance for an individual.

3. A social process can be changed by influencing the actions of those who make the critical decisions which the process calls for. In respect to housing segregation, this means affecting the decisions of those who immediately control access to housing—the builders, mortgage lenders, real estate brokers, and agencies of government.

4. Law can be an effective counterforce against pressures for segregation, especially when efficiently administered and supported by articulate citizen groups. An important function of laws for racial equality is not merely to compel or prohibit, but to give freedom of action to persons who would prefer not to discriminate. This function is particularly important in relation to individual real estate brokers and builders who are constrained to discriminate by the pressures of their business groups and some clients.

By changing the situation, law can influence the factors that shape attitudes and hence, indirectly, the attitudes themselves.

5. To influence private and public decision-makers, as well as legislation, effective organization and mobilization of power by citizens concerned with the problem are indispensable.

6. The majority of people, according to the evidence of attitude surveys, do not have firmly fixed opinions on racial equality. Hence, they may be influenced in their behavior and attitudes by those more concerned with the character of race relations, on one side or the other. This finding further underlines the critical importance of organization and leadership.

7. Association between members of majority and minority

groups in the neighborhood or housing project leads such individuals to have better opinions of each other if contacts are on an equal-status basis, and if the participants are of similar social-class background. Mingling of lower-class minority individuals with middle-class whites is very likely to increase the racial antagonism of the whites.

8. Competition among racial groups (*e.g.,* for dominance of housing areas) tends to increase racial hostility.

9. The most effective means of promoting interracial understanding and acceptance is by creating situations wherein members of different racial groups work together in solving common problems.

10. Efforts to achieve racial equality of access to housing will encounter less resistance and have greater chance of success if they are not confused with proposals to eliminate socioeconomic-group segregation. Some advocates of racial desegregation seem to think it desirable to mingle people not only of different races but of differing economic and cultural levels in the same neighborhood, but this is an unfortunate confusion. It is one thing to ask people of the white middle class to share their neighborhoods with non-whites of similar income, educational level, and social outlook. It is quite a different thing to ask them to associate as neighbors with people of lower income, education, and cultural standards. Socioeconomic segregation is in no way inconsistent with racial integration. Indeed, one of the benefits anticipated from reducing racial discrimination is an enhanced freedom of the minority groups to rise in the class structure of American society.

Gandhi In Greensboro

EDWARD P. MORGAN

SOMEBODY SUGGESTED OVER a drink in Washington recently that what Americans need today is not a good five-cent cigar but a cause. Most of us have, if not as much as we want, at least more than we require of worldly goods. But our comforts are making us uncomfortable. We are squirming and groping for something to live for beyond frozen television tray dinners and motel swimming pools.

Disarmament is a good cause. But it is difficult and in some respects undesirable to become personally engaged with a megaton bomb. The Community Chest is a worthy enterprise. We pay lip and passing pocketbook service to it and then deduct the payment from our income tax. Justice for Tibet! Self-determination for the eastern European satellites! These are goals with which we readily identify ourselves in principle and then lose interest, defaulting, eventually, our support. What about a cause closer to home? The cause of equal rights and human decency, the dignity of that inconsistent, inefficient, irreplaceable piece of machinery, the human individual, including you and me.

Why is it that we cringe a little at these terms, equal rights, decency, and dignity of the individual? Perhaps it is because we have been dignifying the wrong things lately. In a public discussion of morals the other day, Carl Sandburg said we now have an

Currently Senior Correspondent of National Educational Television's new Public Broadcasting Laboratory, Edward P. Morgan was for many years an ABC commentator, whose broadcasts were given a Hillman Prize Award in 1960. He gave this address as the principal speaker at the Prize Award luncheon that year.

Eleventh Commandment: "Do whatever you want to do to be comfortable." So, blessed are the status seekers for theirs is the heavenly kingdom of payola and the fixed quiz show. In this atmosphere of the kickback and influence-peddling, we have forgotten a central truth: people are more important than anything. The fabric of our social system was woven to protect the individual with equal justice, to clothe him with freedom and self-respect. But somehow we have threaded into the garment the fat bulky strands of materialism, the tight dark thongs of selfishness, fear, prejudice, and outright hatred. The garment has been twisted into a degrading shape.

Our cause, I suggest, is to make it fit properly, so that it will once more ennoble the society that wears it. Do we have an inspiration for a pattern? Has anybody been ennobling the human species lately? Down in Greensboro, North Carolina, last February 1, a handsome eighteen-year-old freshman at the state Agriculture and Technical College, named Ezell Blair, Jr., led three schoolmates to the lunch counter in a Woolworth's store and asked for service. Thus, inauspiciously began an auspicious movement, the Negro sit-ins against segregation that have spread to nearly every state in the South. More than 55,000 Negro students and a thousand white undergraduates from 150 college campuses have become directly involved in these demonstrations, and there have been repercussions by sympathetic picketing in some one hundred cities outside the South.

Ezell Blair and his mates didn't know quite what they were starting, but they knew where they got their inspiration. They got it from Mohandas K. Gandhi. "I've never forgotten a television show I saw last year called the Pictorial Story of India," young Blair told a *New York Times* reporter. He was impressed with how the strength of Gandhi's passive resistance seemed to grow each time he was thrown into jail. Blair and his fellows like to think of themselves as part of a movement of "passive insistence."

Many of these current young followers of the Mahatma have already been put in jail. In Petersburg, Virginia, it was for seeking equal access to the public library. Hardly a day goes by in the town where I live, Washington, D.C., especially now that the election campaign season is open, without some aspiring statesman or doom-cracking pundit sounding a warning about the deterioration of the democratic system and the need to do something about it. But while we talk, a Negro teen-ager, not old enough to vote, even if his election board would let him, is doing something about it. With quiet courage, he is daily braving tear gas, fire hoses, truncheons, prison, fines, taunts, spittle, threats, and the gravest bodily harm, because he believes in something as other American revolutionaries did before him.

There is the key. This is a revolution. Here is a new generation of Negroes, well-dressed, college-educated, restrained, determined, asserting its constitutional rights to a freedom promised a century ago but never really fulfilled, North or South. We follow the news from Algiers, from Leopoldville, Capetown, and Johannesburg with excited concern over the latest chapters in the unending history of men's struggle for independence. But to the convulsive developments in a liberation movement rising right under our noses in Miami, Atlanta, Charlotte, Orangeburg, and Baton Rouge, we react with about as much attention as we ordinarily give the National Safety Council's figures on Memorial Day traffic deaths.

And what an astonishing depth there is to the disciplined dedication of these passive insisters.

Acknowledging the teachings of Christ and Gandhi, and looking to the Reverend Martin Luther King for counsel, says one recent newspaper dispatch, "college students in Nashville, Tennessee, drew up the code below to govern student conduct in 'sit-in' protests at lunch counters discriminating against Negroes:

'Don't strike back or curse if abused.
'Don't laugh out.
'Don't hold conversations with floor workers.
'Don't block entrances to the stores and the aisles.
'Show yourself courteous and friendly at all times.
'Sit straight and always face the counter.
'Remember love and non-violence.
'May God Bless each of you.' "

In Chapel Hill, where the unsegregated University of North Carolina is located, the Negro demonstrators made the following declaration of purpose:

"We do not picket just because we want to eat. We can eat at home. . . .

"We do not picket to express our anger or resentment at anyone.

"We do not picket to humiliate anyone or put anyone out of business.

"We do picket to help the businessman make changes that will bring us closer to the Christian and democratic practices. . . .

"We do picket to protest the lack of dignity and respect shown us as human beings."

All twenty-seven ministers of Chapel Hill signed a statement endorsing that declaration.

"We deplore the fact that any group of our citizens is placed in the position of having to ask to be treated with dignity and respect," the statement said in part. "We confess our own responsibility for the existence and toleration of such attitudes and practices as make this request necessary. . . . We commend the leaders of these . . . protests for their dedication to the principles of non-violence. We believe that the right to protest in this fashion is a right generally recognized in our society. . . ."

There is something far more dramatically moving, more deeply convincing to the quiet dignity of this passive offensive than the pathetic belligerence raised against it. This latter answer reflects an anachronistic leadership and the frustrated flatfoot mentality of a country cop, a mentality which the British, with a little more polish perhaps, applied against Gandhi to their everlasting sorrow. And supporting the jungle law of fear and hate is the rabble, The Mob.

One of the voices of the Old Dominion, the Richmond *News-Leader,* sorrowfully described a battle scene of this new conflict recently in these words:

Many a Virginian must have felt a tinge of wry regret at the state of things as they are, in reading of Saturday's "sitdowns" by Negro students in Richmond stores. Here were the colored students, in coats, white shirts, ties, and one of them was reading Goethe and one was taking notes from a biology text. And here, on the sidewalk outside, was a gang of white boys come to heckle, a ragtail rabble, slack-jawed, black-jacketed, grinning fit to kill, and some of them, God save the mark, were waving the proud and honored flag of the Southern states in the last war fought by gentlemen.

Let us not make the disastrous mistake of enshrining the Negroes as a population of paragons. There is evil, lethal delinquency, and tragic corruption of leadership among them too, and you only have to step up the street to Harlem to find evidences of both. But on balance, Negro demagogues do not begin to match the number or viciousness of the bullies of white supremacy and if erring Negro teen-agers have often been brutally violent in their rebelliousness, the duck-tailed delinquents of the white rock-'n-roll set have no prouder record. Indeed with the legacy of repression and prejudice which our Negro citizens have inherited, it is a monumental wonder that they have been able to hold on to their patience and restraint so well.

Ironically, the steadiness of their deportment has inspired some emotional inclination to endow them with certain superhuman faculties, which, when you stop to think about it, involves a sin of racial prejudice in reverse. I have been guilty of this. Shortly after the explosion at Little Rock in the autumn of 1957 I found myself talking to Dr. Alfonso Elder, the Columbia-educated president of North Carolina College, a Negro school in Durham. I told him I had been deeply moved by the high courage of those nine Negro students as they went out utterly alone to run the gamut of hostility and danger and enter Central High. "I am not sure," I said, "that anybody else could have done that."

"You are wrong," Dr. Elder replied rather sharply. "Courage is a human trait, not restricted to any race. If the tables had been turned, white children would have behaved the same."

There, in a nutshell, was the whole lesson. The Negro is simply fighting for full and recognized membership in the human race, with all its inherent strengths and weaknesses. In struggling to break the bonds of his second-class citizenship he is demanding his constitutional rights, nothing more. Let this testimony stand against the absurd, fear-mongering charge of Police Commissioner Eugene "Bull" Connor of Birmingham, Alabama, that the Negro is trying to establish "black supremacy." Let Commissioner Connor look only to the record of the bus boycott in his sister city of Montgomery, to learn the essence of what the racial issue is all about. It is not a sinister conspiracy of black hordes to impress a pagan supremacy on genteel citizens of lighter skin. It is not a swaggering ultimatum, bloodshot with passion as so many seem to fear, that a Negro shall marry your sister. It is the insistence of some of the gentlest souls God ever fashioned to choose their own seat on a municipal bus, to travel afoot or on horseback, in a Cadillac convertible, or to stay at home. In reaching out for these simple rights for himself, the Negro is doing something else for everybody. He is refreshing the roots of the tree of freedom. He is, as Thurgood Marshall so truly said to a thousand students at Yale last month, fighting our battles for us.

There is the cause which I recommend. It is not a narrow cause. It is a cause that has been coursing like a great river through the terrain of history, carrying with it since the beginning of man his fragile but persistent hopes for true freedom. We detach ourselves from this main stream at our own peril. And don't think that the world at large doesn't have the impression that we have already pulled away from it. At a time when the Soviet Union was announcing to the world at large that it would open in Moscow during this year a new university affording free education to thousands of African, Asian, and Latin American students, that great Jeffersonian Democrat, Mississippi's James Eastland, was on the floor of the United States Senate denouncing civil rights decisions of the Supreme Court as "crap." At a time when South African Negroes were being shot down outside Johannesburg and Capetown, American Negroes were being deprived of their rights, intimidated, even terrorized in this country.

We are carelessly inclined to think of the struggle for fulfillment of civil rights as basically a racial problem. It is not. It is a human problem in which every citizen has a stake. As long as a bull-voiced police commissioner in Birmingham can be a law unto himself, conditions are not safe for democracy in Boise or the Back Bay of Boston. No American would be quicker to embrace this truth, none would be more tireless or brave in pushing the cause with which we all must identify ourselves—the rights and dignity of man—than the man we have really come here to honor in memory today, Sidney Hillman.

The Changing Heart
of the South

LILLIAN SMITH

I REALIZE THAT the only enemies we Southerners have are ourselves. The Yankees are not against us, the United Nations are not against us; even Russia is not our Number One enemy. But anxiety is, and the guilt that clings to anxiety, and ignorance, and greed—and above all else, a curious moral blindness that breeds a sick complacency.

It is so true, as I have been saying for a long time, that segregation as belief and practice harms everybody. The white child is injured just as much by the segregated pattern of life as is the Negro child. When one puts up walls outside one's culture, one puts up walls inside one's own mind and heart. And these fragmented children grow into adults, and these adults acquire power. There are evils, a few, that are not contagious; but segregation is a contagious evil and the sickness is felt by everyone, everywhere on earth. When walls fall outside, they must fall inside.

This is why I was so deeply moved by the group of white women I wrote about in the *Ordeal of Southern Women*. I went to New Orleans planning to write quite a bit about those screaming witches, the furies in hair curlers, who gathered in front of the schools frightening the children away. But after I had talked to a

In 1962 the late Lillian Smith, distinguished author, received a Hillman Prize Award for her article in *Redbook Magazine,* "The Ordeal of Southern Women." These excerpts are from the address she prepared for delivery at the Hillman Prize Award luncheon.

few people, I knew that story was only headline stuff and not of real importance. For those benighted women belong to the past. I wanted to catch a glimpse of the future.

The real story, it seemed to me, was the story of the intelligent, warmhearted, sensitive women who were meeting this ordeal of change creatively. I talked, one morning, with thirty such women. The beliefs and attitudes of these women ranged from those opposed to segregation who knew why they were opposed, to those who wanted things to be decent and couldn't bear the bad publicity New Orleans was getting. And there were others who wanted only to do what was right and were not interested in racial ideology.

One young woman from Charleston spoke first. "I have always felt the burden of segregation," she said. "It has weighed on my conscience as a sin. I feel I must accept guilt for what is now happening in our South, although I have had no part in these evil events."

Another answered her heatedly, "Sin? I do not understand you. What does segregation have to do with sin? I see nothing wrong in segregation. I have never harmed a Negro in my life."

"Oh but you have," another said quietly. "You have harmed yourself, too, and your own children by accepting this way of life. It is wrong to humiliate a child; it is also wrong to breed arrogance in a child. We are responsible for what the Ku Klux Klan and Citizens Council do: because we permit it by our silence."

Another woman spoke. "I believe in segregation. I cannot imagine anything else. But I am not willing for any Negro to be hurt. Our church invited a group of Negro women to a meeting. Nobody sat by them; I could not bear it; so I went over and sat with them. But this has nothing to do with my belief in segregation."

Another woman said, "I was a segregationist until last week. I called myself a Christian, too. I was proud of being both. Then I saw those screaming women on television; and I thought, if segregation does this to people, then I am against it. If this is what life in the South has come to, then I'm through with the system. Since then," she said smiling, "I have been an integrationist although I haven't the faintest notion what one is."

Someone mentioned economics. "Ah, but it goes much deeper than that. It has far more to do with your image of yourself—what you think of when you think the words, 'human being.' "

For three hours the talk continued; no one seemed to want to leave. There was the frankest outpouring of anxieties, of conflicts with conscience, of concern for their own children and Negro children. Again and again, the women spoke of needing to understand themselves on deeper levels. "I am not sure I even know what a human being is, I've thought so much in terms of white, white, white," one said.

Another said, "I see it as a spiritual ordeal for us who are white. If we fail to meet this challenge, this plain moral question, *What is right?* then we shall be worse than we were before. I know it is terrible on every level for Negroes, but for whites our very souls are involved."

Then they told me of some of the things they were doing to ameliorate the situation. Highly imaginative acts and some that required real courage. "And of course our telephones ring all night long, with anonymous voices threatening us or our children."

"But the politicians," I said, "How can you outwit them? For they have the power now."

They agreed this was the tough battle ahead of them. But we blame too much on the politicians, several said. If we wouldn't put up with it, they wouldn't do it.

I left New Orleans and wrote my piece for *Redbook*. I could not tell the whole story, it would have required too much space. In it was not much of the terror, although it is there; in it was not much of the vicious greed of the politicians and the brutality they sometimes instigated and always protected. What I was moved by, and deeply excited about, was the fact that these women, some of whom are the social and civic leaders of New Orleans, were at last thinking, at last feeling deeply about all children and their future. This was the real story; for out of their agony of mind and heart will come the new South, the new way of life, and the new values.

And may I add this: all of New York, even Park Avenue and the East Side islands of luxury and security, will be a better place for children when Harlem has been cleaned up. When Harlem is turned into a good place for children to grow, then New York will suddenly flower and become the city it should be, the city we all love and admire and yet which we know, in our hearts, is not a children's city.

As a southern woman, these matters have been of deep concern to me.

As a writer, my special point of view, my personal way of looking at life, has been determined by my experiences with segregation—which is far more than a social or economic or political problem. Segregation is a symptom of a dehumanized way of life that springs from our loss of vision of the human being and his future.

Segregration is a symbol of all we lack, a symbol of hollow men, of emptiness; a symbol of brokenness. We cannot limit this word to race relations. Our entire lives are fragmented; we are split off from the source of wholeness; we are not deeply related even to ourselves.

And yet, although we need and must strive for wholeness, it is the nature of man to be broken. In a philosophical sense, segregation is of the essence of the human condition. For we are all segregated from ultimate knowledge; and birth and death are two forms of segregation which every one of us will experience. These are the Great Separations we cannot alter. And it is out of them, out of the search for meaning, the longing to understand birth and death, the hunger to know the ultimate, that all the great human questions have come: Who am I? Why was I born? Why am I your child? What is eternity? Who is God? Why is death?

Ancient and unanswerable questions; and yet to stay human we must never stop asking them. What is dangerous, what becomes blasphemy is when we dare to give small answers to these great questions. The man who asks "Who am I?" and answers "I am a white man," has lost himself as a human being. This is his fall.

But man has a strange and wonderful way of transcending his weakness. He knows he cannot answer these great questions with surety, so he learns to ask smaller ones, as in science, that he can find answers for. He cannot rid himself of his profound loneliness but out of it come his art and poetry and music; out of this inability to answer what must always be asked, and out of his loneliness has come a new quality of human relations and human awareness. The chasms between man and himself and his world cannot be filled up but they can be bridged; we cannot merge ourselves with others but we can relate.

It is with these matters that I am concerned; the specific, the little, the concrete and the deeper, more symbolic forms.

While I do not want to be too cheerful, I think there is an awakening of the heart in the South; people are searching themselves, separating themselves from that part of the past which cannot be carried into the future. I feel this happening. It is a small thing, now, but it is a good sign, a good omen.

Black and White: The Ghetto Inside

KENNETH B. CLARK

I remember coming home from school, you can guess how young I must have been, and my mother asked me if my teacher was colored or white, and I said she was a little bit colored and a little bit white. . . . And as a matter of fact I was right. That's part of the dilemma of being an American Negro; that one is a little bit colored and a little bit white, and not only in physical terms but in the head and in the heart, and there are days— this is one of them—when you wonder what your role is in this country and what your future is in it; how precisely you are going to reconcile it to your situation here and how you are going to communicate to the vast heedless, unthinking, cruel white majority, that you are here. And to be here means that you can't be anywhere else. I could, my own person, leave this country and go to Africa, I could go to China, I could go to Russia, I could go to Cuba, but I'm an American and that is a *fact*.

—James Baldwin, *The Negro Protest*[1]

THE GREAT TRAGEDY—but possibly the great salvation, too—of the Negro and white in America is that neither one can be free of the other. Each Negro is a little bit white, and every white is a little bit Negro, in the sense that neither is totally alien from the other. Both are caught in a common human predicament. Each needs the other, the white to be free of his guilt, the Negro to be free of his fear; guilt and fear are both self-destructive.

Dr. Kenneth B. Clark, the eminent psychologist and educator, was given a 1965 Hillman Prize Award for *Dark Ghetto: Dilemmas of Social Power* (New York: Harper & Row, Publishers, 1965). This is the concluding chapter of that work.

[1] Kenneth B. Clark (ed.), Boston, Beacon Press, 1963.

72

Yet the psychological distance, the hostility, the wariness, and the ignorance that keep the Negro and the white apart are overwhelming. As the civil rights movement gains in force and the two confront each other increasingly, they see that the courtesy they hid behind in the past was unreal. Beneath the façade lie deep feelings now being released in a torrent of words and responses. Though the expression of these feelings is proving painful to both Negro and white, there can be no healthy relationship between them without this present pain. The anger and bitterness of the Negro has opened many wounds, but his own wounds have been unhealed for what seems like forever. He now feels free—or rather, more free—to reveal the extent of his hurt. The great tragedy will be if the white does not see or listen, with his heart as well as his mind.

A psychologist on the staff of the National Institute of Mental Health, himself white, wrote a revealing account of the Negro protest movement in which he commented on the new relationship between Negroes and whites:

The awesome shame and guilt that might otherwise overwhelm millions of fair-minded and well-meaning whites in both North and South is held in check by ignorance of the shocking facts or assuaged by pernicious rationalizations. It is comforting, self-absolving, to believe that the Negro's innate shortcomings are responsible for his present condition, and hard to acknowledge that the circumstances we force him to live under may be the very cause of this condition.

Another fundamental that must be grasped is the magnitude of the present psychological gulf between whites and non-whites. The growing anger of the more vocal Negroes, fanned and fed by a growing impatience, comes as a surprise to whites who live comfortably and peacefully far removed from the major Negro centers. The Negro and *his* problems never impinge on their thinking, their world, their smooth running democracy. For them "sit-ins" and "stall-ins" and "freedom rides" are evidence of irresponsibility, of unreasonableness, of lawlessness, of radicalism that reinforce all the myths they have learned to believe. On the other hand, when such whites do come face to face with the Negro world they discover in themselves an entirely new response: fear. They sense the Negro's envy of the "privileged caste," they sense some of his bitterness. They see sometimes the flaring anger that injustice breeds. They realize for the first time how far most Negroes have been forced into a world apart, a world so unfamiliar to the average white that it could as well be in a foreign land. And in this alien world they discover a complement to the white man's rejection: the Negro's distrust. For the failure of the white man thus far to deal honestly and fairly with his non-white fellow citizens has bred a suspicion so deep that very few whites are ever trusted. And out of this recognition of distrust springs an unreasoned, and often unacknowledged fear.

The people who know this best of all perhaps are the young whites currently working in the Freedom Movement. Sometimes the ambivalence of their young Negro co-workers in the Mississippi COFO project last summer was hard to conceal ("If any heads get smashed down there this summer, I hope it'll be that blonde rich kid's, not mine"). At least in the beginning, some Negroes felt the whites had joined the dangerous venture "for kicks." The distrust is so pervasive that *Ebony* magazine recently reflected it in a feature article on the ten white men Negroes trust most. Not respect, not admire, but *trust*. The gulf that exists is wide and deep. Bridging it will not be easy.[2]

Although the plight of the Negro in the ghetto and the chance of his escape from his predicament depend on his own strength, they depend also upon the willingness of the white to accept that strength. Negroes alone cannot abolish the ghetto. It will never be ended as long as the white society believes that it needs it.

For generations Negroes and whites alike have been blinded by fantasies which have kept both races apart and added to frustration and impatience even as they seem to project their opposites. An important first step is to examine these fantasies as the false comfort and delusions they are.

The fantasy of *accommodation* or *acceptance,* which used to be the primary pretense of Negroes, still affects some, particularly certain successful Negroes who surround their lives with typical middle-class daydreams. Just as the white of threatened status may trace his lineage to the "Mayflower" and seek refuge in the Daughters or Sons of the American Revolution, so the Negro may boast that his family were freed Negroes earlier than others were, or that his parents "had money." Or, as one successful Negro professional, who lives in a beautiful home, is wont to say: "All Negroes need to do is prepare themselves, save money, invest properly, buy decent homes, and then there would be no more prejudice." A common fantasy is to deny one's own identification with the racial

---

[2] William F. Soskin, "Riots, Ghettos and the 'Negro Revolt,'" Staff paper, Office of Planning, National Institute of Mental Health, 1964.

dilemmas: "I have no racial problem; I get along with all whites."
So, too, a single Negro or a few Negroes on a prestige campus or in
a church or a profession may "fit in beautifully," indirectly reas-
suring the institution that it is satisfactorily color-blind. The truth
is that every Negro has a racial problem, repressed or otherwise,
and that no American social institution is truly color-blind—to be
color-blind in a society where race is relevant is not to be free but
insensitive. Negroes themselves may encourage this fantasy, re-
sponding to the safety of the oasis, not sure whether it is a mirage
and generally careful not to challenge the dream for fear of wak-
ing. But as long as whites take special pride in having "a Negro
friend" or boast of inviting Negroes to their parties, as long as it is
considered daring and "liberal" on campuses to have an interracial
affair, the dream is a dream.

The fantasy of *acceptance* is a form of another pretense, the
fantasy of *denial*. The Negro or white may seek to repress painful
racial problems or conflicts. The white may deny any knowledge
that Negroes are excluded from renting or buying homes in certain
neighborhoods or that Negroes are prohibited from registering and
voting in parts of the South or that the absence of Negroes in
certain executive and management jobs reflects anything other
than natural selection of the "best" applicants. Some middle-class
Negroes tend to share these pretenses with their "white friends,"
hoping to avoid conflict and discomfort. To believe that one is
a living example of the proposition that there is no racial problem
for the hard-working, successful, sophisticated person of either
race does bring some measure of satisfaction. Yet, to the extent
to which either the Negro or white believes this and behaves
accordingly, the psychological distance between Negro and white
is increased even if it may, on the surface, appear to be otherwise. No genuine friendship can be based on a lie, even a congenial
lie.

Acceptance and accommodation are no longer the most prevalent fantasies among Negroes. Today it has become fashionable,
instead, as the civil rights movement grows in fervor, to move from
appeasement to a stance of defiance, a new fantasy of *militancy*,
though many Negroes who are now in the forefront of militancy
were among the most accommodating yesterday, little interested in
the patient, determined progress of groups like the NAACP.

But random defiance, no more than meek accommodation, is

based on the facts of life. The pretense of the Muslims who call for a separate black state, and of the extremists who threaten to close down the public schools if immediate and total integration is not forthcoming, have in common a failure to face the truth. It is clear—or ought to be—that American society would not sustain a separate black nation. It is clear—or ought to be—that immediate and total integration of the schools is not possible in cities with large and growing Negro populations. It is clear that white middle-class parents will not endure "reverse busing," the transporting of their children into the heart of the ghetto to schools that Negroes themselves have said for years are inferior. For Negroes to justify any such demands on the grounds alone of militancy is to attempt to deal with a disturbing reality by wishful fantasy. Yet it has become fashionable to demand and to expect the unreal, and the fact that a particular strategy does not make sense is considered irrelevant to its virtue. Those Negroes who oppose extreme militancy run the risk that their commitment to justice will be called into question, that they will be derided as "Uncle Toms" who do "the bidding of the white man." If they try to point out that it would be more useful to consider strategies that will divide rather than unite the opposition, they are suspected of irresolution in their devotion to civil rights. This automatic separation into sheep and goats by those who have arrogated to themselves the right of such judgment reduces the range of realism available to both. Fewer alternatives of action are judged acceptable; there is less flexibility to adapt strategy to changes in circumstances and to take advantage of openings; there is less personal grasp on reality itself. Anyone who raises questions threatens this fantasy of *militancy*. But if there are fewer questions, there will inevitably be fewer answers.

The basic delusion of the American white, on the other hand, is the fantasy of *aristocracy*. The basic myth of racism is that white skin color brings with it superiority—that the white is more intelligent, more virtuous, more sexually controlled by the mere fact of being white. In the integration of schools, the white child is believed, automatically, to be ahead of the Negro child in performance and in potential. The movement of Negroes into a white community is considered to be a prelude to poorly kept lawns, raucous parties, lowered property values. When a white thinks of himself in relation to the Negro, he need not appraise his own strengths and weaknesses, but enjoy membership in a homogeneous and superior white group in which ethnic and class differences are erased. It is no accident that the whites most ready to accept the assumption of social superiority are generally those of the lower middle class, who are struggling to improve their own economic and social status.

The delusion of the "white liberal" is superiority of another kind—not of origin, or of status, but of the spirit. He takes pride in the fact that he is free from prejudice. The fantasy of *tolerance,* which a decade ago was, for the liberal conscience, adequate support, has been superseded by the fantasy of *purity.* The crowning insult which anyone can pay to an intelligent Northern white is to suggest that he might be motivated to some action, decision, or plan by racial considerations. He responds somewhat as follows: "We do not keep racial records. We do not even know the color of Mary or Jim. He is just like one of us." Northerners find it more difficult or more painful than Southerners to face their prejudices. For the liberal it is a matter of self-respect to be considered free of bias. Yet when brought to the test by the stark and seemingly extreme demands of Negroes, this confidence often gives way to a resentment and anger at the Negro, an anger accompanied by guilt: "These Negroes, whose friends we are, are now going too far; they are breaking the bounds of our tolerance." The white liberal, who thought he considered Negroes as "we," may now address them as "you people." If he is sensitive, he may be shaken to discover in himself new feelings of alienation and even hostility.

One is forced to ask the further question, disconcerting to anyone who teaches or writes, whether fantasy also afflicts those Negroes and whites who believe it is possible for race to be transcended, those who consider that what they think is actually relevant to power, those who have confidence that rational communication between whites and Negroes in America can affect the real decisions of society. It is the wish but, more than that, the belief of those who teach and write that intelligent, rational planning can and will determine the direction of events. Yet it is surely possible that this direction will be charted rather in response to emotion than to rational strategy.

The Negro thrust out of the ghetto has imposed upon white public officials and liberal whites in the North a struggle which in many respects presents a more complex level of racial turbulence than the conflict between Negroes and obvious segregationists. This struggle, in the final analysis, may be even more pivotal to the direction and rate of the civil rights movement in America than the solution of the South's own problems. The key to meaningful resolution is in the hands of that large majority of whites who conceive of themselves as liberal, moderate, and decent human beings. It is a cold, hard fact that the many flagrant forms of racial injustice North and South could not exist without their acquiescence.

On issues of social justice other than race—on the rights of labor, on civil and political liberties—an initially small and committed minority of whites worked incessantly to win over the uncommitted majority. Their role in abolishing child labor at the turn of the century is an example of the social effectiveness of a small group working in concert with the uncommitted majority. The difference between these crusades and race is that in race one's own status needs are at stake. No significant minority of white liberals can work in a totally committed manner for racial justice for long without coming in conflict with conscious or unconscious anxieties.

White liberals believe that if the right to vote, the right to an education, the right to a job, the right to a decent home, the right to ordinary courtesies, the right to protection of government are denied to anyone; they are protected for no one. But many liberals stop short, disturbed and apologetic, when the principle is appealed to in behalf of sexual equality and intermarriage. Guilt, insecurity, and anxieties are easily associated with the problems of race. It is not accidental that sex is the most powerful argument for maintaining the *status quo,* when all others fail. Among the most powerfully stated and unstated rationales for the maintenance of segregated schools is the insistence that Negro children are sexually precocious and will contaminate the otherwise "normal" white children. The implication of this argument along with the academic retardation theory is that Negroes are academically retarded, and white children are sexually retarded, and that it would, therefore, be catastrophic to mix them in integrated schools. Without regard to the validity of such contentions, it remains an overriding fact that the demands for equality before the law and the insistence that rights not be qualified by race cannot be curtailed or postponed *because* of the fear of whites that if Negroes are granted these rights, whites may find them sexually attractive. The problem for the white liberal is to choose his own sexual partners; curtailment of this important personal freedom— as important to his own freedom as to a Negro's—cannot be determined by restrictions of the civil rights of Negroes.

The liberal position, when applied to race, has been, for a multiple of reasons, somewhat tainted. In those areas of life where liberals are powerful—labor unions, schools, and politics—one is forced to say that the plight of the Negroes is not significantly better than it is in areas where liberals are not dominant. Labor unions are not "better" than management. In fact, Wall Street and industrial leaders appear to be more realistic about race than are rank-and-file workers. During the most effective period of political liberalism in this century, the Roosevelt New Deal era, when the oppressed without regard to race gained some measure of economic security, Negroes had to threaten to embarrass the Administration by demonstrations and a march on Washington in order to achieve an executive Fair Employment Practices order. Perhaps it is impossible for any person, any organization, any political party, to be consistently and totally liberal.

Again, in the schools—on the primary, secondary, and collegiate level—where one finds strong declarations against prejudice, there is overwhelming evidence of a devastating form of oppression, perhaps second only in contemporary society to discrimination in housing. Colleges and universities, the citadels of American liberalism, are devoted to the freeing of the mind from narrow restrictions and from error; yet when one looks at the faculties of interracial colleges, one finds fewer than three hundred Negroes, and probably no more than two or three in the position of department chairman; there are no Negro deans and no Negro presidents. Recently these colleges have gone out of their way to recruit Negroes—another revelation of the fact that race is still a dominant aspect in all areas of American life. The continued existence of Negro colleges, with their predominantly Negro faculties and administration, reassures whites and Negroes that there is equal professional opportunity for Negroes. Negroes are ambivalent about Negro colleges; even at best, they are ashamed of them, for such colleges are an anachronism: that they need to exist to give Negro students an education can only emphasize the fact that integration has not come to American education at any level.

Negroes are dismayed to discover that even when liberals are in apparent control of an organization, not only do they not rally their groups for an effective role in the fight against racial discrimination; they even tolerate a measure of discrimination within their own jurisdictions. Loren Miller, a Los Angeles attorney and a vice president of the NAACP, points out that because the liberal's historic concern has been with individual rights, he sees progress in the admission of a few Negro children to a hitherto white school; while the Negro, who also wants individual rights, nevertheless regards the raising of status of the group "to which he has been consigned" as his own immediate problem and spurns the evidence of individual progress as mere tokenism.

The problem is multisided. The liberal often is less in control of the political or other institution than the Negro thinks he is. Doubtless because many organizations, churches, and political platforms have frequently taken the liberal stance, Negroes have been misled into believing that liberals set the standards for society as a whole. But often, power groups have allowed liberals to have the satisfaction of the words while they kept for themselves the satisfaction of the deeds. Liberalism, because of its close relationship to the world of the intellect and the world of language, often assumes that the word *is* the deed. Politicians and industrialists and business leaders know better. For liberalism to be really effective, and to regain the allegiance of the Negroes, which it has in some measure lost, it will need to move from the verbal level to the actual level of power.

The ambivalent role of white liberals must be understood also in terms of the power of their own conflicting loyalties—their desire to maintain the liberal democratic image of themselves and their desire to maintain their identity in their "in-group," their friends, their family, their social cliques, who do not necessarily share all of their own liberal attitudes. The conflict between the individual and the groups to which he belongs is transferred to the individual himself; his own conscience is in conflict with his timidities. In some this conflict is resolved by a self-protective rejection of the Negro as "too impatient" and by the conviction that the good of the total society requires a more measured, gradual approach.

One of the dangers in the present white liberal ambivalence toward the Negro is that it has caused many Negroes to reject the "liberal" label as a designation for themselves. For a number of Negroes "liberal" has come to mean "white." They, too, are ambivalent, for they do not wish to feel alien to the liberal tradition with which they associate the concept of justice. Yet the liberal has become a curious and troublesome adversary, often harder to deal with than the bigot who, at the least, states his position honestly in unmistakable terms. The bigot will react with contempt and hatred to Negro criticism, but the liberal looks hurt and expresses his continuing and forgiving friendship, thereby creating in his Negro counterpart a sense of frustrated rage and guilt that adds to the psychological burden already difficult to bear—a burden seemingly doubly unjust. When a Negro responds with anger to an act or attitude that seems to him discriminatory, he is often regarded as having violated the rules of conduct among gentlemen. He has not been amiable. He would seem, therefore, to have no way out. The choice is to alienate his friends or to suffer a sense of self-alienation.

In a round-table discussion on "Liberalism and the Negro," conducted by *Commentary* magazine and reported in its issue of March 1964, James Baldwin tried to explain to a group of distinguished, mostly white liberals why the term "liberal" had begun to pall. The liberal, he said, was an "affliction" to the Negro:

What I mean by a liberal is someone . . . whose real attitudes are revealed when the chips are down . . . someone who thinks you are bitter when you are vehement, who has a set of attitudes so deep that they're almost unconscious and which blind him to the fact that in talking to a black man, he is talking to another man like himself.

In a provocative article, "Farewell to the Liberals, A Negro View," in the *Nation,* October 20, 1962, Loren Miller said that the liberal could be defined as one who sees "both sides" of issues, one who is "impatient with 'extremists' on both sides."

The Negro is outraged at being an extremist. Since he takes the position that the Constitution confers complete equality on all citizens, he must rest his case on the proposition that there is only one side; his side, the constitutional side. Whoever opposes, or even doubts, that doctrine is cast in the role of a foe, whether he calls himself conservative or liberal. The middle ground on which the traditional liberal has taken his stand is being cut from beneath him.

Whites, as well as Negroes, are caught up in conflict and ambivalence about race. They have been required to learn the language and behavior of prejudice at the same time that they learned the words and ideals of democracy. One obvious way to cope with the contradiction between the ideal and the real is to deny the existence of the real. White officials, confronted by Negro demands in Northern urban areas, often say with bewilderment that there is no policy of exclusion of Negroes, that "some of our best friends, in fact, are Negro," or that no Negro has "ever applied for a job in our firm." Such beliefs ironically can create the very reality they assert. In professions where Negroes have felt unwelcome by whatever means—advertising in the "white" rather than the Negro press, relying on employment agencies in white neighborhoods, hiring by word of mouth from friend to friend—few, if any, Negroes *do* apply; and the failure to apply, in turn, convinces the employer that Negroes are unqualified for or uninterested in his business. Nor is an open-door policy in a church or club in itself generally sufficient to attract Negroes; in a society in which race is a dominant influence, those who have in the past been excluded assume they are "not wanted" until the evidence to refute this assumption is forced upon them.

So, too, many liberal whites believe that Negroes prefer to live together, that they are drawn to each other as the Chinese may be in Chinatown, because of a shared culture. No one will ever, in fact, know whether Negro culture *does* bind its members together until Negroes have the freedom others have to live anywhere. A conspiracy of white-controlled financial and real estate interests has effectively blocked any significant outward movement from the ghetto in spite of the fair-housing laws or other concessions to democratic ideology. Every Negro who seeks to move outside of an all-Negro community is required to fight and insist upon this right; for while the law protects his right, it does not allow him to take for granted in the first instance that he will be justly treated. The law asserts that the legitimate and verbal power of society is not on the side of exclusion. It does permit those willing to make the test to do so; and offers assurance that the law will not be used against them. In the South the law has been used as an instrument for the perpetuation of racial *status quo*. In the North, the law neutralizes exclusion; it does not, however, prevent it. The law sometimes penalizes injustice when injustice can be proved, but the burden of proof is on the Negro.

In many all-white suburbs, human relations committees and fair housing committees have now been organized by liberals to break down the housing barriers. Such campaigns are a fascinating illustration of the fact that the Negro is forced to consider himself special—otherwise, why would campaigns be needed to permit him to exercise the rights which the law assures him?

White liberals have been having a frustrating time finding Negroes who will offer themselves as test cases. For one thing, it is not particularly comfortable to be a test case. For another, middle-class Negroes who break out of the ghetto are often themselves convinced that they are already accepted by whites—to be a test case would be to allow race to become salient again in one's life, to bring the ghetto nightmare along when all one has sought is effective escape. When whites learn that hosts of Negroes are not poised and eager to take advantage of their new hospitality, when white human relations committees search in vain for a Negro (a search Negroes often regard with ironic humor) they tend to take this failure as evidence that Negroes really do want to live "with each other" after all. Furthermore, job discrimination has reduced the proportion of Negroes who can afford to pay the high rents or purchase price of good suburban housing. Generally Negroes are able only to move into those communities where whites themselves have minimum social and economic status; in those lower-income areas, economic and psychological status is already so tenuous that whites cannot allow their security to be jeopardized voluntarily. When Negroes move in, such whites feel they have sunk a bit themselves. They fight back in self-defense, in the phenomenon known as the "white backlash." As the civil rights pressure increases, the identification whites feel with their own group, through the "neighborhood" (previously downgraded in Northern cities, now suddenly rediscovered), through fraternities, churches, social clubs, is reinforced. The mobilization of the white community to protect itself through organizations like the Parents and Taxpayers groups in New York City must necessarily increase as the pressure to take sides increases. This stark confrontation, even when hostile and terrifying, has at least the important virtue of honesty.

It is easy to forget the rather obvious fact that whites are competitive and hostile among themselves, among and within the various ethnic groups which comprise the dominant "white" population. This quiet but pervasive intrawhite competitiveness is merely intensified and considered normal when Negroes insist upon sharing the rewards and status symbols. Whites then tend to close ranks in what seems to Negroes to be a solid wall of resistance to their demands. There is a temporary decrease in rivalry among whites and a joining of forces. The Parents and Taxpayers group included whites of varying political and religious views and ethnic origin; Jews and Gentiles; Catholics and Protestants; Italians, Irish, Polish, and others.

Whites who are reluctant to join this protective homogeny are subjected to social coercion, ridicule, and harassment, and in extreme cases, to the forms of violence, like bombings, ordinarily employed only against Negroes. The appearance of a formidable coalition of white resistance forces demands a compensatory defense alliance between middle-class and workingclass Negroes, ordinarily suspicious of each other—the middle-class Negro escaping reminders of the ghetto, the workingclass Negro apathetic and cynical about the motives of the middle class. For when a middle-class Negro's home in a white neighborhood is bombed, all Negroes are angry. When a workingclass Negro adolescent is shot by a white policeman, all Negroes are bitter, although only marginal Negroes might actually protest through rioting in the streets. Any homogeneous white resistance to Negroes tends to cause Negroes to close ranks.

When liberals say that the Negro is ungrateful and insensitive to the predicament of less secure lower-middle-class whites, who do have much to lose by integrated housing and schools, Negroes understand that they are to permit the rate of change in their status to be determined by the willingness of whites to accept them as human beings. This is the heart of racism: when one accepts race as a relevant criterion for decision about when, under what conditions, and how fast the lower-status race should be granted equality. Any Negro who agrees to accede to the majority's power to decide his rights for any reasons other than purely strategic has already been damaged psychologically in subtle, tragic ways.

The liberal has often felt righteous in his role as protector of the Negro. He talked of freedom and therefore successfully separated himself from involvement in the restrictions on freedom. He did not face his own role as accessory. He wrote serious articles on race in *Partisan Review, Commentary, New Leader,* and other magazines. He invited Negro intellectuals to discuss their common problems with him. He lived in accordance with the ritual of commitment and concern but ordinarily without the substance. Negro intellectuals have often played the game with the same *élan.* Some became pets of the whites. But if they took the game seriously, they were lost. Many were saved by protective cynicism; some, by the ability to exploit their position.

Negroes generally felt that white liberals did not understand, for if there had been a real relationship between them, they would have joined in an anguished outcry, beating their own heads against the walls of power in a demand for justice. Whenever a *New York Times* editorial questions the democracy of laws against discrimination in housing, whenever a *Partisan Review* writer takes moral relativism seriously, whenever a Norman Podhoretz explores his hostility toward Negroes in the pages of *Commentary,* a Negro may praise the honesty which permits such free expression but he must also question the serious concern for him.

Perhaps it has been more important psychologically than the white liberal knew for him to serve as surrogate and spokesman for the disadvantaged. The liberal's compassion and pity for the underdog, particularly the Negro, has led to a role of symbiosis and interdependence between the white liberal and the Negro. Perhaps it was inevitable that as the Negro came to reject the role of underdog and sought to be treated as peer, he would increase the psychological distance between himself and the white liberal, and stimulate in his earlier white benefactor both resentment and alienation, which, in turn, would cause the Negro to feel contempt for the white liberal.

Negroes are now insisting on being their own spokesmen; they are asking the whites to join them, either as equals or even in subordinate roles; but it is abnormal in our society for whites to be in a passive or subordinate or even equal role with Negroes, and extremely awkward for many of them to make the necessary psychological readjustment.

The present question is whether the relationship between the white liberal and the Negro, who have needed each other in the past, will survive the test of transformation of roles from the dependence of the advantaged and disadvantaged upon each other to a common commitment to mutually desired goals of justice and social good.

If the civil rights struggle is going to be successful, it will require white participation and commitment, even though a number of Negroes believe the white is no longer relevant. The simple fact of arithmetic decrees otherwise. Negroes are one-tenth of the American population. Without white support and without the white power structure the civil rights struggle is doomed to failure. As Gunnar Myrdal, at the *Commentary* conference noted earlier, replied to James Baldwin, who had spoken, "Nevertheless, Mr. Baldwin, you will have to rely upon the liberals because, as somebody said before, it's not the conservatives who are going to fight for the bigger reforms which must be made . . . you will have to rely on the liberals—even if sometimes they are not too clear and too courageous, and even if they sometimes need you to give them a push. I think the most encouraging thing which has happened in America in recent years is the rebellion of the Negro group, because that rebellion will help the liberals to get into power and do the job that has to be done."

The white liberal must be prepared, in this turbulent period of transition, to accept the fact that even his closest Negro friends will feel some hostility toward him. For if the white liberal can delude himself into believing himself color-blind, the Negro of insight and sensitivity cannot. To a Negro, every white person is, in a sense, a symbol of his own oppression. Almost every Negro who has white friends and associates suffers from feelings of ambivalence; every relationship of respect and affection that seems to transcend the racial and to be merely human causes the Negro to feel some sense of guilt and betrayal just because it does bring an experience of liberation from the bonds of inferior racial identification other Negroes have not been able to achieve. Many Negroes are caught in a gnawing sense of doubt, hostility, and guilt that interferes with any genuine affirmative relationship with whites— and even with Negroes themselves. The Negro tends to justify his own anxieties and ambivalence in self-protective ways, fearing to yield to the temptation to become a "show friend," ascribing to the white an inability to be a friend to a Negro. It would be too painful to realize that the guilt of unfulfilled friendship is in some measure his own. He may tell himself: I needn't feel guilty because my white friend is not really free to be my friend.

Subtle tensions may result when whites themselves who harbor deep feelings of guilt about Negroes attempt prematurely and with exaggerated warmth to establish close relationships with them. This puts a strain on the Negro and makes it difficult for him to adjust normally. If the Negro rejects the overture as an invasion of his individuality, the whites, in turn, may be bewildered and hurt, and regress to a safe level of hostility and alienation. Few, if any, are capable of racelessness. But whites who try to be free must have the courage to accept the inevitable chaos and confusion of a changing society. There will be inevitable irrationalities in any move to a higher stage of rationality and justice. Above all, one must not retreat in the face of pain. Anyone who cringes, who retreats to the insidious conviction that things were more peaceful and, therefore, better when the Negro knew his place may find temporary security, but he has chosen the way of the past and instability.

The mistake is to seek for purity at all, and the white liberal no more than the Negro ought to expect of himself a superhuman response. Original innocence, if such a thing has meaning, can never be regained; in contemporary society, no one, Negro or white, can be totally without prejudice. No one should expect purity of himself or others. Any genuine relationship between Negro and white must face honestly all of the ambivalences both feel for each other. Each must identify with the other without sentiment. The white must resist the tendency to attribute all virtue to the underdog; he must respond insofar as he is able with a pure kind of empathy that is raceless, that accepts and understands the frailties and anxieties and weaknesses that all men share, the common predicament of mankind.

Any white who dares to be free of the myths of race faces awkwardness and risk and a need to defend himself, even ironically, against Negroes themselves. For many Negroes prefer, unconsciously or not, a continuation of the double standard; their preference sometimes wears the guise of an insistence on interpreting lack of prejudice as itself evidence of prejudice. Negroes are so accustomed to prejudice that many find it easier to deal with it than with a single standard of judgment for all men. It requires strength and courage for whites to persist in the face of such rejection. It is a temptation to retreat into sentimentality instead, and to be caught in the net of condescension, to say, "I would not want to hurt you because you are a Negro," and to suffocate the Negro with respect. Any white who refuses to be trapped into such an escape, and reaches the point of total liberation, will see and understand and act freely. He can never retreat, no matter what the threats, either to the sentimental lie or to the traditional racist lie; for the Negro is watching and waiting, despite his cynicism and his suspicion, with the beginning of trust.

Those whites who are really committed to civil rights can make it clear to society at large that a significant minority of Americans will no longer accept equivocation and procrastination. But it is far easier to deal with racial problems by writing letters to congressmen than to demonstrate one's own freedom. Every individual who rises above the constrictions of race is a demonstration that this is really possible. Every time a Negro sees a group of secretaries—white and Negro—chatting over lunch; or children—white and Negro—walking together to school, he feels that hope is possible. Every time his white friend shows he is not afraid to argue with him as with anyone else, he sees that freedom is possible, that there are some for whom race is irrelevant, who accept or reject a person not as a Negro or a white, but in terms of himself. Only so can the real confinements of the ghetto be broken. The Negro alone cannot win this fight that transcends the "civil rights struggle." White and Negro must fight together for the rights of human beings to make mistakes and to aspire to human goals. Negroes will not break out of the barriers of the ghetto unless whites transcend the barriers of their own minds, for the ghetto is to the Negro a reflection of the ghetto in which the white lives imprisoned. The poetic irony of American race relations is that the rejected Negro must somehow also find the strength to free the privileged white.

Human Rights in 1966

ROY WILKINS

IN 1966 THE CIVIL rights movement has been checked, but its forward progress has not been halted.

The outstanding event of the year in this field was the setback occasioned by the failure of the Congress to enact the Civil Rights Bill of 1966. Violence, too, played its role in the year's civil rights history.

But neither the setback on the civil rights bill nor the violence has deterred the Negro. He pressed his campaign right into and through the November election, emerging from that a more significant political factor than ever before.

What slowed him and his cause was not the violence directed against him but the persistence of two myths: (a) the Negro is going too fast, and (b) the Negro is getting too much help from government. Undeniably these contentions were bolstered in the minds of their eager believers by the ill-advised riotous outbreaks by young Negroes in a dozen cities, with strategically bad ones in Oakland, Calif., and in Chicago, Illinois.

But the two myths did not need the underscoring of the riots. The "going too fast" story was given dignity in 1956 by the late William Faulkner in a *Life* article. For the millions of white people unacquainted with the facts, this slogan has been their thinking and acting guide.

Compared to anything except to his own glacier-like progress in

In 1966 Roy Wilkins, Executive Director of the National Association for the Advancement of Colored People, gave this lecture, sponsored by the Hillman Foundation, at Oakland University in Michigan.

the past, the Negro has been merely crawling. Other Americans outdistance him in nearly every area of living. It will be useful, in assessing where we are and where we go from here, to scan Negro life and progress. Is there any validity to the assertion that he has gone "too fast?"

In the important area of employment the two salient facts to remember are that his rate of unemployment, even in these affluent times, is twice the national rate and that the working Negro, from laborer to executive, averages only 55 per cent of the annual income of white workers.

Of 6,600,000 employed Negroes at the last census, 4,500,-000 were in the low-paid categories of unskilled farm and nonfarm labor, household workers, and other service workers.

Since 1935 Negro workers have entered the ranks of organized labor largely through the industrial union door. They are in some craft unions, but have always had difficulty with these. The attitude of craft union leaders on Negro membership, particularly of those at the top, has changed. But the actual admission of Negroes has been slow. In too many cases Negroes have been shut out despite top policy.

Where Negroes are in unions they have a battle in many of them over separate seniority lines, restricted categories, apprenticeships, and promotion to supervisory posts. Out in Cleveland, where a training program has been underway for apprentice applicants, three hundred Negro boys have passed a written test, but not one has survived the oral examination given by the union.

More than one thousand complaints on racial discrimination in employment have been filed by the NAACP with the President's Commission on Equal Employment established under Title 7 of the 1964 Civil Rights Act. It is true that some progress has been made on professional, technical and white collar levels. Recruitment is proceeding by big corporations on the campuses of Negro colleges. The federal government, largest employer of Negroes in the nation, has managed to upgrade a noticeable number of them past the $7,500 grade and a smaller number past the $12,000 grade.

The sobering fact remains, however, that almost uniformly throughout the country, the Negro workers are concentrated in the menial, low-paid categories. The quick excuse that they lack the required education and training is too often just a quick excuse. It is true, too, that fewer Negroes receive in-plant training than whites. Certain it is that in this field the cry of "too fast" has little validity.

As for housing, around which has swirled such emotional currents, the Negro in the sixties has met organized and well-financed opposition from the real estate business as well as from highly partisan citizens committees, civic associations and others, including, I regret to say, some church congregations.

The basic fact is that of all new housing built in the country since the end of World War II, less than 2 per cent has gone to Negroes. Not only have they been shut out of new housing, but their attempts to purchase used housing has been hindered by a myriad of customs, regulations, codes, mortgage restrictions, and plain, old-fashioned mob violence.

Crime, disease, immorality, and drug addiction flourish in the slums. These, coupled with a Negro teen-age unemployment rate of 32 per cent, breed a young Negro who, in the words of sociologists, "can't be reasoned with." He is skeptical of anything from the outside world and is ready for any "tear-it-up" adventure that anyone may suggest. His elders, long ago discouraged by discrimination on a dozen fronts and made cynical by broken promises and backward steps in the democratic process, make no effort to stop him and only half-heartedly condemn him.

It is clear that speed has not marked the housing field, but in no area is the falsity of the "too fast" slogan more evident than in that of public education.

Those who bothered to do even casual research and those non-Southerners who came into contact with the products of the Southern legally segregated school system knew something of the gross inequalities. There has been a great deal of noise, considerable court action, and some feverish political maneuvering on school desegregation in the Southern states, but the pace of desegregation has been token and painfully slow. There are still more than two million Negro children in racially segregated schools twelve years after the United States Supreme Court ruled such schools unconstitutional.

Today Southern politicians and officeholders are waging a wide campaign against the school desegregation guidelines issued by the

Office of Education of the Department of Health, Education and Welfare. Title Six of the 1964 Civil Rights Act provides for cutting off federal grants to states wherever such monies are used in a racially discriminatory manner. HEW is simply carrying out the law, but the Southerners want to keep the Federal money and keep segregation, too. In effect, they seek to repeal, administratively, the Civil Rights Act of 1964.

While the Southern conditions were known, no one, except well-informed sophisticates, was prepared fully for the subtle and deeply intrenched *de facto* racial segregation revealed in the Northern schools.

Too many Northern school boards have remained adamant on the adoption of plans to desegregate their schools. Others have taken tentative and merely palliative steps. The heart of the problem seems to be not so much in the vociferous and emotional white parents groups, but in the School Establishment itself—the teachers, principals, superintendents, and administrators. They don't want to change a system that promises them promotion and security, and many of them are not convinced that Negro children can be educated.

The latest and most shocking study, made for the Department of Health, Education and Welfare and reported in 1966, shows that Negroes attending segregated schools in the North lag behind white children, the gap widening year by year until it reaches 3.3 years in grade twelve!

Yet wherever sincere efforts have been made at integration, and especially where care has been used in teacher selection and in teaching methods, the results have been good.

All the evidence is that our country has not yet come to grips with segregated education. Far from proceeding too fast, we have been criminally slow. It could well be that the lack of meaningful dialogue between disenchanted Negroes and their white fellow citizens is directly traceable to the failure in the very first instance to teach democracy in a democratic school system.

Police-minority relations, as a part of the administration of justice, have not improved at such a rate as to be branded as "too fast." Indeed, the police remain high on the list of factors which make for racial unrest.

The McCone Report on the Watts riot of 1965 placed major

emphasis on the improvement of police-minority relations if communities wish to avoid trouble. All except one of the riots of 1964 were triggered by police action.

Civilian review boards to consider complaints against the police have been bitterly combatted by police organizations who want no "outside" opinion judging police actions. The slogan, "Stop Violence in the Streets," is regarded by Negroes as a euphemism for controlling the Negro community.

Some enlightened police officials are including human relations and minority problems in police institutes and a slowly-growing number of Southern officials are changing. In general, however, the police are not doing all they might do to build the kind of sentiment that eliminates racial violence.

At year's end it is possible to state that the Negro, despite sporadic diversionary urgings, has reiterated his determination to struggle, as he has always, for his inclusion, on a full partnership basis, in American citizenship.

As proof of this attitude, he voted more heavily than ever before in the November election. He helped choose more than 120 Negroes as members of state legislatures, ten of them in Georgia. He has six members of the House and now one senator. White Massachusetts voters who refused to be stampeded by "white backlash" sentiment voted with him to elect a Republican to the United States Senate—the first Negro in that chamber since Reconstruction days.

A Negro sheriff was elected in Alabama and a school board member in Jefferson County, Mississippi. Negro voters helped elect Republican governors in Arkansas, New York, and Michigan, a liberal Democratic senator in Virginia and a liberal Republican senator in New Jersey.

In the South, where the "Black Power" cry, with its implied separatism, was first raised, 2,660,000 Negroes were registered to vote, the greatest total in history. This number represented 52 per cent of the eligible Negroes as against the white percentage of 70. This figure and the Negro vote in the North suggest strongly that the Negro population is bent upon using the ballot and legislation to win its way to first-class citizenship.

The Negro has continued his choice of nonviolence as a tactic and has shown a willingness, even an eagerness, to use all the traditional American methods to achieve his ends. There will be no let-up in his demands for the correction of inequities. Indeed, these will be accelerated, for the record which I have cited shows clearly that he is entitled to swift action across the whole civil rights spectrum.

In a very real sense, the fate of racial peace is in the hands of white Americans, not those of Negroes. The theory, advanced in some quarters, that Negro leadership and Negro private organizations ought to be able to "control" Negro urban concentrations is extremely unrealistic. When murderers of Negroes go free, when police mistreatment is glossed over, when civil rights legislation is killed and the enforcement of existing laws is hamstrung, when housing, employment and school policies represent stubborn standpatism, no honest Negro leadership can ignore the cold facts and seek to generate confidence in a zero.

If, as some predict and others fear, we are to have a "conservative" Congress, then the maintenance of racial peace will present problems. Contrary to the popular tale, the Negro is now so far down in all categories that any slowdown imposed on his forward movement will be in effect a complete halt. In this space age he cannot afford to halt or he will die. And he does not propose to permit suicide to be forced upon him.

PART TWO

Civil Liberties

/\/\/\/\/\/\

In postwar periods, as wartime cohesion wanes and wartime hopes begin to fade, it has become an unhappy habit of the United States to drown its frustrations in a hunt for scapegoats—heedless of our democratic heritage or Constitutional guarantees. It happened after World War II, during a grim period named after the chief huntsman, U.S. Senator Joseph McCarthy. Throughout the period, a number of men helped maintain our heritage and our guarantees—occasionally at considerable risk to themselves. Alan Barth is one of the most understanding of the nation's civil libertarians, and one of the most articulate. His fellow worker on the Washington *Post*, Herbert Block, is equally expressive, in another medium. Using a different style but in the same vein was Daniel Fitzpatrick.

Two of McCarthy's most fervent opponents were also from Wisconsin—publishers William T. Evjue, who attacked him from a long background in the Progressive movement, and Morris Rubin, who devoted a stunningly documented issue of *The Progressive* to the Senator's life and works. However, the man who probably made the greatest impact of all was Edward R. Murrow. His *See it Now* programs were seen by millions and gave style and weight to TV's early years.

As the McCarthy period waned, the U.S. Supreme Court emerged as one of the most active defenders of our civil liberties. The late Edmond Cahn was one of the principal legal scholars writing in support of the Court's new attitudes.

Today McCarthy is dead and scorned, the nation hopefully better able to withstand the efforts of those who still try to exploit McCarthy techniques. One of our contemporary problems is conformity, which was exposed so dramatically in the WCAU program. Another is the attack on academic freedom, opposed so firmly by Francis Keppel. Others are touched on by several of the pieces in the section on foreign policy.

The Utility of Freedom

ALAN BARTH

Liberty is to faction what air is to fire, an ailment without which it instantly expires. But it could not be less folly to abolish liberty, which is essential to political life, because it nourishes faction, than it would be to wish the annihilation of air, which is essential to animal life, because it imparts to fire its destructive agency.[1]

INDIVIDUAL FREEDOM PRESUPPOSES a tolerance of ideas which are thought to be mistaken, disloyal, and even dangerous. Tolerance of opinions which are thought to be innocuous is as easy as acts of charity that entail no sacrifice. But the test of a free society is its tolerance of what is deplored or despised by a majority of its members. The argument for such tolerance must be made on the ground that it is useful to the society.

The proposition to be proved, in short, is that free societies are better fitted to survive than closed societies. This is a proposition peculiarly relevant to the present struggle between the United States and the Soviet Union. Here the struggle is between a nation committed to the idea of individual freedom, and therefore to the principle of tolerance, and another nation which, in effect, denies the significance of the individual personality and the value of freedom.

Tolerance of diversity of opinion gives rise, undoubtedly, to what Madison called the spirit of faction. As long as men are

---

Alan Barth, editorial writer for the Washington *Post,* was given a 1951 Hillman Prize Award for his book *The Loyalty of Free Men* (New York: The Viking Press, Inc., 1951). This is the final chapter.

[1] JAMES MADISON, in the tenth essay of *The Federalist.*

permitted to express diverse opinions they will do so. As long as they are permitted to join in voluntary associations for the advancement of purposes they hold in common, there will be jostling for group advantage, pressure for special interests. Such conflicts are in greater or less degree disruptive. The resolution of them is the business of the democratic process. It is a process that has worked effectively for the American people in the past and can be counted upon to work in the future, so long as there is general acceptance of certain fundamental values and an underlying mutual trust among members of the society.

It is true that opinions challenging fundamental values and corroding mutual trust present a threat to social stability. To tolerate an organization like the Communist Party, which operates outside the democratic process and would destroy that process if it ever came to power, is to tolerate what must seem a seed of destruction. Similarly, to countenance the nihilism of a Senator McCarthy is to countenance methods that ignore standards of decency and poison the springs of confidence. Undoubtedly national unity—and therefore national security—suffers from such attacks on either side. But, paradoxically, loyalty in a free society depends upon the toleration of disloyalty. The loyalty of free men must be freely given —which is to say, that those who give it must be genuinely free to withhold it. Nothing is more fundamental to freedom than that this choice be a real one. The premise on which every free society rests, the American society more explicitly than any other, is that only through such freedom can loyalty be evoked and counted on to endure.

Moreover, to forbid disloyalty is to let it triumph. At bottom, the Communists and the Americanists are frighteningly similar: they are believers in the suppression and punishment of dissent. That they would suppress and punish different sorts of opinion is less significant than that, alike, they would suppress and punish. At bottom, they are alike also in being sick men: they are men who would relish a chance to use whip and club. It is necessary, therefore, to keep whips and clubs out of their hands—that is, to enforce the laws forbidding acts of violence, whether by them or against them. It is, however, equally necessary to enforce the laws which guarantee them the right to speak as they please. To suppress and punish their opinions is to embrace their opinions; it is to practice what they preach; and the end of that practice is the destruction of all diversity.

If tolerance of diversity involves an admitted element of risk to national unity, intolerance involves a certainty that unity will be destroyed. Unity does not grow out of uniformity; it grows out of resolved conflict. "Like the course of the heavenly bodies," Mr. Justice Brandeis once observed, "harmony in national life is a resultant of the struggle between contending forces. In frank expression of conflicting opinion lies the greatest promise of wisdom in governmental action; and in suppression lies ordinarily the greatest peril."[2]

While speech can be silenced by authority, and silence may give the appearance of assent, thought cannot be wholly controlled by any instrument of suppression yet devised. Thought that is silenced is always rebellious. It can be won to an acceptance of contrary opinion only if it has been accorded a chance to be heard and assured of a future chance to win acceptance for itself. Majorities, of course, are often mistaken. This is why the silencing of minorities is necessarily dangerous. Criticism and dissent are the indispensable antidote to majority delusions. Afforded free expression, they serve as the self-regulating mechanism of a democratic community.

There is a persistent and prevalent myth that totalitarian societies are somehow more efficient than free societies. A dictatorship can move more swiftly, it is true, than a government which depends upon the voluntary consent of the governed. This is merely to say that the policies of irresponsible leaders are more speedily translated into action—which may be disastrously mistaken—than the policies of democratic leaders. Leadership is as necessary in a democratic as in a totalitarian state; and when leadership is lacking or inept or misguided, the consequences may be very costly. But free men have a means of correcting mistakes by a change of leadership. The incorrigible defect of dictatorship lies in the absence of any remedy for error on the part of the dictator.

This defect was revealed in numerous ways in the course of the war. For all its vaunted efficiency in the techniques of total war, Germany never fully mobilized its resources or its people. There

[2] *Gilbert* v. *Minnesota,* 254 U.S. 325 (1920).

was nothing like the all-out effort of Britain. Neither the industrial capacity nor the manpower of the country was ever wholly integrated. Unnecessary consumer goods were produced in plants that might have been converted to war production; the luxury of domestic servants was widely enjoyed throughout the war, especially

"Help! I'm Being Followed" [3]

Oct 51

FROM *The Herblock Book* (Beacon Press, 1952)

by Nazi Party officials. The United States Strategic Bombing Survey, which conducted an intensive study in 1945 of the impact of the air war on the German economy and German morale, made these significant findings:

. . . Measured by the standards of other belligerents, there was no "total mobilization" and no long-term planning to bring the war effort to its attainable maximum. The production of civilian goods was only restricted to a moderate extent; there was no further mobilization of women and no great transfer of labor from the nonessential to the essential industries. Even in the face of reverses, the German leaders were still hypnotized by their belief in their own infallibility. . . . German armament industries with few exceptions worked only single

[3] This and the other Herblock cartoons in this section are from *The Herblock Book* for which Herbert Block, the cartoonist of the *Washington Post*, won a 1952 Hillman Prize Award.

shifts throughout the war, and the great capacity reserve that would have been available from double- or triple-shift operations was never completely utilized. . . . While Britain, in the course of the war, increased the proportion of women in whole- or part-time work (outside agriculture) from 40 to 56 per cent, the number of German women mobilized remained practically unchanged throughout the war. The number of German women in domestic service fell only slightly—from 1.5 to 1.3 millions between May 1939 and May 1944. In Britain, over the same period, the number of domestic servants was cut from 1.2 to 0.5 million. . . . Whether mobilization of women, movement of labor into the war industries, or the length of the working week be taken as the test, it is clear that Germany did not mobilize its labor force as fully as she might have, not even after the much advertised manpower drives in 1943 and in the summer of 1944.

These fatal inefficiencies in German mobilization grew directly out of the nature of totalitarian rule. There was no one to tell the Führer that the war effort was not being administered satisfactorily. To have questioned his wisdom would have been tantamount to treason. The mistakes therefore went uncorrected and in the end proved disastrous to the German people. The Strategic Bombing Survey reached the conclusion that these mistakes were rooted in a fundamental miscalculation about the strength of the nations ranged against Germany:

. . . The conclusion is inescapable that Germany's war production was not limited by its war potential—by the resources at its disposal—but by demand; in other words, by the notions of the German war leaders of what was required to win. The Germans did not plan, nor were they prepared for, a long war. . . . After the occupation of France, England, though not invaded or brought to heel through aerial bombardment, was no longer considered an immediate threat. Possible intervention by the United States was not taken seriously. The attack on Russia was started in the confident expectation that the experience of the earlier campaigns was to be repeated; Russia was to be completely subjugated in three to four months.

Faulty intelligence produced faulty planning all along the line in Germany. The belief that victory could be achieved quickly and cheaply produced an emphasis, in the composition of the German air force, on fighters and bombers of a type suitable to close co-operation with ground armies; Germany lacked, in consequence, the long-range bombers necessary to win the Battle of Britain. The development of jet planes, in which German technicians pioneered, was "much hindered," according to the Strategic Bombing Survey, "by Hitler's insistence that the aircraft be used as a fighter bomber." The assumption that Britain and the United States could mount only a limited air attack—"Allied production figures were disbelieved"—resulted in totally inadequate civilian-defense precautions. And when the mass air raids struck Germany, their psychological impact was compounded by Nazi propaganda which had stressed the infallibility of the Führer. A government based on coerced consent and the suppression of diversity lacked the capacity of a government based on voluntary consent to call for all-out effort and sacrifice on the part of the governed. It could command no comparable loyalty. It could achieve no comparable unity. It possessed no resiliency in disaster, comparable to that of the British after Dunkerque or the Americans after Pearl Harbor, to correct errors and restore confidence.

The validity of what has been said here is not lessened by the fact that totalitarian Russia was among the victors and democratic France among the vanquished in the war. The Soviet dictator demanded, and received, heroic sacrifices from the Russian people; no nation waged war so totally. Russia mobilized tremendous strength, although wastefully in many respects; and her soldiers and civilians alike stood with magnificent fortitude at Stalingrad and Moscow, rallying after losses that, to the world outside, seemed catastrophic. But this qualification should be noted: the Russians were invaded, and by an enemy so stupidly ruthless as to leave them no alternative to resistance save extermination; even so, great numbers in the Ukraine and elsewhere showed themselves willing to join the Germans in fighting against their own government. In the vast unconquered land mass of the Soviet Union, however, the Nazi attack solidified devotion to leaders whom the people had no choice but to follow; and no doubt this attack from the outside forged a loyalty, beyond anything the Communist propagandists had been able to create, to a political system which with all its faults was their own.

France collapsed for a variety of reasons, perhaps the most fundamental of which was that she lacked in the 1930s the acceptance of common values and the underlying mutual trust which

have been suggested as prerequisites to the working of the democratic process. The French people were united only in
devotion to France as a geographical entity. They were rent
by a political factionalism that went beyond mere rivalry for public
office or mere conflict as to policy; the Cagoulards and the Croix
de Feu and the Monarchists and the Catholics and the Socialists
and the Communists reflected deep cleavages respecting the nature
of French society and the role of the State. There was no agreement
among them as to first principles; agreement had to be forged, at
last, through the anguish of defeat and regeneration. There is a
profound warning for Americans in the French experience.

It has not been intended to suggest here that free societies are
necessarily and invariably stronger than totalitarian societies. The
point is simply that freedom is a source of strength if it is used
wisely. It cannot provide a guarantee against ruinous mistakes; but
it can provide a means of correcting mistakes, a means denied to
those who live in a society where dissent is silenced.

There were many blunders, of course, in both British and American planning of the war effort. They were subject, however, to
unremitting and caustic criticism. Gradually, as a result, they were
overcome. The harnessing of American industry was begun under
the National Defense Advisory Council; when that agency proved
unsatisfactory, it was replaced by the Office of Production Management, which in turn gave way to the Supply Priorities and Allocation Board. The bludgeoning of critics, who, in Germany, would
have been considered traitors, forced this to yield at last to the
War Production Board, which measured up to the gigantic job
pretty well. The process commonly called "trial and error" is peculiarly democratic; it can work successfully only where opposition
parties and the press individuals are free to expose error, and where
trial is always open to protest. Criticism is liable to seem captious
or crackpot or disloyal to those in authority, and often, no doubt,
they are quite right about it; but it is an invaluable goad and tonic
all the same. For all its excesses and inconveniences, societies that
tolerate criticism unconditionally tend to be stronger and more
stable than those that do not.

The contrast between the German and American experiences in
the development of atomic energy affords perhaps the most dramatic illustration of the pragmatic uses of tolerance. Some of the

most brilliant German scientists, driven from their homeland because they were Jewish or because they were politically unorthodox,
found asylum in the United States and in Britain and made important contributions to our primacy in perfecting an atomic bomb.
German science, once pre-eminent, was crippled even more by the
tendency to entrust authority over research to politically "reliable"
scientists—to scientists who were more political than scientific.
Doctrinaire insistence on Nazi fetishes of race supremacy accelerated the deterioration. The outcome, in strictly practical terms,
was to impair German national security.

A similar process seems to be taking place today in the Soviet
Union. In a number of fields, science is being cramped by orthodoxy. There is no reason to think that purges will promote efficiency there any more than they did in Germany. Moreover, the
Russians, like the Germans, appear to be victims of their own
doctrinaire assumptions. It is a part of Russian doctrine—as it was
so mistakenly a part of German doctrine a decade ago—that the
United States is hopelessly divided and decadent. No one who
reports on conditions in this country dares, therefore, to call the
doctrine into question. Intelligence is bound to be faulty when the
bearer of bad tidings fears that he will fall into disfavor; and faulty
intelligence is likely to produce mistaken policy.

There is a lesson for us in this too. We are in danger of allowing
prejudice to distort our estimates of Soviet strength—as we did in
1941 when our military experts took it for granted that the Wehr-
macht would destroy the Red Army in a matter of weeks. If we
allow men like Owen Lattimore and John Service to be slurred and
silenced because they say what we do not wish to hear, we shall
end by formulating policy on the basis of fancies instead of facts.
Nothing could be more perilous to national security. There is no
sense in emulating the errors of our enemies.

Democracies may unconsciously embrace their own peculiar
form of totalitarianism through extra-legal pressures for conformity. If their members all talk alike and think alike, they run
the serious risk of being plunged alike into disaster. The Gadarene
swine had their own species of democracy when they rushed down
the hillside together into the sea—acting with perfect unanimity,
all agreeing, none contradicting.

From the point of view of national security, tolerance of diversity has proved itself to be a powerful asset. It has been the real "secret" of American strength. It has welded the diverse elements of the American people into a union in the genuine sense of the term; and, more than any other single factor, it has kept that union invulnerable to outside attack. The whole of the American experience refutes the notion that tolerance is a luxury to be enjoyed only in untroubled times. It is the genius of American growth. It is needed most, and most urgently, precisely in times like the present when the nation is subject to extraordinary stress. It may well be that for a long time to come we shall find ourselves ranged against the Soviet Union in a conflict of endurance which is not war in the conventional sense but which involves, nevertheless, a test of the survival value of the two societies. Those who hold that time is against us and therefore urge an immediate attack on Russia— preventive war is the phrase in fashion—betray a loss of faith in our own institutions. The American society—if it remains free— possesses a greater capacity for growth, a greater resourcefulness in meeting new problems and changing situations, than any closed society. Time is not against us; it is on our side. In the long run, the free have triumphed over the enslaved. We shall grow in strength as we exploit our freedom.

Tolerance of diversity is now being vitiated in ways dangerous to national security. Fear—and a diminution of faith in our own institutions—has led us into a condition of panic threatening self-destruction. The condition is depicted in Shelley's terrifying image:

> 'Tis we who, lost in stormy visions, keep
> With phantoms an unprofitable strife,
> And in mad trance strike with the spirit's knife
> Invulnerable nothings. . . .

Certainly there are real dangers to be faced. Espionage and sabotage are not imaginary threats to national security. They need to be countered by careful, realistic screening of government personnel, by systematic controls over classified communications and data, by watchful police or military protection of all vital installations. There are disloyal men, especially among the Communists. But to see disloyalty everywhere, to suppose that the Communist

Party in the United States is a powerful octopus with tentacles reaching into every avenue of American life, is to strike at invulnerable nothings. Communist propaganda is undoubtedly aimed at the subversion of American values. But the antidote is not repression: it is free and unlimited discussion.

Let us face the real dangers with the techniques of freedom. These techniques have kept us safe and made us strong. To forsake them now is to forsake the most vital element of national defense.

This discussion of freedom has been in utilitarian terms—in terms of its value for the security of the United States. But there is no disposition here to ignore its significance from the point of view of the individual. If, as we profess to believe in the United States, the nation exists only as an instrument to promote the welfare of its citizens, tolerance of diversity is imperative, because without it, without the personal liberty and individualism that flow from it, life would lose its savor. Progress in the arts, in the sciences, in the patterns of social adjustment springs from diversity and depends upon a tolerance of individual deviations from conventional ways and attitudes. The totalitarian society is not only less efficient than the free society in terms of its own survival; it is also stultifying and degrading to the human beings who live in it. Freedom gives a release to the human spirit, provides the indispensable condition for the realization of its limitless potentialities.

Individual freedom, is then, a means, an invaluable means, toward national security and survival. But it is an end as well—the supreme end which the government of the United States was instituted to secure. Faith in freedom as a means and as an end must be the ultimate touchstone of American loyalty, of the loyalty of all free men.

The Weapon of Fear

WILLIAM T. EVJUE

TODAY, COMMUNISM HAS become the perfect scare-word with which the entrenched order can club the American people into submission and conformity. Millions of people have been denied the right of free speech through fear of being branded as disloyal. The press, radio, television and the movies have cringed before the assault that has been made on the printed and the spoken word. Boycott has been urged by the political demagogues who have sought to still criticism by threatening to pin the label of communism on an offender. Confidence of the people in their government has been threatened by casting the shadow of disloyalty over thousands of honest and conscientious persons. A campaign of hate, suspicion, distrust, confusion and character assassination has been let loose at a time when there is a great need for unity, confidence and a united front to meet a world menace.

This has been made possible, in large part, by the consummate demagoguery of the Senator from my state. In 1949, he knew that he was a dead duck politically unless he could find some way to divert the attention of the people from his miserable record. It was then, upon the advice of shrewd friends in Washington, that he decided to ride the issue of communism. Ever since, he has been fiercely using communism as a weapon with which to place a question mark on the loyalty of those who have dared to criticize

William T. Evjue, editor and publisher of the *Capital Times,* Madison, Wis., addressed the 1952 Hillman Prize Award luncheon. These are the concluding paragraphs of his address, which was adapted for the Foundation Reprint Series.

his record. I am proud to say that the *Capital Times* has been No. I on his newspaper list. You know the record—the New York *Post* did a great job in exposing him—the $10,000 from Lustron, the $20,000 wangled out of a sugar lobbyist to support Mc-Carthy's $72,000 loan in a Wisconsin bank, the $5,000 contribution from a Texas oil millionaire. McCarthy voted for the Kerr gas bill and tidelands oil. Isn't it strange that 500,000 citizens in Wisconsin voted for a man who has had to be prodded to pay taxes to support the government that has supported him during the major part of his adult life? Isn't it appalling to think that a man with his record is being accepted by millions of people as the leader who will save us from communism?

Communism is the giant problem facing a free world today. Disaster is sure to come if we allow political demagogues to represent us in this great emergency. It is a problem that will not be solved by the scheming politician on an un-American committee seeking a new headline in the afternoon edition by plastering some innocent person with the label of Communist. The menace of communism cannot be met by chucking a few Communists in jail. Reason must supplant demagoguery in meeting this problem.

If communism ever comes to this country, do you know where it will come from? Another depression. Communism will come when millions of people are hungry and out of jobs, when millions of farms and homes are being lost through mortgage foreclosures and when business is paralyzed because people do not have the money with which to buy the necessities of life. This is what Moscow is banking on. They know that mass hunger and poverty have been the allies of communism in its parade across the face of the earth.

It was the centuries old exploitation by a corrupt nobility and mass hunger and poverty that brought communism to Russia. It was the centuries of landlordism, colonialism, corruption and their accompanying mass poverty and hunger that brought communism to China. We are foolish enough to be quibbling over the responsibility of a few generals and diplomats in China as though they could have stopped the mighty avalanche of social discontent that swept over China. If all there is to this problem of communism is to expose and put in jail the Communists who have wormed themselves into places in government, how is the growth of communism in Italy, under the shadow of the Vatican, to be explained? It is to be explained in the hunger, poverty and denial of land among millions of peasants. Why aren't we realistic? Why aren't we willing to accept what we know is a fact—that a social revolution has been sweeping the world during the past 30 years, a revolution brought on because millions of people in all parts of the world are

"Always Happy To Take The Word Of A Lady"

FROM *The Herblock Book* (Beacon Press, 1952)

no longer willing to accept hunger, poverty, landlordism, colonialism, epidemic and disease as the way of life that has been ordained for them? Communists were smart enough to get on the side of the people in this great revolutionary struggle and to make hunger and poverty its allies as it made millions of converts each year.

The future safety of this country against the aggressions of communism lies with a patriotic, constructive, informed leadership that holds to the idea that the best insurance against communism is the American family that is well housed, well fed and with a reasonable prospect of security for the future. The future safety of this country must depend on leaders who realize that hunger, poverty, unemployment, the loss of homes and farms paves the way to communism. The political demagogues who have appropriated the issue of communism to serve their political ends, McCarthy, Hickenlooper, Jenner, Cain, Byrd and others in the Republican-Democratic coalition, are poor reeds to lean on in a fight against communism. These are the men who will be found continually voting on the side of the powerful special interests. They seized communism as an issue with which to divert the attention of the people from their service to pelf and privilege. Meanwhile, they can always be depended upon to vote against all measures to make life better for more people and to insulate them against communism— protection against dependency in old age, unemployment and occupational hazards, protection for their life savings, decent housing, medical care at a price they can afford to pay, farm price supports based on the knowledge that a healthy agriculture is potent insurance against communism, the blessings of electricity on the farm, the right of labor to bargain for a fair share of the wealth it helps to create and the extension of educational opportunity. Have you ever seen any evidence of any devotion to this type of insurance against communism on the part of McCarthy, Jenner and their interest-serving colleagues in the Senate?

See It Now:
The Radulovich Case

EDWARD R. MURROW

EDWARD R. MURROW: Good evening. A few weeks ago there occurred
a few obscure notices in the newspaper about a Lieutenant Milo
Radulovich, a Lieutenant in the Air Force Reserve and also something about Air Force Regulation 35-62. That is a regulation which
states that a man may be regarded as a security risk if he has close
and continuing association with Communists or people believed to
have Communist sympathies. Lieutenant Radulovich was asked to
resign. He declined. A Board was called and heard his case. At the
end, it was recommended that he be severed from the Air Force,
although it was also stated that there was no question whatsoever as
to the Lieutenant's loyalty. We propose to examine, insofar as we
can, the case of Lieutenant Radulovich. Our reporter, Joe Wershba:
JOE WERSHBA: This is the town of Dexter, Michigan . . . population
1500.
EDWARD R. MURROW: This statue is at the head of Ann Arbor Street.
"Erected by the citizens of Dexter to the heroes who fought and the
martyrs who died that the Republic might live." This is the story of
Milo Radulovich . . . no special hero, no martyr. He came to Dexter
one year ago after ten years in the Air Force . . . won a general
commendation for working on a secret weather station in Greenland.
Now he is a senior at the University of Michigan eight miles away.

In 1953 the late Edward R. Murrow was given a Hillman Prize Award
for his coverage of two civil liberties cases on *See It Now*, his CBS TV
series. These excerpts are from "The Radulovich Case," first broadcast
October 20, 1953.

His wife works nights at the Telephone Company. They live at 7867 Ann Arbor Street. This is Milo Radulovich.

MILO RADULOVICH: The Force does not question my loyalty in the least. They have reiterated that on several occasions. They have presented me with allegations against my sister and father that they have—to the effect that my sister and dad have taken—have read what are now called subversive newspapers, and that my sister and father's activities are questionable. That's the specific charge, or allegation I prefer to call it, against them. Against me, the actual charge against me is that I had maintained a close and continuing relationship with my dad and my sister over the years. I had spent the last seven years studying or actually working in meteorology. That is weather forecasting—and now for the past approximately year and a half or two I have been studying Physics at the University of Michigan. Well, I think I am being a realist about it. Anybody that is labeled with a security risk in these days, especially in Physics or Meteorology, simply won't be able to find employment in his field of work. In other words, I believe that if I am labeled a security risk—if the Air Force won't have me—I ask the question —who else will?

EDWARD R. MURROW: This is Selfridge Field, Headquarters of the Tenth Air Force, where the Radulovich hearing took place. There was a Board made up of three Colonels whose recommendation was that Radulovich be separated from the service as a bad security risk, quote, for having maintained a close, continuing association with your sister and your father, unquote. The Board also stated, "No question as to your loyalty is involved." No reporters were permitted at the hearing and the Air Force refused to provide us with a transcript of the hearing. (It was unclassified, however).

EDWARD R. MURROW: Lieutenant Radulovich was defended by Attorney Charles C. Lockwood, and this is his report on the hearing.

CHARLES C. LOCKWOOD: When this case started, the President of the Hearing Board placed a sealed envelope in front of him and said: "These are the allegations. Now proceed to exonerate yourself." There were twelve charges made by the Air Force—eight of them against the sister and four of them against the father. We put in several disinterested witnesses who testified definitely and positively upon the allegations made by the Air Force. These witnesses gave unchallenged testimony and they gave it under oath. The Air Force did not produce a single witness. We were not told who the accusers were. We have no right to confront them or cross-examine them. But at the conclusion of the trial, although we had met the allegations, the Air Force made findings at the conclusion of the hearing that every single allegation was true. They disregarded every bit of testimony we introduced and the statements of all our witnesses. As a matter of fact, we have had no hearing at all. We have had no day in court. In all the thirty-two years that I have been a practicing attorney in Detroit, I have never witnessed such a farce and travesty upon justice as this thing has developed. Now this whole theory of

"I Don't Need You To Protect Me, Junior"

FROM *The Herblock Book* (Beacon Press, 1952)

guilty by relationship is something that was adopted back in the thirteenth and fourteenth century and then abandoned as being inhuman and cruel. It was later revived in Germany under Hitler and Himmler and it died when they did. Now the Air Force, for some unknown reason, has revived this intolerable guilty by relationship and the whole country is shocked as a reason—by reason thereof.

EDWARD R. MURROW: This is the transcript of the hearing. It is not classified. We got it from the Lieutenant's lawyers. I would like to read you just a bit of it. The lawyer says: "This whole proceeding is taken over objection." The President of the Board says: "That is understood and adequately shown in the record. Will the Recorder

"Say, What Ever Happened To 'Freedom-From-Fear'?"

FROM *The Herblock Book* (Beacon Press, 1952)

introduce the government's evidence."

RECORDER: I would like to introduce into evidence as Exhibit F, the classified investigative file.

PRESIDENT: It will be received and will be considered by the board.

THE LAWYER: Is it being received as a closed envelope?

PRESIDENT: It is a confidential investigative file.

LAWYER: It is a report to the Air Force by someone or some agency, is that right?

PRESIDENT: It is a consolidation of reports by various investigative agencies of the government.

THE LAWYER: Of which the respondent is not informed, does not see and has no way of knowing what it is except as found in the statement of reasons?

PRESIDENT: That is correct.

MURROW: Later the President says: "It is not in a sealed envelope in a strict sense."

MURROW: The lawyer replies: "May the record show it is an envelope approximately 9 x 12 inches with a rubber band placed around same and scotch tape along the edges which have been broken up, that is the scotch tape, which we can fully see from where we are sitting, with no right to examine it."

MURROW: Then the lawyer says to the President of the Board: "Do you think we all have the right to transmit our views and publish them?"

MURROW: And the President of the Board replies: "I might decline to answer that question in that I am not on trial for my views and my personal views might not be the views of the Air Force."

MURROW: Perhaps you will permit me to read a few sentences just at the end because I should like to say rather precisely what I mean. We have told the Air Force that we will provide facilities for any comments, criticism, or correction it may wish to make in regard to the case of Milo Radulovich. The case must go through two more Air Force Boards routines and channels before it reaches Secretary Talbott who will make the final decision. We are unable to judge the charges against the father or the Lieutenant's sister because neither we nor you nor the Lieutenant nor the lawyers know precisely what was contained in that manila envelope. Was it hearsay, rumor, gossip, or hard, provable fact backed by creditable witnesses; we do not know. There is a distinct difference between a loyalty and a security risk. A man may be entirely loyal, but at the same time be subjected to coercion, influence, or pressure, which may cause him to act contrary to the best interests of national security. In the case of Lieutenant Radulovich, the Board found that there was no question of his loyalty, but that he was regarded as a security risk. The Security Officers will tell you that a man who had a sister in Warsaw might be entirely loyal, but would be subjected to pressure as a result of threats that might be made against his sister's security or well being. They contend that a man who has a sister in the Communist party in this country might be subjected to the same kind of pressure, but here again, no evidence was adduced to prove that Radulovich's sister was a member of the party, and the case against his father certainly was not made. We believe that "the son shall not bear the iniquity of the father," even though that iniquity be proved beyond all doubt, which in this case, it was not. But we believe, too, that this case illustrates the urgent need for the Armed Forces to communicate, more fully than they have so far done, the procedures and regulations to be followed in attempting to protect the national security and the rights of the individual at the same time. Whatever happens in this whole area of the relationship between the individual and the state, we do ourselves—it cannot be blamed upon Malenkov, Mao Tse Tung, or even our Allies. It seems to us that—that is to Fred Friendly and myself that that is a subject that should be argued about endlessly.

McCarthy:
A Documented Record

MORRIS RUBIN

MCCARTHYISM HAS BEEN defined in a variety of ways, none of them flattering to the man who gave his name to the ism. Perhaps the most effective method of evaluating McCarthy and McCarthyism is to observe them in action.

One of the most criticized ingredients in McCarthyism is the ruthless smearing of individuals who happen to hold views on foreign policy or other issues which McCarthy finds objectionable.

The *Michigan Catholic,* official publication of the archdiocese of Detroit, skillfully caught this characteristic of McCarthyism in an editorial (*Sept. 20, 1951*) which conceded McCarthy's right to fight his foes on foreign policies, and then went on:

"But that is quite a different matter from exposure of covert Communist influence. It is an issue that ought to be fought on its own merits, and not as a smear campaign that seeks to discredit what are apparently honest motives."

When charged with conducting a smear campaign, as he has

Morris Rubin supervised the preparation of *The McCarthy Record* when it was first issued during the Senator's re-election campaign in 1952. In April, 1954, an up-dated and expanded version was printed as a special issue of *The Progressive,* of which Rubin is editor, and was subsequently given a Sidney Hillman Prize Award. The two following excerpts summarize a few highlights.

118

been, not only by Catholic publications but by spokesmen of virtually every religious denomination, McCarthy habitually denies the charge with a statement like:

"All right, what innocent person have I injured? I've asked that question lots of times—on forums and in speeches—and nobody ever tells me. I've never yet had anyone give me the name of a single innocent person who has been hurt by my methods." (*New York* World Telegram and Sun, *June 13, 1953.*)

Americans who have the facts have no difficulty driving McCarthyites to cover when this question is asked. The official records and the reports of the country's most reliable newspapers show the extent to which McCarthy has smeared individuals. Suppose we look at a few of the better-known cases.

On June 14, 1951, speaking to an all but empty Senate chamber, McCarthy delivered a 60,000-word attack on one of the most distinguished of Americans, George C. Marshall, former Secretary of Defense, former Secretary of State, former Chief of Staff, a five-star general, and subsequently (1953) winner of the Nobel Prize for Peace.

Although McCarthy has since offered a variety of interpretations of what he recalled saying on that occasion, the record is clear that he accused Gen. Marshall of treasonable conduct.

In his bitter outcry against Marshall, McCarthy went on to say:

"Gen. Marshall is at the head of our Armed Services. Quite apart from the destructive nature of his public acts since the beginnings of World War II, I ask in all gravity whether a man so steeped in falsehood who has recourse to the lie whenever it suits his convenience is fit to hold so exalted a place where he must be a model to the officers and men of our Armed Services." (*Congressional Record, June 14, 1951, p. 6752.*)

In his book-length attack on Marshall, *America's Retreat From Victory,* McCarthy professes to see in Marshall's activities "a pattern which finds his decision maintained with great stubbornness and skill, always and invariably serving the world policy of the Kremlin."

And yet McCarthy continues to insist that "no innocent person has been hurt by my methods." If Marshall has not been hurt by McCarthy's smear attack, the only reason can be that Marshall is too great a figure and too patriotic an American to be affected by McCarthy's calculated attempt at character assassination.

The conservative Washington *Star* characterized McCarthy's tirade against Marshall as "an adaptation of Hitler's big-lie technique."

In 1953 when Gen. Marshall was awarded the Nobel Prize for Peace, McCarthy was asked if he had anything to say on the award in view of his bitter attack on Marshall's loyalty. "No comment," was all he would say.

Another prominent American smeared by McCarthy—and vindicated by the evidence—was Dr. Philip C. Jessup, professor of international law at Columbia University. Dr. Jessup has held a number of government posts during the past 25 years, starting in the Justice Department during the Coolidge Administration.

In 1950 McCarthy charged that Jessup "has an unusual affinity for Communist causes." (*Congressional Record, Mar. 30, 1950, p. 4464.*) On another occasion McCarthy said, "For some reason or other, you find Jessup always is following the Communist Party line."

McCarthy persisted in his smear of Jessup despite clear-cut evidence to refute his charges.

Hiram Bingham, former Republican Senator from Connecticut, then head of the Federal Government's Loyalty Review Board, wrote Sen. John Sparkman of Alabama in response to a query:

"My dear Senator: With further reference to your letter of Sept. 24 requesting information as to the status of Philip C. Jessup, a panel of the Loyalty Review Board has now put its seal of approval on the action of the Loyalty Board of the State Department in finding *there is no reasonable doubt of his loyalty.*" (Italics ours.)

Said *The New York Times* editorially:

"In making a political career of mud-slinging and Red-baiting, Sen. McCarthy has launched irresponsible, unprovable, and ridiculous charges against so many respected citizens that his attacks have become almost an accolade.

"Sheer disgust and weariness of his demagogic tactics impel fair-minded men to rise to the defense of his victims . . .

"In the case of Dr. Philip C. Jessup, this newspaper has sharply disagreed on occasion with his views and his attitudes on matters

of public policy. He is a liberal whose good impulses have sometimes confused and misled him. But we have never had the slightest doubt of his loyalty or his patriotism."

Another ingredient of McCarthyism is the practice of shooting
first and asking questions later, of rushing into print with sensa-
tional charges and then, after a while, looking around for some

"WE NEED JOE IN OUR BUSINESS" [1]
D. R. Fitzpatrick in the St. Louis *Post-Dispatch*

evidence that might support those charges.

A notable case involved McCarthy's shameless attempt to imply
that former President Harry Truman had deliberately concealed
from the FBI a list of some 150 Soviet spy suspects received from
Canadian authorities.

McCarthy's statement hit the front pages with big, black headlines, as he knew it would. Then, according to the Associated
Press, "McCarthy fired off a letter to Atty. Gen. Herbert Brownell
asking if the Justice Department ever got such a list from Truman.
He called this a first step toward deciding whether to ask the
investigation's subcommittee to call Truman as a witness."

---

[1] Daniel R. Fitzpatrick won a 1954 Hillman Special Prize Award for his
editorial cartoons in *The St. Louis Dispatch*.

Two weeks later, McCarthy reluctantly revealed that the FBI had assured him Mr. Truman had not withheld any information he had received from Canada—a fact which inevitably received far less prominence in the press. McCarthy, of course, could have acquired the necessary information by picking up a telephone or writing his letter to the Department of Justice before he rushed into print with his original statement.

Still another ingredient of McCarthyism is the sly use of innuendo to plant doubts about the integrity and loyalty of Americans of unassailable character and patriotism. One of the shabbiest examples of this McCarthy treatment involved Nathan Pusey, the new president of Harvard University.

In the summer of 1952, Dr. Pusey was president of Lawrence College, located in Appleton, Wis., McCarthy's home town. Dr. Pusey joined with a group of distinguished citizens, among them bankers, industrialists, clergymen, educators, doctors, and lawyers in sponsoring *The McCarthy Record*. Throughout the campaign of 1952, when he was seeking reelection to the Senate, McCarthy refrained from attacking *The McCarthy Record* or its sponsors, and refused to challenge in any way that documented analysis of his record.

In the summer of 1953, when Pusey was appointed to the presidency of Harvard, Neal O'Hara, columnist for the Boston *Traveler,* asked McCarthy for an estimate of his fellow-townsman. In his reply, McCarthy said:

"I do not think Dr. Pusey is or has been a member of the Communist Party." The use of this language to create a doubt where none was justified was bitterly denounced by the paper which is closest to and most enthusiastic about McCarthy's operations, his home town Appleton *Post-Crescent,* as a *"gutter-type approach."*

In his statement to the Boston *Traveler,* McCarthy went on to say of Dr. Pusey:

"His activities could well be compared to the undercover Communist who slaps at the Communist Party in general terms, cusses out the thoroughly well-known Communist, and then directs his energy toward attempting to destroy those who are really hurting the Communist Party by digging out the dangerous undercover members of the party, who parade as loyal to the country which their conspiracy is attempting to destroy.

"What motivates Pusey, I have no way of knowing. He is what could best be described as a rabid anti, anti-Communist."

McCarthy's attempt to smear Dr. Pusey infuriated some of the Senator's best friends in his home town—people who knew Dr. Pusey well and who were thus exposed first-hand for the first time

ALL IN THE NAME OF SECURITY

D. R. Fitzpatrick in the St. Louis *Post-Dispatch*

to McCarthyism in action.

The most outraged response came from the Appleton *Post-Crescent* quoted above, whose managing editor, John Reidl, was listed number one among "McCarthy's Wisconsin newspaper backers" by Richard Wilson, chief of the Cowles correspondents in Washington (Look, *Dec. 1, 1953*).

After noting that McCarthy had been fighting "a two-front battle against the machinations of the enemy, and against the doubts of his fellow Americans as to the fairness of his methods," the *Post-Crescent* went on to say:

"The Senator has multiplied those doubts by his gratuitous and completely uncalled-for attack on Dr. Nathan Pusey. Dr. Pusey is known to us all here in Appleton for his integrity, his devotion to American ideals, his exemplary personal life, and his leadership in the liberal arts movement that is just as important in fighting Communism as McCarthy's exposures.

"The only motive for the Senator's statement appears to be Dr. Pusey's opposition to him in last fall's election. If this is the case, McCarthy is running way out of bounds. Dr. Pusey, like any other loyal citizen, has a perfect right to take whatever stand he pleases in a political campaign, and should not be subjected to personal slaps for so doing."

McCarthy's use of innuendo in the case of Dr. Pusey is paralleled by a similar device he used in attempting to smear *The Commonweal,* the distinguished Catholic magazine which has been critical of many of McCarthy's methods. Here is what happened:

In August 1953 the North American Newspaper Alliance, a national press syndicate, released to its member papers a four-part interview with McCarthy. In it the Senator was asked to comment on his habit of labelling critics as "Communists."

McCarthy replied, "I'd have to know what critics you have in mind."

When *The Commonweal* was mentioned, McCarthy said, "I never said *The Commonweal* was Communist. I just said that, in front of the Jenner Committee, one of its writers refused to say whether he is a Communist or not. From that you can draw your own conclusions."

The editors of *The Commonweal* asked McCarthy to identify the writer to whom he had referred. Five weeks later McCarthy "replied" by asking the editors "what connection Thomas Davin has with *The Commonweal*—whether he writes for it, whether he has any voice in determination of policy, etc."

The Commonweal reported in its issue of Nov. 27, 1953:

"We . . . assured Sen. McCarthy that Mr. Davin had never at any time written a single line for *The Commonweal,* that he has never had the slightest voice in determining the magazine's policy, and that, previous to the present incident, four of the present five editors had never heard of him. We therefore ask the Senator to make a public correction of his own statement (with its dark innuendo: 'from that you can draw your own conclusions') and to bring this correction to the attention of the North American Newspaper Alliance."

A recurring McCarthy device is to play fast and loose with the record, even in cases where the record can be easily checked.

An example and one which is a revealing study of Mc-Carthyism in action came in a speech McCarthy gave in Milwaukee, Sept. 3, 1952, during his primary campaign for reelection. McCarthy said in the course of his address:

"There are those who say, 'But there are no longer Communists in government.' I am not going to ask you to take my word for that. I have in my hand the brief prepared by seven lawyers of the Justice Department dated July 28, 1952. Let me read to you from it:

" 'Illegal passports have been used to expedite travel in foreign countries by members of the Communist Party. Plans have been discussed by leading members of the party and agents of the Soviet secret police to obtain blank American passports from Communists employed in the State Department.'

"For the benefit of the press, that's on page 91 of their very excellent and lengthy brief."

Two days later, on Sept. 5, the Associated Press reported from Washington that Atty. Gen. James P. McGranery had exposed the distortion McCarthy had made of the Department report. Mc-Granery said that Paul Crouch, an acknowledged former Communist, had testified that in 1928 he had met a man identified as the head of the Russian secret police in the United States and learned from him that a plan was afoot to obtain blank passports from Communists employed in the State Department.

"His [McCarthy's] reference to 'plans' discussed to obtain blank American passports from Communists employed in the State Department does not mean that there were Communists employed in the State Department," McGranery said.

In other words McCarthy used a quotation from the Department's report which referred to a condition that was alleged to exist 24 years earlier under the Administration of Calvin Coolidge, to support his charge that there were Communists in government in 1952!

The recent uproar generated by McCarthy's violent clash with the U.S. Army—a case in which he accused high Army officials of "coddling Communists"—is perhaps the best recent example of McCarthyism in action. The background:

Dr. Irving Peress, a New York dentist, was called to duty as a captain Jan. 3, 1953. In the routine loyalty inquiry that followed, he invoked the Fifth Amendment in refusing to answer questions. In June, 1953, the commandant at Camp Kilmer, N. J., where

Peress was stationed, recommended that the dentist be dismissed. This was more than six months before McCarthy took a hand.

But as a result of the Army's "hurry up and wait" delays known

BIRD FROM AN ALIEN NEST

D. R. Fitzpatrick in the St. Louis *Post-Dispatch*

to every GI, Peress was not dismissed then. In a completely separate action Peress received an automatic promotion to major in October under the law requiring advancement of medical men according to age and professional experience. On Feb. 2, 1954, he was given his honorable discharge.

Army officials, *The New York Times* reported Feb. 26, 1954, "admit certain aspects of the case have been poorly handled . . ." But, they were quick to point out, they "had no feasible legal alternative but to grant the dentist an honorable discharge under Defense Department directives. . ."

The case began to command frontpage headlines when McCarthy summoned Gen. Ralph W. Zwicker, new commandant at Kilmer, to a secret hearing. McCarthy's treatment of Zwicker angered Army officials. The official transcript shows that Zwicker, a combat veteran much decorated for heroism, had declined to answer some questions because a Presidential order forbade Army officials from revealing details of loyalty investigations. Zwicker's steadfast insistence on following Presidential orders enraged Mc-Carthy into using language of this kind:

"General, let's try and be truthful." . . . "I cannot help but question either your honesty or your intelligence." . . . "Don't give me any of that double-talk." . . . "Anyone with the brains of a five-year-old child can understand that question." . . . "Any [General] who says, 'I will protect another General who protected Communists' is not fit to wear that uniform."

Afterward, McCarthy said, "I was too temperate."

The violence of McCarthy's attack on Army officials created a front-page sensation throughout the world and measurably lowered American stature everywhere people could read. Even papers usually friendly to McCarthy were critical of his behavior.

Summarizing the whole case for the Republican New York *Herald Tribune* Feb. 27, Walter Lippmann expressed the conclusion of countless middle-of-the-road newspapers and citizens when he said:

"Manifestly, McCarthy's purpose . . . was to demonstrate his power to intimidate the Army, to show that he was so powerful that he could reach over the head of the Commander-in-Chief and terrorize individual officers. . . .

"This is the totalitarianism of the man: his cold, calculated, sustained, and ruthless effort to make himself feared. That is why he has been staging . . . demonstrations, each designed to show that he respects nobody . . . and no institution in the land, and that everyone at whom he growls will run away."

McCarthy sought, as always, to reserve the last word for himself. He issued a statement sneering at the "silly tempest in a teapot" and characterized the criticism as "unprecedented mud-slinging . . . by the extreme left-wing elements of the press and radio . . ." McCarthy did not make it clear whether this designation was meant to include the Chicago *Tribune,* the Hearst press, and the scores of ultra-conservative dailies and radio commentators that had condemned his conduct.

* * *

The dominant reality that emerges from the documented record of McCarthy in action is the fact that this man who has made anti-

Communism his political career has contributed dangerously to strengthening the Communist cause. If the Kremlin could succeed in planting one of its own agents in the Senate of the United States, it could hardly hope for greater results in creating doubt, disunity, and fear in America than it has gained from McCarthy's operations.

If this judgment seems harsh and extreme, we can only reply that the hard facts make it clear that—

McCarthy has struck violently at the very principles of freedom and fair play which distinguish democratic self-government from Communist regimentation.

McCarthy has sown seeds of suspicion and disunity among the nations of the free world at the very moment they most need unity against the threat of Communist aggression.

McCarthy has flagrantly demoralized the civil and military establishments of our government at a time of unparalleled world crisis.

By substituting headlines and hysteria for facts and evidence, McCarthy has so successfully harnessed Hitler's concept of "The Big Lie" to his own purposes that many decent Americans actually believe he has exposed a Communist plot in our government and rescued the Republic from betrayal by traitors.

Many Americans who share this belief say they find McCarthy's methods repulsive, but they feel that in tense times like ours we need someone to do "the dirty work" of exposing the subversives in our midst.

This widely held feeling might be more understandable if McCarthy were in fact exposing Communists in government and saving us from a Red plot. But fact piled relentlessly on fact shows that the evidence does not in any way support such a conclusion.

In the pitifully rare cases that he has focused his sights on what may have seemed like a worthwhile target, McCarthy has so totally distorted the evidence and overplayed his hand as to render his "revelations" less than useless. In his eyes honest mistakes, misjudgments, or misunderstandings become part of a sinister pattern of conspiracy.

The evidence seems to us overwhelming that if we overlook methods because it is results we say we want, McCarthy has not in any measurable way contributed to strengthening the security of our country against spies and saboteurs. More than four years of hit-and-run accusations have yet to produce a single conviction of a Communist in government on evidence uncovered by McCarthy.

Some Americans who know of no specific achievements in McCarthy's record of Red-hunting are still loath to criticize because they think his activities have been worthwhile in dramatizing the evils of Communism and alerting the nation to the menace. However, as Elmer Davis so crisply put it recently, "This amounts to saying that nothing brings the danger of fire more to the attention of the public than turning in false alarms all over town."

But means and methods *are* important to people who love liberty and cherish principles of tolerance and fair play. It is the contrast between our means and methods, and those of the totalitarians, whether Communist or Fascist, which mark one of the great gulfs between them and us.

Allan Nevins, one of our foremost historians, summed this up with great clarity recently when he said:

"The fact is that in the protection of basic human rights, method is everything. The Spanish Inquisition justified torture on the ground that it was in a good cause, and was a mere matter of method. The Russian secret police justifies the knock on the door at 3 a.m., the summary sentence, and the pistol shot or deportation to a slave camp on the ground that all this is in a good cause and is a mere matter of method."

The right of Congressional committees to investigate and the need for the most comprehensive surveillance in guarding the nation's security are not at issue; what is at stake is the urgent necessity for exposing and combating the dangerously un-American character of McCarthy's one-man show before it completes the corruption of what is finest in the American system of law and justice.

Learned Hand, one of the wisest of American jurists, who has retired as Chief Judge of the Federal Circuit Court of Appeals after 42 years on the bench, warned his countrymen of this very danger in a memorable address a year and a half ago. Said Judge Hand:

"I believe that that community is already in the process of dissolution where each man begins to eye his neighbor as a possible enemy, where non-conformity with the accepted creed, political as well as religious, is a mark of disaffection; where denunciation without specification or backing takes the place of evidence; where orthodoxy chokes freedom of dissent; where faith in the eventual supremacy of reason has become so timid that we dare not enter our convictions in the open lists, to win or lose.

"Such fears as these are a solvent which eat out the cement that binds the stones together; they may in the end subject us to a despotism as evil as any that we dread; and they can be allayed only insofar as we refuse to proceed on suspicion, and trust one another until we have tangible ground for misgiving."

In his nightly newscast Feb. 24, 1954, Edward R. Murrow quoted David Schoenbrun, CBS chief in Paris, on precisely this point. Commenting on the shocked reponse of our friends in Europe to the capitulation of the U.S. Army to McCarthy, Schoenbrun told Murrow: "They [our friends] don't think a line can be drawn between objectives and methods, particularly when methods, as in the McCarthy case, are so spectacular and destructive that they obviously achieve objectives far removed from the avowed one.

"It is a case of burning down the barn to catch a rat, one French editor told me, pointing out that it is ridiculous to say you approve rat-catching, although you deplore the fact that the barn burned down. You cannot separate the two, any more than you can say that you approved Hitler's aims while deploring his uncouth methods. Hitler's aims may have been to eradicate Communism in Germany and destroy the Soviet Union, but what his *methods* did in fact accomplish was to eradicate democracy in Germany and destroy France—not Russia."

We live in a dangerous age, and surely one of the greatest dangers that confronts us is the counterfeit philosophy of Communism and its appeal to the underprivileged of humanity. But we do not begin to meet that menace by burning books, by crushing dissent, and by creating an atmosphere of hysteria.

"How can we defeat Communism," President Eisenhower asked at Dartmouth last year, "unless we know what it is? What it teaches— why does it have such an appeal for men? . . . . We have got to fight it with something better."

Here is the heart of our problem in this dangerous age—the challenge to oppose Communism with something better. This we can never hope to do if we abandon our most cherished democratic principles and embrace the very methods we abhor in Communism. This process of diluting precisely those qualities which distinguish us from those we oppose is dangerously far advanced in McCarthyism. McCarthy's daily activities carry us perilously close to the Kremlin concepts that trial by jury must be replaced with trial by mere accusation; that honest, human error of judgment is equivalent to criminal offense; that dissenters are traitors, and that every friendly foreign nation must become our regimented satellite or suffer our wrath and reprisals.

The first battle in the struggle against Communism is within ourselves—to strengthen our own dedication to democracy by living its compelling principles in our daily lives.

If we are to be true to ourselves and effective in action with others, ours must be more than a mere negative adherence to anti-Communism. A fighting faith in freedom, not cringing fear of Communism, alone will qualify the United States of America to lead the free world in the historic clash of ideologies that is the dominant fact of life in our time.

Can the Supreme Court Defend Civil Liberties?

EDMOND CAHN

WHEN THE ANNALS of our time come to be written, the future historian is bound to regard us with amazed admiration. Here are the American people of the postwar decade, a people full of kindness, generosity and solicitude for the welfare of their neighbors and all mankind. Here are a people who have lavished untold billions on the poor and needy in every continent. Here are a people responsive to a seemingly endless list of charitable and benevolent appeals—a people who can be made to weep by a picture of a little girl whose doll is broken. What a good-hearted people we are!

When the future historian has finished admiring us for our benevolence and humaneness, he will begin a new chapter to record our extraordinary and unparalleled ingenuity. Being such a humane people we could not possibly do to other people, whether citizens or aliens, one tenth of the things that apparently have been done if he believes our statute books, the records of our administrative agencies and the reports of our courts. If we are so tender-hearted, how did all these seemingly cruel and unjust things come about? How were they possible? Our future historian will see the

For several years the Hillman Foundation sponsored one-semester courses on civil liberties at The New School for Social Research. In 1956 the late Edmond Cahn, legal scholar and professor at New York University Law School, as one of the visiting lecturers, gave this lecture, which was later used as a Hillman Reprint.

answer without trouble. All these things were made possible by our inventiveness and ingenuity, adapted scientifically to the fields of government and law. Since our tender hearts would never permit us to be unjust or cruel to other human beings, we applied our world-famous ingenuity to the task of de-personalizing and de-humanizing our victims. Rarely, if ever, has a task been executed with so much imagination and ingenuity.

I don't mean to suggest that there were no historic precedents for what we have done. We are not the only people who have spared their sensitive feelings in some such way. I think, however, we do deserve the palm for having applied the process of de-humanization with superlative skill and ingenuity.

You know how we did it. We de-humanized first the crime or offense, second the trial or hearing, and third the punishments. Let us take first the nature of the crime. We think too highly of human dignity in the United States to hold anyone guilty by mere association, or to penalize anyone for his thoughts or opinions, or the causes he advocates. In fact, in this blessed country you have to be guilty of overt anti-social conduct before the law interferes with your liberty. If we allowed people to be punished for anything other than overt conduct, we should be violating our most cherished traditions. These we never violate. We invariably respect human dignity. Naturally, if someone is charged with conspiracy to advocate overthrowing the government by force, it is not our fault that he has chosen to withdraw from the human species.

We used to think that only the top leaders of the Communist Party had handed in their resignation, but soon we found that a considerable number of smaller fry had also chosen to abandon participation in genus homo. Having got this far, the exodus did not stop. In two recent cases, which are apparently on their way to the Supreme Court, the so-called "membership clause" of section 2 of the Smith Act has been invoked for the first time. Our government claims that membership or affiliation with any subversive society, group or assembly, "knowing the purpose thereof," is a crime in and of itself, and the government knows it can rely on the overwhelming majority of American juries not to be too exacting about proof of "knowing the purpose thereof." According to these cases, you not only don't have to do anything, you don't have to advocate anything, you don't even have to conspire to advocate anything; all you have to do is "affiliate" in some way or other, "knowing the purpose thereof."

Consider how ingeniously we've de-humanized the trial or hearing. As part of our ideal of human dignity, we Americans have scornfully rejected inquisitions held *in camera,* invasions of homes and families and personal privacy, resort to secret files, reliance on testimony of anonymous informers, and all the other vices that we associate with the Star Chamber and the Spanish Inquisition. We are not like other nations in these respects; we would never consider resorting to such methods. Of course, it is true that if the individual involved is an alien, he can be deported in 1956 for having been a member of the Communist Party for a few years in the 1920s. If the individual involved is a government employee, it is true that he can lose his job and be stigmatized permanently as disloyal without having the elementary safeguards we would furnish him if he were charged with parking on the wrong side of the street. It is also true as shown in Adam Yarmolinsky's "Case Studies in Personnel Security" that if you work for a corporation that does business with the government and the business is of a kind that involves security regulations, you may be discharged and branded with disloyalty, not disloyalty to your company but disloyalty to your native land, and still not have the slightest idea about the so-called evidence against you. These incidents may prove very inconvenient to the individuals involved, but they should not complain that they have been deprived of due process of law. We have been inventive enough to develop a distinction between a constitutional right and a mere privilege, a distinction between a privilege and a mere "matter of grace," a distinction between a criminal trial and a civil proceeding, a distinction between a citizen and a resident alien, a distinction between a resident alien who is in the country and one who has been indiscreet enough to leave it for travel, a distinction between a rule of law and the discretion of the attorney general, a distinction between justiciable issues and political issues, and a distinction between evidence obtained illegally by Federal officers and evidence obtained illegally by anyone else. If these distinctions do not suffice, more and even subtler ones will be produced. We are an ingenious people.

In the third place, we have done a thorough and complete job of de-humanizing the punishment. Branding individuals as security risks, taking away the citizenship of persons who have been naturalized, deporting resident aliens: these make only part of the story. Perhaps the cleverest display of our dialectical virtuosity is the Expatriation Act of 1954. In this legislation we have surpassed even ourselves. The legislation creates no new crimes and imposes no new punishments. At least we have been too ingenious to call them punishments. All we do is take away the American citizenship of everybody, including native-born Americans, who may be convicted of advocating subversion. This is in addition to all other penalites. Of course, we don't consider it a punishment, because we say on behalf of these individuals, whether they want us to say it or not, that they have chosen to renounce the priceless right of American citizenship. True, this may leave them in a strange position. They become entirely stateless, whereas even the aliens in our midst have a claim to nationality somewhere. Many experts say it is a violation of international law and of the United Nations charter to reduce people to a level of statelessness. There is not a nation on earth that believes more sincerely in the principles of the United Nations than we do. Can the future historian blame us because these individuals have chosen of their own free will and accord to renounce their American citizenship and become stateless? Do you really think he can?

The picture I have been painting makes part of our national portrait. I have not presented the whole picture, nor etched in the details, most of which are all too familiar and repetitious. I've said enough to identify the specific problem. Given the framework of the American Constitution, given the ideal of human dignity that we claim to revere, given the history of the past ten years during which we have been de-humanizing the concept of crime, the concept of trial or hearing, and the concept of punishment; given all these things, what can the Supreme Court of the United States do about them? That is our problem.

In recent years, innumerable speeches and articles, not to mention Justice Robert H. Jackson's posthumous book, have been devoted to contending that the Supreme Court can do little or nothing. Most of this literature sounds like the querulous excuses of a hypochondriac. Back in 1935 and 1936, the court drank some raw wine and woke up with a bad headache in 1937. You would think the hangover would have ended by now, but such is not the case. On the contrary, the memories of the 1930s still haunt many of the justices. They keep wringing their hands over the court's impotence, while they tell us that unlike Congress, it must sit and wait for cases to come before it, that unlike Congress it cannot launch its own investigations, and that it must depend on other branches of the government to define its appellate jurisdiction and enforce its decrees. Justice Jackson said that no court decree could have stopped the downfall of the French monarchy or the onslaught of the French Revolution, as though he believed that our conditions were similar to those of Paris in 1789 and as though our Secretary of Agriculture had looked unsympathetically at some starving employees of General Motors and said "Let them eat cake."

Of course, the Supreme Court must function like a court; it cannot perform the operations of a legislature. Of course, like all governmental institutions, there are limits to its powers. But Congress and the President do not refuse to perform their duties just because they cannot also act like a court. We know and the court knows it *can* act forcefully and courageously when it wills to. It has done so on many occasions, for example, in the Steel Seizure case and very recently in the School Segregation cases.

A hypochondriac can gradually convince himself that day by day he is able to do less and less. Then, if he is a really imaginative hypochondriac, he will find a complicated variety of ways to say "No, I can't." There are at least four technical ways for the Supreme Court to say "no" without appearing to do so. (1) It can say the party who is trying to present the question to it has no standing to sue. In other words, the question may be an important question, but the party who poses it is not the right party. (2) The court can say the proceeding is not a true "case or controversy" and is, therefore, not within its power under the Constitution. (3) It can say the question in the case is a "political question," which means that the executive or legislative or perhaps the electorate must find the answer, not the courts. (4) In the majority of instances, the Supreme Court can simply refuse to take the case at all, without publishing any explanation. Most of the Supreme Court's appellate jurisdiction is taken or refused at the justices' option by granting or denying a writ of certiorari.

Some experts would like to see the Court liberalize its policies on standing to sue or the scope of "case or controversy" or the defining of political questions or the frequency of granting certiorari. Other experts are not too eager to have the Court take more cases as long as it continues to decide them the way it has in recent years. They prefer no decision to what they consider a wrong decision. All this goes only to show that you cannot take a practical position, even on such an apparently technical question as the standing to sue, without finding yourself involved sooner or later in a clash between disparate conceptions of American government. The technical policies are important, but mainly as by-products. Ultimately, wherever we take hold of our subject, we must confront two rival philosophies of government, each of which has a set of answers to the questions of judicial technique. What the Supreme Court can or ought to do depends, in final analysis, on a choice between two fundamentally different political philosophies.

When a speaker says he is going to present two separate and distinct philosophies, one naturally expects him to dramatize the difference between them. Usually, as he describes the philosophy which he prefers he will seem to press a button on one side of the platform so that from above a sort of heavenly vision descends as in the old morality plays. Then, turning to the other philosophy, he presses a button on the opposite side, and we see a trapdoor opening (over there), we get a whiff of sulphur and brimstone, and some repulsive demon rises gradually before our eyes. If I have created any such expectations, I'm sorry but they will be disappointed. I do not conceive of constitutional law in terms of a calendar of saints or a study of demonology; nor do I believe, when a judge seems mistaken, that he is necessarily a hypocrite or a tool of the corporate interests. The gap between our two philosophies of law does not consist in attributing good faith to one and bad faith to the other.

The division between them goes back to the time of the founding fathers. In point of fact, James Madison on one side and Thomas Jefferson on the other saw the issue of our era so clearly and debated it so well with each other that we can afford to stay with their thought and avoid getting entangled with present-day judges and personalities. For our immediate purposes, I'm going to call Madison's philosophy "majoritarian" and Jefferson's philosophy "libertarian."

You may remember that Thomas Jefferson was representing this country in Paris during the entire period when our Constitution was framed and adopted. Meanwhile, young James Madison, at that stage of his career a strong nationalist, attended the Convention in Philadelphia in 1787. There he contributed more than anyone else toward drafting the Constitution. When, some time later, Jefferson received a copy of the Philadelphia document, he was shocked to see that it contained no bill of rights. He wrote Madison that "a bill of rights is what the people are entitled to against every government on earth." In the correspondence between Madison and Jefferson from 1787 to the middle of 1789, the two philosophies stand boldly opposite each other.

Madison, like Hamilton and other leaders of the federalist group, saw no need or occasion for a federal bill of rights. He believed that since the real power under a republican form of government resides in the people, it is they who are the main source of danger to freedom. Those who insisted on a bill of rights were looking in the wrong direction. The menace came not from the government, but from passionate and self-seeking factions among the people. Madison hoped, however, that the enormous territorial expanse of America and the strong framework of the federal government might keep the problem of civil liberty within manageable bounds.

The political situation changed in the spring and summer of 1788 when the various state conventions met to vote on the new Constitution. Several of them, including Madison's own Virginia, demanded and obtained a firm promise that amendments would be adopted promptly to declare the people's fundamental liberties. When the first Congress under the new Constitution would convene in the spring of 1789, Madison knew it would be watched with suspicion and distrust until the pledge was redeemed and amendments were submitted to the states. The enterprise was to be his. He would be the leader in the House of Representatives, to examine all the proposals for clauses in a bill of rights, to organize them in a rational order and guide them through.

It was high time to write Jefferson in Paris that his demand for a bill of rights would be met. On October 17, 1788, Madison composed a long letter of self-examination and self-revelation. In it he proceeded to conduct a search for the principles he would use to guide his course in the forthcoming Congress.

He still believed that, under a republican form of government, freedom depends primarily on the minds and hearts of the people and that, just as they are the main source of support for freedom, they are also the main source of danger to it. Solemn declarations of human rights still seemed to him like mere "parchment barriers." Well then, would it be a fraud and a farce if he kept the promise he had made to the Virginia Convention, if he recommended a bill of rights in the Congress? Addressing Jefferson on the other side of the Atlantic and his own conscience at the same time, Madison wrote:

What use then it may be asked can a bill of rights serve in popular Governments? I answer the two following which, though less essential than in other Governments, sufficiently recommend the precaution: 1. The political truths declared in that solemn manner acquire by degrees the character of fundamental maxims of free Government, and as they become incorporated with the national sentiment, counteract the impulses of interest and passion. 2. Altho. it be generally true as above stated that the danger of oppression lies in the interested majorities of the people rather than in usurped acts of the Government, yet there may be occasions on which the evil may spring from the latter source; and on such, a bill of rights will be a good ground for an appeal to the sense of the community. Perhaps too there may be a certain degree of danger, that a succession of artful and ambitious rulers may be gradual & well timed advances, finally erect an independent Government on the subversion of liberty. Should this danger exist at all, it is prudent to guard agst it, especially when the precaution can do no injury.

Here we have the Madisonian or majoritarian philosophy. According to it, while our Bill of Rights may serve other incidental purposes, its main objective is to educate the popular community and to rally public resistance against "the impulses of interest and passion." When Madison presented the proposed amendments to the first Congress, he told the House of Representatives candidly that he still considered the popular community as the locus of greatest power, hence of greatest danger, in a republic. He went on to express the hope that a bill of rights might at least improve public opinion and inculcate respect for basic liberties.

Let us see what follows when the Supreme Court of the United States applies this majoritarian philosophy. One of our basic political principles is obedience to the will of the majority. The majority have expressed their will by electing the members of Congress and the president. The majority never have a chance to vote for justices of the Supreme Court. If Congress, representing the majority, passes a law, should not that law be upheld unless it is grossly and utterly unreasonable? Moreover, who are the justices of the Supreme Court to charge the people's representatives with being unreasonable? The president, the cabinet officers, the executive agencies, the Congress, have much more intimate knowledge of the need for a law, say, a law like the Communist Control Act or the Expatriation Act of 1954, than the nine jurists of the United States Supreme Court. Doesn't the mere fact that the law was proposed, debated, and voted by the Congress and signed by the president demonstrate its reasonableness? This is the majoritarian approach. In a period like ours, it means that the Supreme Court is not the place to look for a very vigorous redeemer of liberty.

Well, would we expect a different philosophy from Thomas Jefferson, whose gospel was confidence in the wisdom and judgment of the common people? In Jefferson's very first letter on reading the new Constitution, he announced that he was less in favor of giving energy to the government than information to the people:

Educate and inform the whole mass of the people, enable them to see that it is their interest to preserve peace and order, and they will preserve it, and it requires no very high degree of education to convince them of this. They are the only sure reliance for the preservation of our liberty.

Having this deep and enduring confidence in the people, Jefferson certainly accepted the Madisonian philosophy as far as it went. But, in his judgment, it did not go nearly far enough.

When he received Madison's letter assuring him that the demand for a bill of rights would be complied with, it was already March of 1789 and the first Congress was scheduled to convene very soon. He replied quickly. Here is what he wrote on March 15, 1789:

In the arguments in favor of a declaration of rights, you omit one which has great weight with me; the legal check which it puts into the hands of the judiciary. This is a body, which, if rendered independent and kept strictly to their own department, merits great confidence for their learning and integrity. In fact, what degree of confidence would be too much, for a body composed of such men as Wythe, Blair and Pendleton? On characters like these, the [frenzy of the citizens bidding what is wrong] would make no impression.

Now this was the very first time in the long transatlantic correspondence that either of them had even alluded to the judiciary as an instrument to enforce the Bill of Rights. The concept was of superlative constitutional importance. But would Madison receive the letter in time to place Jefferson's concept before the Congress along with the proposed Bill of Rights?

In New York where Congress was sitting, Madison was suffering from impatience and anxiety. Aware that the people would never trust the new government until Congress voted on the amendments, he was in a great rush to have them considered and passed. Nevertheless, Congress, which was not in a rush, continued from day to day discussing every other subject but a bill of rights. Madison had no choice but to wait. Meanwhile, Jefferson's letter, with the significant message which Madison could not possibly anticipate, reposed in the Embassy's official pouch on a vessel moving slowly across the Atlantic. By arrangement, Madison was due to address the House of Representatives on the 8th day of June. Jefferson's letter arrived in New York on June 2nd—just in time to influence Madison's speech and thus to establish the constitutional dignity of the Bill of Rights. When Madison rose to address the House on June 8th, 1789, he said:

If [the fundamental rights] are incorporated into the Constitution, independent tribunals of justice will consider themselves in a peculiar manner the guardians of those rights; they will be an impenetrable bulwark against every assumption of power in the legislative or executive; they will be naturally led to resist every encroachment upon rights expressly stipulated for in the constitution by the declaration of rights.

Thus, the first United States Congress was frankly and explicitly informed that the illustrious sponsors of the Bill of Rights expected the judges to consider themselves in a peculiar manner the guardians of our basic rights.

Now we see how the Jeffersonian or libertarian philosophy includes everything affirmative in the Madisonian. Jefferson did not consider for a moment that the Supreme Court was the sole guardian of liberty. He pointed out, you will remember, that the judges must not only "be rendered independent" but must be kept "strictly to their own department." He required them to be men of the very loftiest intellectual stature and moral integrity. If the Government and the people of the United States conducted themselves and their affairs as Jefferson hoped they would, the Bill of Rights would need to serve only a Madisonian purpose, that is, the purpose of educating the public conscience. But if either the Government or the people should fall into a frenzy and demand things that were depraved and wrong, then the judges must impose a firm, courageous legal check.

On the present Supreme Court, there is comparatively little disagreement about the constitutionality of federal economic and social legislation; that is no longer the problem. But when a case involves freedom of personal and political expression, that is to say, a right under the first Amendment, then philosophy clashes against philosophy. The majoritarian justices acknowledge that the First Amendment is couched in absolute and categorical terms, forbidding *any* abridgement of free expression, whether reasonable or unreasonable. Nevertheless, majoritarian justices take a neutral, laissez faire attitude toward laws abridging free expression if they can find some "reasonable" ground for the legislation.

The libertarians emphasize the absolute language of the First Amendment, which says that Congress shall make "no law" abriding these freedoms. They say that there are three basic reasons why this language is so very absolute: (1) Some of the rights of free expression, such as worshipping God and forming one's private opinions, cannot become the proper business or concern of any government; (2) without active exchange of information and ideas, a society stagnates and ultimately loses its freedom; and (3) representative government needs the criticism of a free press and free debate so that the people may be able to make informed decisions. This is the libertarian philosophy.

In one important field of constitutional law, the Supreme

Court's majoritarians do follow the principles of the libertarians. I refer, of course, to the rights of Negroes to equal protection of the laws. We have made such magnificent, though—Heaven knows— belated, strides toward. racial equality in the past generation be- cause on this front the *whole* court has adopted a libertarian view. As libertarian justices see it, this record shows that the court need not surrender fundamental American ideals, or follow a laissez faire policy, or exhibit an abject humility when it comes to deal with the enemies of freedom. If, in the teeth of prejudice and passion, the court can uphold equal protection of the laws, why is not the Jeffersonian philosophy likewise applicable when First Amendment liberties are attacked, or when security procedures violate elementary standards of fairness?

There is another string to the majoritarian bow. They like to point to the superiority of the English system, under which parlia- ment is supreme and the courts possess no right of constitutional review. The majoritarians claim that Americans rely too much on the Supreme Court to protect their liberties, and thus become lazy and flaccid. In England, we are told, they order these things better. Since Englishmen cannot turn to the courts to invalidate an act of parliament, the newspapers speak up more actively and the House of Commons is peculiarly sensitive to any infringement of liberty or miscarriage of justice. Thus, it is claimed, the English system reposes genuine trust in the people.

I think those who subscribe to the American libertarian philos- ophy should not shy away from this challenge, but meet it head on. Some English lawyers and law professors do not find the grass of liberty so green in England as it may appear to Americans. For example, they tell me that Hyde Park is so very free for oratory, mainly because the oratory there is so very futile. But let us assume that free expression (except in religion of course, because Ameri- cans would scarcely consider that they had religious freedom under an established church) let us assume that free expression is well protected in England.

The difficulty with the majoritarians is that they are trying to graft an incomplete slice of the English system on ours. They don't say, "Let us change to a parliamentary government, headed by a prime minister who will be subject, along with the other heads of departments, to regular scrutiny at a 'question hour.' " They don't say that, if the legislature censures a minister's action, the whole government will resign. Thus the majoritarians are proposing to take away one of our major protections—the Supreme Court's intervention—without putting anything in its stead. After a century and a half of relying on the Supreme Court as one, though of course not the only, means of defense, why should we acquiesce in its abandoning the function unless we are provided with some equivalent shield for our rights?

Finally, which philosophy puts more trust in the people? The majoritarians claim it is theirs, because they follow a policy of laissez faire toward the people's elected representatives, and refuse to accord a preferred position to First Amendment freedoms. Here I think is the very nucleus of their error. When a problem arises under the First Amendment, it may appear on the surface as though the majoritarians favor deferring to the people and the libertarians favor defying the people.

On deeper analysis, we discover precisely the contrary. For what happens when a majoritarian court yields to legislative excitement in a First Amendment case? The restrictive law or administrative order becomes effective and reduces the people's access to information and opinion. What happens when a libertarian view prevails and such a law is struck down? Then the channels of information and persuasion are kept open, and the people remain free to examine, evaluate, and decide for themselves. Real confidence in the people will give them credit for capacity to reject Communist propaganda and Communist advocacy. If the mass of Americans were so myopic that they could not be trusted to see the conspicuous folly and falsity of Communist advocacy, the republic would indeed be in a hopeless state. It is the libertarians who have a genuine and robust faith in the people and in the republic.

On these grounds, we are entitled to reproach the majoritarian justices of the Supreme Court with trusting us too little and with straining to be reasonable when they ought to be adamant. We are entitled to tell them respectfully: "If your Honors feel a compulsive need to be reasonable, then be reasonable with an angry tiger, or with a tropical hurricane, or with an epidemic of cholera. But be not reasonable with laws and executive orders that contemn American liberty. Be not reasonable with inquisitions, anonymous informers, and secret files that mock American justice. Be not reasonable with punitive denationalizations, ex post facto deportations, labels of disloyalty, and all the other strategems for outlawing human beings from the community of mankind. These devices have put us to shame. Exercise the full judicial power of the United States; nullify them, forbid them; and make us proud again."

Conformity

JOHN KEATS

NARRATOR (HARRY REASONER): Here, in these quiet, orderly streets, look-alike people live in look-alike houses. All hold more or less the same kind of jobs. They all earn roughly the same salary; drive the same kinds of cars; shop in the same stores; buy the national brands. They raise the same number of children; read the same paper; wear the same clothes. Perhaps they all have the same blood type. This is communism, of a kind.

A French philosopher remarked, "It is not what separates the United States from the Soviet Union that should frighten us, but what they have in common . . . those two technocracies that think themselves antagonists, are dragging humanity in the direction of dehumanization." Here is the real danger. The work a man does now is apt to be the least important thing about him, and he increasingly finds his identity with a group, rather than within himself. In this sense, we are becoming dehumanized, changing ever more swiftly from a land where individual difference was prized into a nation of drones, who swarm from their hives to work at fractional tasks in a uniform world. The danger is that we will become a think-alike people, and indeed, we encourage the process. In fact, we teach group-think in many of our schools.

INSTRUCTOR: Be seated. Good Morning, Class.

CLASS: Good morning, Sir.

INSTRUCTOR: This morning, we are going to discuss why Athens fell. Take out your textbooks. Turn to page 143. Now, as you can see,

---

In 1962 WCAU-TV in Philadelphia produced a program on the subject of conformity. Writer John Keats, producer George Dessart and director David E. Wilson received Hillman Prize Awards for this program, of which these quotations are excerpts.

your textbook gives you three reasons why Athens fell. What is the first reason? Pierre?

PIERRE: The first reason that Athens fell is lack of leadership.

INSTRUCTOR: Good. Lack of leadership. Thank you. And what is the second reason? Fred?

FRED: The second reason why Athens fell was slave labor.

INSTRUCTOR: Good. The second reason. And the third reason? What is the third reason? Peggy?

PEGGY: The third reason that Athens fell is individualism.

INSTRUCTOR: Good. Individualism. The third reason why Athens fell. Good. Now, then we have three reasons, don't we, why Athens fell. Yes, Bob?

BOB: But couldn't you say that the Greeks were weak because of their lack of individualism, and that they cut down their industry and strangled it because they wouldn't let nonconformist foreigners become citizens. And, didn't Socrates die because he was an individualist?

INSTRUCTOR: These are good ideas, Bob, but does the textbook say anything about lack of individualism being a reason for the fall of Athens? I think we can pretty much rule that out don't you? After all, the authors of our text have had much more time to think about these problems than we have. I think we better accept their judgment. Now, let's remember then the three reasons for the fall of Athens; lack of leadership, slave labor, and individualism. Memorize those reasons for tomorrow and be prepared to state them on the test that I will give you.

NARRATOR: This is not education, this is indoctrination in conformity. Given this sort of schooling, it is no great step from the child to the man. Here is the end result.

PTA PRESIDENT: Well, as we all know, this is our last meeting of the year. Before we adjourn, there is just one thing I want to say. I want to say we can all be proud of the fact that this year no controversial issues came up.

NARRATOR: Surrender of personal taste to group demands, sacrifice of personal conviction on the altar of agreement, surrender of personal responsibility and refuge in regulations are not the qualities that conquered the wilderness and built the nation. Rather, they are the essential ingredients of conformity. And from conformity, it is only a small step to oppression. Inevitably, a think-alike nation produces thought police.

CITIZEN: You admit the book is about adultery.

CITIZEN: Do you think children should read about this?

LIBRARIAN: This book is not a course in adultery. *The Scarlet Letter* is an American classic. It is in every library.

CITIZEN: It's a classic. . . ?

LIBRARIAN: Now before we talk about what *The Scarlet Letter* actually says, let me ask you this; What would you say about a book about a high-ranking general—a married man—who seduces the wife of one of his captains? He gets her pregnant. He is afraid the captain will find out. More than that, he is so infatuated with the woman that he is jealous of her husband. So the general sends the captain into the toughest combat situation he can find. He sends secret instructions to the battlefield commander to make sure that the captain is sent on a hopeless mission. When the general learns the captain has been killed, he brings the woman into his house, the house in which his wife also lives—to be his mistress. . . .

CITIZEN: I suppose you call that a classic, too. . . .

LIBRARIAN: I call it Holy Scripture. That is the story of David, Bathsheba and Uriah the Hittite. Do you mean the Bible has no place on our shelves?

CITIZEN: Tell me one thing: Are you a Communist?

NARRATOR: Tell me, Sir, what was your opinion of tonight's meeting?

SERENE CITIZEN: Well, as I saw it, it wasn't a matter of censorship. I think we're all against that. I think Harry was wrong when he called the librarian a Communist. Of course, everybody knows that a lot of teachers and librarians and intellectuals are Reds, but I wouldn't say Mr. Smith was, although you never know. But as I saw it, Mr. Smith was wrong to get books that just get everybody all stirred up. I mean, there must be other—just as good books—that don't get people all upset; that don't have all that stuff in them. So I went along with the decision to fire Mr. Smith. We have a good man in mind, and we're going to set up a committee to choose the books. . . .

(Cut to footage of the late Senator McCarthy going full cry after a headline.)

MCCARTHY: We must get out of any department of the government anyone who was serving the Communist cause. Now I give this man's record, and I want to say Mr. Welch labored in government long before he became a member—as early as 1944.

MR. WELCH: Senator, may we drop this: (Fade Under)

NARRATOR (Voice Over): The important fact about Senator McCarthy is not that he is dead, but that his spirit is still alive. Indeed, his spirit has been present in all societies of man, at all times everywhere. We hear his voice most loudly in troubled times, and it has its greatest effect, in time of trouble and doubt, in a land where people do not, or will not think for themselves, but prefer agreement and order.

IST WATCHER: I'm not sure I like his methods, but I sure agree with what he's trying to do!

2ND WATCHER: Don't worry about his method. You have to fight fire with fire.

NARRATOR: Somebody said America was the place where they beat you to death with feathers. And so it does, if one unthinkingly accepts the plenty that America offers. That is, one dies in that one fails to live, for life demands conscious choice. But, because what America offers is generally so good—after all, it *is* cake, and not a crust—the death does not seem to be a death. It is not painful to accept. Yet each question of value, even the smallest, is bound up in the question of human survival—of survival of the individual in an increasingly abstract, dehumanized society.

This nation was established by men who refused to accept things as they were. Above all things they prized the necessary right of free, unlimited inquiry. They considered it the precondition of any government that would be responsible to the governed. If there is virtue to their experiment, it is reflected in our accomplishment to date, and if we wish to accomplish more, the experiment must continue. Indeed, when we fail to question, we fail to be responsible to ourselves, and then we shall most certainly deserve exactly the kind of government we shall most certainly get. Then, indeed, will diversity give way to uniformity; freedom, to inevitability; democracy, to dogma; tolerance, to conformity. All wisdom begins when someone says *No,* and someone else asks, *Why not?* In simplest terms, if anyone would claim to be alive, it is necessary for him to question the value of everything. To be, or not to be? To be, or not to be human in this Year of Our Lord. Jesus was King among Men. He was, incidentally, a nonconformist. He asked questions, and they killed him. Who would say the sacrifice was in vain?

Freedom Is More Than Academic

FRANCIS KEPPEL

IN THIS MORNING of renewal of your educational promise, I would like to talk on an old yet durable theme. It has drawn the attention of the academic world from the days of man's first academy of learning. It is as contemporary as tomorrow morning's newspaper, which in this particular time and place is as likely as not to present another pointed and possibly disappointing illustration of my topic.

My theme is academic freedom—the root and trunk on which education, leaf and branch, must always grow—and what we must do to assure its continued growth and flourishing. In this college and in other colleges, other universities, this old objective of academic freedom remains fundamental to the life of inquiry and the transmission of learning.

Here in California as elsewhere—wherever academic freedom is challenged—freedom is more than academic. This is because if freedom is lost or damaged here, in such institutions as yours, it is endangered everywhere else in our land. And wherever academic freedom is endangered, our free and open society is sapped and diminished.

Today, as we speak of academic freedom, there is no doubt that

In 1964, while he was U.S. Commissioner of Education, Francis Keppel spoke at California State College. This adaptation of his speech was used in the Hillman Reprint Series.

we in education are faced by the most challenging problems in generations, by strains and stresses of considerable scope.

In our schools, we are undergoing a long postponed struggle to make education open and equally available to all our citizens, regardless of race or color or creed. We are called to make good what we have always said—that educational opportunity in our country must be truly universal.

In our colleges and universities, we are expecting more than 7 million students by 1970—almost twice the number at the start of this decade. But higher education is not a numbers game. We may succeed in expanding our physical plants to accommodate these students, but we will assuredly fail unless we extend and preserve the quality of education as well.

In our society, we have come to a day in which education is no longer regarded as peripheral, but as indispensable to our economic and social progress. Education, we have long said, is a national resource. Now, again, we are taken up on our words. As society increases its demands on education, we may expect increasing support, which will be a blessing. But with increased public dependence on education, we can expect an increased public concern for what goes on in our schools and colleges and this, if misdirected, could lead to increasing external pressures that would control and censor and limit the educational process.

It is against the background of these strains and stresses that I speak of academic freedom—first, of the forces that endanger it from outside the educational community and, second, of the responsibility for defending it from within.

In discussing academic freedom, let us be clear at the outset that we are talking of a special freedom, a unique position which the teacher and the educational institution occupy. There is no law or Constitutional provision for academic freedom. It embraces freedom of speech and the press and goes on to assure the absence of any pressure which inhibits free thought. It preserves the right to challenge, to dissent, to expound ideas honestly arrived at no matter how much they may be at odds with conventional thought and opinion, or even at odds with the views of the academy itself. It preserves these rights because freedom of inquiry is impossible without them. Academic freedom entails the risks that all new ideas present and it must be struggled for in every generation.

Now how may we best define and identify the external hazards to academic freedom today? What are their sources, what is the nature of their threat? To what ends are they bent?

One might enumerate persons and organizations that presently constitute or generate threats to the integrity of the academic enterprise. But these are notoriously changeable and different from place to place. Or one might mention sources of power or influence in our society from which these threats to academic freedom have frequently come. But here again we limit our diagnosis.

It will be more to the point, I think, to identify the dangers to academic freedom in terms of certain states of mind. The forces against academic freedom may change their points of attack, their strategy, or their paramount concerns, but the traits that animate them remain fairly permanent features of our social landscape, mounting or dwindling in influence as circumstances make us more or less vulnerable to their attack. These states of mind are always with us. And they are always in need of being watched.

Among those which most endanger academic freedom, I would underscore three. They are *bigotry . . . conformity . . .* and *fear.* Like many troubling states of mind, they often tend to run together. But we can delineate them, recognize them, see them for what they are.

The *first* is *bigotry,* the noisiest and gaudiest of the three. Often, but not always, it assaults the academic community from the right flank, wearing a masquerade costume of flags and patriotism and sounding off at the top of its lungs. Its exponents elect themselves as peculiarly and solely the guardians of American virtue. Strident and vituperative, they seek to drown out the voices of dissent, even the thoughts of dissent.

In an era of profound change at home and abroad, the forces of bigotry would batten down the hatches against change, or even the exploration of change. In a day of exploding knowledge, they read history and economics, sociology and science in terms of what has been, rather than what is or what can be. They wait in the snug harbor of America's past, bombarding every landing party of the present or future.

But we would err if we think of this danger of bigotry as thundering against us from the right flank alone. It also marches from other directions, shouting other slogans. When the super-liberal would outlaw the views he opposes in the name of liberty, he is no less a bigot than the super-patriot of the right. Academic freedom is in jeopardy whenever the critical examination of our society is thwarted or blocked from any flank. The self-styled "liberal" who limits inquiry for the sake of his own cluster of causes is also a dismaying and dangerous foe of academic freedom, almost more dangerous because he waves the flag of liberalism as he crushes out dissent.

The *second* enemy of academic freedom is *conformity*. It arrives in drab protective clothing, whispering rather than shouting, and it rarely makes the headlines or draws attention of any sort. It argues its case with a variety of spurious reasons—such as "prudence," as "good taste," as "no-sense-in-rocking-the-boat."

But conformity is no less deadly than bigotry when, in its quiet fashion, it reduces dissent, divergence and difference within the scholarly community. It succeeds whenever a faculty member is discharged because his views are unpopular. It strikes at academic freedom whenever a book is removed from the shelves of a library because its ideas fail to conform to prevailing sentiment.

Academic freedom distinguishes great colleges and universities and great scholars by their very failure to conform, by their restless, often courageous insistence on moving back the borders of ignorance, by uprooting the well-rooted idea, the conventional and the accepted and the approved, by a constant and salutary re-examination of even those tenets we hold most dear. The academy of conformists, on the other hand, is no academy at all. It is an assembly line.

So if we would guard academic freedom, we must guard against conformity, a state of mind that is deadening to education and to free inquiry upon which learning ultimately rests. We must protect non-conformity which leads to the ceaseless seeking of the *why* of things, not merely the *so-what* of things. Unless we do so, the conformists will move in quietly and quickly to fill the vacuum.

The *third* enemy of academic freedom is *fear,* and this is the overriding danger. When I denounce fear as an enemy, I do not want to be misunderstood. A common retort of the fear-mongers when their works are condemned is to insist that there is indeed something to fear. They are right, of course. There are causes for anxiety and concern today. But we should be fearful of one thing above all—and that is the whirlwind of panic which they themselves sow.

We live in a time of real dangers, real perils. We are living in a period that has been truly called a race between civilization and catastrophe. In a world of uncertainty, we are called on for wisdom and leadership unmatched at any time in our history. We cannot provide this leadership out of fear. We can provide it out of a quality of mind which is open and exploring and free.

In education, we are confronted by domestic dangers that become increasingly visible—when we look at the wave of unemployed youth coming toward us . . . at the millions of high school students who are dropping out of school in this decade and entering the ranks of the unemployed because they lack employable skills . . . at the explosion of knowledge and technology which education must grasp and prepare our people to comprehend.

But when we look at these challenges, where do we find the fear-mongers? What do they tell us?

The fears they would post in our nightmares are vague and general and diffuse—fears about hidden enemies so secret that we can't hope to see them, about ideologies so insidious that they are said to infect Presidents and Supreme Court justices and teachers in your neighborhood high school classrooms. These are the panic-born fears that the fear-mongers would peddle, while keeping the silence of the dead about the true dangers in our society, the dangers to our domestic strength and vitality and our leadership abroad, the dangers of smugness and indifference and complacency.

Now how shall we defend ourselves from these forces against academic freedom—bigotry, conformity, fear? How shall we preserve the strength of education which, so long as it is free, can light our way to knowledge and accomplishment? Where shall we look for the defenders of academic freedom?

Sometimes we find them among the public generally and, when we do, they deserve our highest esteem. They are the public's "teachers-at-large"—the civic leader, the newspaper editor, the politician with the courage to stand up for the school teacher under fire, the library book under attack. The courageous leader in a town can teach more to the young people of that town about the spirit of freedom by his example than all the courses in high school put together.

When the teacher whose views do not meet the standards of the self-anointed critics is condemned and loses his job and no one stands up for him, then the youth who witness this can only conclude that freedom does not pay and that conformity is the wisest behavior. Even if it is inevitable that a non-conforming teacher will lose his job, it is vitally important that knowledgable voices are heard—so that the younger generation at least knows that an important issue exists, that the issue is not abandoned without a struggle, that it is worth struggling for.

We have not yet come to the end of attacks and assaults on academic freedom. The forces of bigotry, conformity and fear will continue to make their thrusts. There will be many skirmishes, many battles within our public schools and in higher education.

But today we draw strength for the encounters to come from the vitality of institutions such as this one. And we continue to depend on the university as a fortress of freedom in our time of challenge and hope.

PART THREE

Public Welfare

/\./\./\./\./\

The two decades covered by this volume saw the flowering of the Roosevelt Revolution and our first groping efforts to develop new answers to problems old and new. In the immediate postwar years, public opinion and Congress still feared federal involvement in economic affairs. Today the issue is not whether but how much and in which direction the government should apply its resources.

Leon Keyserling is a leading economist linking the New Deal period with today. His recommendations of the early 1950s still have relevance.

A landmark work of the period was *The Affluent Society,* by John Kenneth Galbraith, who suggested that our society would strengthen itself by using more of its resources to meet public needs rather than private gratification. Another was *The Other America,* by Michael Harrington, who described that part of society which affluence had passed by when much of the nation was climbing into the middle classes. His message—which was the stimulant for the federal war on poverty—was in turn given momentum by an incisive critique by a veteran political observer, Dwight Macdonald.

One of the principal factors separating the poverty classes from those above is automation, which is rapidly making unskilled labor obsolete. Secretary of Labor W. Willard Wirtz, whose department is largely responsible for meeting the consequences, summed up our prospects and goals at a time when the nation was just awakening to the problem.

Our newest crisis, embracing a community of needs, is the plight of our cities, which have not developed the resources to meet the rising expectations of growing populations. One of the most cogent observers is Paul Ylvisaker, who described the options facing urban planners and the penalties for non-planning.

Economic Policies for Full Employment and Full Production

LEON KEYSERLING

OUR BASIC ECONOMIC task is to raise the standard of living of the average American family enough to keep up with our burgeoning productive power. The question naturally arises as to what devices we have available to lift the standard of living of the average American family.

First of all, there is tax policy. What is taxation? Taxation operates very substantially to redirect the flow of national income. Some people prefer not to look at it this way; but every time the government takes a dollar out of a person's pocket in taxes, it is taking a dollar of income away from him; and whenever the government spends that money—no matter whether for the purpose of financing a war, distributing social insurance benefits, or building schools—we have, in effect, a *redirection* in the flow of income, and someone's income is increased.

This does not mean that all taxation has as its overt purpose the redistribution of income. Its overt purpose, at times, may be to prevent inflation, although the process of inflation itself does redis-

In 1954 Leon Keyserling gave three lectures at Howard University entitled "Economic Policies for Full Employment and Full Production." These excerpts from the lectures, which were sponsored by the Hillman Foundation, summarize his principal points.

tribute income. Nonetheless, one of the major purposes of a progressive tax system in general is to impose the burden according to ability to pay, and to spend the revenues in accord with national needs. Obviously, this is a neutral and pleasant way of saying that one of the major purposes of taxation is to redistribute income along lines which benefit the economy and the people as a whole.

It does not follow that all sound tax policy at all times must shift income from higher-income groups to lower-income groups. For example, if during a great war when government spending was extremely high it was decided to impose a very large part of the burden upon relatively high-income families already paying much higher tax rates than others, it might conceivably be desirable when the war was over to accord to these people a somewhat higher amount of tax reduction than others. And sometimes tax reductions or incentives may well be used to stimulate business investment, to encourage new industries, to help small business, and for a variety of other purposes which do not fall directly within the traditional concept of progressive taxation. Nonetheless, my analysis of our current and prospective economic problems leads me to the conclusion that the principle of progressive taxation needs to be honored and in some respects extended.

A second item of economic policy which we now hear much about is monetary policy. This is too technical a subject for full discussion here, but I want to say something about it. Public policies can expand or contract the money supply in many ways, by enlarging or reducing direct public loans and credits, by enlarging or reducing public guaranties or insurance of private loans, by enlarging or reducing the size of the requirements for bank reserves as a base for commercial loans, by regulation of marginal and installment buying, by varying the interest rates on public and private borrowing, by other shifts in methods of managing the national debt and supporting the government bond market, by variations in taxing and spending, and in other ways. The standard or prevalent general theory is that the government should contract the money supply when there are inflationary trends, and reduce the money supply when there are deflationary trends.

While this general theory has many valid applications, it has tended in my judgment to oversimplify our economic problems and to neglect or underestimate the importance of the distribution of the money supply as distinguished from its size. While generalizations on this matter are dangerous, I will hazard this one: Viewing American economic history as a whole, those in favor of limiting the money supply have generally been the spokesmen of powerful private interests, while those in favor of expanding the money supply have generally been the spokesmen of the average producer and consumer. There have been few occasions, if any, in this century when the money supply has been too large to meet the needs of a full economy; and I think that in the recent years now under review, and for our immediate future needs, the money supply has tended to be too small rather than too large. A larger money supply, among other things, would facilitate the management of the national debt, but this is too complicated an issue to pursue further at this moment.

Social security is another weapon that is capable of providing vast improvement in the lot of the average American family. We are moving into a long era where each year more and more people are reaching an advanced age. Vastly increased millions of people, partly voluntarily and partly for reasons beyond their control, will want retirement, and be entitled to it if they want it. Our retirement systems, both public and private, are adjusted to the size of our economy years ago. They bear little relationship to the productive power of our current economy; little relationship to what we can afford in all fairness to provide to retired people; little relationship to the amount of purchasing power and consumption which our economy demands of these retired millions in order that we may fully absorb the output of our expanding productive power.

As a very rough indication, I think that we should point as rapidly as possible toward changing the average retirement benefit throughout the economy as a whole from the neighborhood of a fifty-dollar average to an average of two hundred-two hundred-fifty dollars. Some people may call this pie-in-the-sky or what have you. But when we objectively quantify our economic problems—our productive power on the one side and our consumer needs on the other—it appears clear that a prompt and enormous increase in the flow of income to retired people is essential to keep the wheels of enterprise rolling.

This calls for broadening the coverage of social security to include practically everybody, enlarging the benefits, and improving the financing of the system. The enlargement of retirement benefits —and although I have not had time to speak of them here, other social security benefits, such as unemployment insurance, should also be enlarged—is by no means the only public spending which should now be expanded. In fact, any kind of honest and efficient public spending for useful end products is preferable to excessive unemployment of manpower and other resources. Consequently, even if the federal budget is unbalanced, the level of honest and efficient public spending is too low when unemployment is too high, unless there are immediately practicable alternative ways to restore full employment and full production.

But in thus talking about the need for expanded public spending to restore full employment and full production, let us never forget that the most basic of all the purposes of public spending in our kind of society is to provide for the people the goods and services they need and can afford, but which, in the words of Lincoln, they cannot provide in their separate and individual capacities. Quite apart from the immediate economic situation, there are now great educational shortages, whether measured by school buildings, numbers of teachers, or teachers' pay. There are great inadequacies in health services, whether measured by facilities, doctors, nurses, or the relationship between the cost of medical care and the resources of many millions of families. There are great gaps in the development of our natural resources and of power, measured against our potentials, particularly in river valley areas, and measured against shortages such as that of water along the West Coast and elsewhere. Our highway systems are in no condition to reduce accidents or to carry expanding traffic. I believe, also, that our outlays for national defense, and especially for economic assistance to underdeveloped areas, have been responsive to false concepts of economy rather than to true appraisals of need. Looking at this whole picture, even the amount by which the federal government would need to increase its outlays to help restore full employment and full production would fall far short of what could wisely be used further to build our human and natural resources.

While all of the measures that we have had under discussion can help to improve the lot of low-income families, the composite of these measures will not alone be enough. There is need in addition for a special set of programs, trained with great particularity upon low-income families. Minimum wage legislation is very important, along with rehabilitation and retraining programs. Insofar as a substantial portion of low-income people are beyond economic rehabilitation, due to age or physical handicaps or other factors, public assistance programs for these groups should be brought more nearly into line with the economic capabilities of the country.

The major barrier to our doing what is imperative, both at home and abroad, is the misplaced concern that we cannot afford what we must afford. As a nation, we must draw a clear line of distinction betwen real economic costs and money costs. The real economic capacities of our country are based upon our manpower and skills, our natural resources and plants and tools, and our free institutions and good will. By these tests our looming problem now is not that we may excessively strain these resources, but rather that too many of them are idle and unemployed. This looming problem is racing forward with the accelerated march of our technology—much more so than most of us realize. Under current and foreseeable conditions the economic policies that expand employment and production opportunities are wise and sound. The economic policies that sacrifice this objective, in the thought that its pursuit would weaken the federal budgetary situation, are unwise and unsound. The main issue is not whether the federal budget is in balance, but rather whether the whole economy is in balance. The main point of concern is not the books of the Treasury, but rather the books of the average American family. So long as we maintain this perspective, we can prosper and progress as a free and expanding nation.

The Theory of Social Balance

JOHN KENNETH GALBRAITH

It is not till it is discovered that high individual incomes will not purchase the mass of mankind immunity from cholera, typhus, and ignorance, still less secure them the positive advantages of educational opportunity and economic security, that slowly and reluctantly, amid prophecies of moral degeneration and economic disaster, society begins to make collective provision for needs which no ordinary individual, even if he works overtime all his life, can provide himself.

—R. H. TAWNEY[1]

THE FINAL PROBLEM of the productive society is what it produces. This manifests itself in an implacable tendency to provide an opulent supply of some things and a niggardly yield of others. This disparity carries to the point where it is a cause of social discomfort and social unhealth. The line which divides our area of wealth from our area of poverty is roughly that which divides privately produced and marketed goods and services from publicly rendered services. Our wealth in the first is not only in startling contrast with the meagerness of the latter, but our wealth in privately produced goods is, to a marked degree, the cause of crisis in the supply of public services. For we have failed to see the importance, indeed the urgent need, of maintaining a balance between the two.

This disparity between our flow of private and public goods and

---

John Kenneth Galbraith's *The Affluent Society* (Boston: Houghton Mifflin Company, 1958), considered one of the most important books of our times, was given a 1958 Hillman Prize Award. This chapter contains one of the central ideas of the book.

[1] *Equality* (4th revised ed.), pp. 134-35.

services is no matter of subjective judgment. On the contrary, it is the source of the most extensive comment which only stops short of the direct contrast being made here. In the years following World War II, the papers of any major city—those of New York were an excellent example—told daily of the shortages and short-comings in the elementary municipal and metropolitan services. The schools were old and overcrowded. The police force was under strength and underpaid. The parks and playgrounds were insufficient. Streets and empty lots were filthy, and the sanitation staff was underequipped and in need of men. Access to the city by those who work there was uncertain and painful and becoming more so. Internal transportation was overcrowded, unhealthful, and dirty. So was the air. Parking on the streets had to be pro-hibited, and there was no space elsewhere. These deficiencies were not in new and novel servies but in old and established ones. Cities have long swept their streets, helped their people move around, educated them, kept order, and provided horse rails for vehicles which sought to pause. That their residents should have a nontoxic supply of air suggests no revolutionary dalliance with socialism.

The discussion of this public poverty competed, on the whole successfully, with the stories of ever-increasing opulence in pri-vately produced goods. The Gross National Product was rising. So were retail sales. So was personal income. Labor productivity had also advanced. The automobiles that could not be parked were being produced at an expanded rate. The children, though without schools, subject in the playgrounds to the affectionate interest of adults with odd tastes, and disposed to increasingly imaginative forms of delinquency, were admirably equipped with television sets. We had difficulty finding storage space for the great surpluses of food despite a national disposition to obesity. Food was grown and packaged under private auspices. The care and refreshment of the mind, in contrast with the stomach, was principally in the public domain. Our colleges and universities were severely over-crowded and underprovided, and the same was true of the mental hospitals.

The contrast was and remains evident not alone to those who read. The family which takes its mauve and cerise, air-conditioned, power-steered, and power-braked automobile out for a tour passes through cities that are badly paved, made hideous by litter, blighted buildings, billboards, and posts for wires that should long since have been put underground. They pass on into a countryside that has been rendered largely invisible by commercial art. (The goods which the latter advertise have an absolute priority in our value system. Such aesthetic considerations as a view of the countryside accordingly come second. On such matters we are consistent.) They picnic on exquisitely packaged food from a portable icebox by a polluted stream and go on to spend the night at a park which is a menace to public health and morals. Just before dozing off on an air mattress, beneath a nylon tent, amid the stench of decaying refuse, they may reflect vaguely on the curious unevenness of their blessings. Is this, indeed, the American genius?

In the production of goods within the private economy it has long been recognized that a tolerably close relationship must be maintained between the production of various kinds of products. The output of steel and oil and machine tools is related to the production of automobiles. Investment in transportation must keep abreast of the output of goods to be transported. The supply of power must be abreast of the growth of industries requiring it. The existence of these relationships—coefficients to the economist— has made possible the construction of the input-output table which shows how changes in the production in one industry will increase or diminish the demands on other industries. To this table, and more especially to its ingenious author, Professor Wassily Leontief, the world is indebted for one of its most important of modern insights into economic relationships. If expansion in one part of the economy were not matched by the requisite expansion in other parts—were the need for balance not respected—then bottlenecks and shortages, speculative hoarding of scarce supplies, and sharply increasing costs would ensue. Fortunately in peacetime the market system operates easily and effectively to maintain this balance, and this together with the existence of stocks and some flexibility in the coefficients as a result of substitution, insures that no serious difficulties will arise. We are reminded of the existence of the problem only by noticing how serious it is for those countries—Poland or, in a somewhat different form, India—which seek to solve the problem by planned measures and with a much smaller supply of resources.

Just as there must be balance in what a community produces, so there must also be balance in what the community consumes. An increase in the use of one product creates, ineluctably, a requirement for others. If we are to consume more automobiles, we must have more gasoline. There must be more insurance as well as more space on which to operate them. Beyond a certain point more and better food appears to mean increased need for medical services. This is the certain result of the increased consumption of tobacco and alcohol. More vacations require more hotels and more fishing rods. And so forth. With rare exceptions—shortages of doctors are an exception which suggests the rule—this balance is also maintained quite effortlessly so far as goods for private sale and consumption are concerned. The price system plus a rounded condition of opulence is again the agency.

However, the relationships we are here discussing are not confined to the private economy. They operate comprehensively over the whole span of private and public services. As surely as an increase in the output of automobiles puts new demands on the steel industry so, also, it places new demands on public services. Similarly, every increase in the consumption of private goods will normally mean some facilitating or protective step by the state. In all cases if these services are not forthcoming, the consequences will be in some degree ill. It will be convenient to have a term which suggests a satisfactory relationship between the supply of privately produced goods and services and those of the state, and we may call it social balance.

The problem of social balance is ubiquitous, and frequently it is obtrusive. As noted, an increase in the consumption of automobiles requires a facilitating supply of streets, highways, traffic control, and parking space. The protective services of the police and the highway patrols must be available, as must those of the hospitals. Although the need for balance here is extraordinarily clear, our use of privately produced vehicles has, on occasion, got far out of line with the supply of the related public services. The result has been hideous road congestion, an annual massacre of impressive proportions, and chronic colitis in the cities. As on the ground, so also in the air. Planes collide with disquieting consequences for those within when the public provision for air traffic control fails to keep pace with private use of the airways.

But the auto and the airplane, versus the space to use them, are merely an exceptionally visible example of a requirement that is pervasive. The more goods people procure, the more packages they discard and the more trash that must be carried away. If the appropriate sanitation services are not provided, the counterpart of increasing opulence will be deepening filth. The greater the wealth the thicker will be the dirt. This indubitably describes a tendency of our time. As more goods are produced and owned, the greater are the opportunities for fraud and the more property that must be protected. If the provision of public law-enforcement services do not keep pace, the counterpart of increased well-being will, we may be certain, be increased crime.

The city of Los Angeles, in modern times, is a near-classic study in the problem of social balance. Magnificently efficient factories and oil refineries, a lavish supply of automobiles, a vast consumption of handsomely packaged products, coupled with the absence of a municipal trash collection service which forced the use of home incinerators, made the air nearly unbreathable for an appreciable part of each year. Air pollution could be controlled only by a complex and highly developed set of public services—by better knowledge stemming from more research, better policing, a municipal trash collection service, and possibly the assertion of the priority of clean air over the production of goods. These were long in coming. The agony of a city without usable air was the result.

The issue of social balance can be identified in many other current problems. Thus an aspect of increasing private production is the appearance of an extraordinary number of things which lay claim to the interest of the young. Motion pictures, television, automobiles, and the vast opportunities which go with the mobility, together with such less enchanting merchandise as narcotics, comic books, and pornographia, are all included in an advancing gross national product. The child of a less opulent as well as a technologically more primitive age had far fewer such diversions. The red schoolhouse is remembered mainly because it had a paramount position in the lives of those who attended it that no modern school can hope to attain.

In a well-run and well-regulated community, with a sound school system, good recreational opportunities, and a good police force—in short a community where public services have kept pace with private production—the diversionary forces operating on the modern juvenile may do no great damage. Television and the violent mores of Hollywood and Madison Avenue must contend with the intellectual discipline of the school. The social, athletic, dramatic, and like attractions of the school also claim the attention of the child. These, together with the other recreational opportunities of the community, minimize the tendency to delinquency. Experiments with violence and immorality are checked by an effective law-enforcement system before they become epidemic.

In a community where public services have failed to keep abreast of private consumption things are very different. Here, in an atmosphere of private opulence and public squalor, the private goods have full sway. Schools do not compete with television and the movies. The dubious heroes of the latter, not Miss Jones, become the idols of the young. The hot rod and the wild ride take the place of more sedentary sports for which there are inadequate facilities or provision. Comic books, alcohol, narcotics, and switchblade knives are, as noted, part of the increased flow of goods, and there is nothing to dispute their enjoyment. There is an ample supply of private wealth to be appropriated and not much to be feared from the police. An austere community is free from temptation. It can be austere in its public services. Not so a rich one.

Moreover, in a society which sets large store by production, and which has highly effective machinery for synthesizing private wants, there are strong pressures to have as many wage earners in the family as possible. As always all social behavior is part of a piece. If both parents are engaged in private production, the burden on the public services is further increased. Children, in effect, become the charge of the community for an appreciable part of the time. If the services of the community do not keep pace, this will be another source of disorder.

Residential housing also illustrates the problem of the social balance, although in a somewhat complex form. Few would wish to contend that, in the lower or even the middle-income brackets, Americans are munificently supplied with housing. A great many families would like better located or merely more houseroom, and no advertising is necessary to persuade them of their wish. And the provision of housing is in the private domain. At first glance at least, the line we draw between private and public seems not to be preventing a satisfactory allocation of resources to housing.

On closer examination, however, the problem turns out to be not greatly different from that of education. It is improbable that the housing industry is greatly more incompetent or inefficient in the United States than in those countries—Scandinavia, Holland, or (for the most part) England—where slums have been largely eliminated and where *minimum* standards of cleanliness and comfort are well above our own. As the experience of these countries shows, and as we have also been learning, the housing industry functions well only in combination with a large, complex, and costly array of public services. These include land purchase and clearance for redevelopment; good neighborhood and city planning, and effective and well-enforced zoning; a variety of financing and other aids to the housebuilder and owner; publicly supported research and architectural services for an industry which, by its nature, is equipped to do little on its own; and a considerable amount of direct or assisted public construction for families in the lowest-income brackets. The quality of the housing depends not on the industry, which is given, but on what is invested in these supplements and supports.

The case for social balance has, so far, been put negatively. Failure to keep public services in minimal relation to private production and use of goods is a cause of social disorder or impairs economic performance. The matter may now be put affirmatively. By failing to exploit the opportunity to expand public production we are missing opportunities for enjoyment which otherwise we might have had. Presumably a community can be as well rewarded by buying better schools or better parks as by buying bigger automobiles. By concentrating on the latter rather than the former it is failing to maximize its satisfactions. As with schools in the community, so with public services over the country at large. It is scarcely sensible that we should satisfy our wants in private goods with reckless abundance, while in the case of public goods, on the evidence of the eye, we practice extreme self-denial. So, far from systematically exploiting the opportunities to derive use and pleasure from these services, we do not supply what would keep us out of trouble.

The conventional wisdom holds that the community, large or small, makes a decision as to how much it will devote to its public services. This decision is arrived at by democratic process. Subject to the imperfections and uncertainties of democracy, people decide how much of their private income and goods they will surrender in order to have public services of which they are in greater need. Thus there is a balance, however rough, in the enjoyments to be had from private goods and services and those rendered by public authority.

It will be obvious, however, that this view depends on the notion of independently determined consumer wants. In such a world one could with some reason defend the doctrine that the consumer, as a voter, makes an independent choice between public and private goods. But given the dependence effect—given that consumer wants are created by the process by which they are satisfied—the consumer makes no such choice. He is subject to the forces of advertising and emulation by which production creates its own demand. Advertising operates exclusively, and emulation mainly, on behalf of privately produced goods and services.[2] Since management and emulative effects operate on behalf of private production, public services will have an inherent tendency to lag behind. Automobile demand which is expensively synthesized will inevitably have a much larger claim on income than parks or public health or even roads where no such influence operates. The engines of mass communication, in their highest state of development, assail the eyes and ears of the community on behalf of more beer but not of more schools. Even in the conventional wisdom it will scarcely be contended that this leads to an equal choice between the two.

The competition is especially unequal for new products and services. Every corner of the public psyche is canvassed by some of the nation's most talented citizens to see if the desire for some merchantable product can be cultivated. No similar process operates on behalf of the nonmerchantable services of the state. Indeed, while we take the cultivation of new private wants for granted we would be measurably shocked to see it applied to public services. The scientist or engineer or advertising man who devotes himself to developing a new carburetor, cleanser, or depilatory for which the public recognizes no need and will feel none

2 Emulation does operate between communities. A new school or a new highway in one community does exert pressure on others to remain abreast. However, as compared with the pervasive effects of emulation in extending the demand for privately produced consumer's goods there will be agreement, I think, that this intercommunity effect is probably small.

until an advertising campaign arouses it, is one of the valued members of our society. A politician or a public servant who dreams up a new public service is a wastrel. Few public offenses are more reprehensible.

So much for the influences which operate on the decision between public and private production. The calm decision between public and private consumption pictured by the conventional wisdom is, in fact, a remarkable example of the error which arises from viewing social behavior out of context. The inherent tendency will always be for public services to fall behind private production. We have here the first of the causes of social imbalance.

Social balance is also the victim of two further features of our society—the truce on inequality and the tendency to inflation. Since these are now part of our context, their effect comes quickly into view.

With rare exceptions such as the post office, public services do not carry a price ticket to be paid for by the individual user. By their nature they must, ordinarily, be available to all. As a result, when they are improved or new services are initiated, there is the ancient and troublesome question of who is to pay. This, in turn, provokes to life the collateral but irrelevant debate over inequality. As with the use of taxation as an instrument of fiscal policy, the truce on inequality is broken. Liberals are obliged to argue that the services be paid for by progressive taxation which will reduce inequality. Committed as they are to the urgency of goods (and also, as we shall see in a later chapter, to a somewhat mechanical view of the way in which the level of output can be kept most secure) they must oppose sales and excise taxes. Conservatives rally to the defense of inequality—although without ever quite committing themselves in such uncouth terms—and oppose the use of income taxes. They, in effect, oppose the expenditure not on the merits of the service but on the demerits of the tax system. Since the debate over inequality cannot be resolved, the money is frequently not appropriated and the service not performed. It is a casualty of the economic goals of both liberals and conservatives for both of whom the questions of social balance are subordinate to those of production and, when it is evoked, of inequality.

In practice matters are better as well as worse than this statement of the basic forces suggests. Given the tax structure, the revenues of all levels of government grow with the growth of the economy. Services can be maintained and sometimes even improved out of this automatic accretion.

However, this effect is highly unequal. The revenues of the federal government, because of its heavy reliance on income taxes, increase more than proportionately with private economic growth. In addition, although the conventional wisdom greatly deplores the fact, federal appropriations have only an indirect bearing on taxation. Public services are considered and voted on in accordance with their seeming urgency. Initiation or improvement of a particular service is rarely, except for purposes of oratory, set against the specific effect on taxes. Tax policy, in turn, is decided on the basis of the level of economic activity, the resulting revenues, expediency, and other considerations. Among these the total of the thousands of individually considered appropriations is but one factor. In this process the ultimate tax consequence of any individual appropriation is *de minimus,* and the tendency to ignore it reflects the simple mathematics of the situation. Thus it is possible for the Congress to make decisions affecting the social balance without invoking the question of inequality.

Things are made worse, however, by the fact that a large proportion of the federal revenues are pre-empted by defense. The increase in defense costs has also tended to absorb a large share of the normal increase in tax revenues. The position of the federal government for improving the social balance has also been weakened since World War II by the strong, although receding, conviction that its taxes were at artificial wartime levels and that a tacit commitment exists to reduce taxes at the earliest opportunity.

In the states and localities the problem of social balance is much more severe. Here tax revenues—this is especially true of the General Property Tax—increase less than proportionately with increased private production. Budgeting too is far more closely circumscribed than in the case of the federal government—only the monetary authority enjoys the pleasant privilege of underwriting its own loans. Because of this, increased services for states and localities regularly pose the question of more revenues and more taxes. And here, with great regularity, the question of social balance is lost in the debate over equality and social equity.

Thus we currently find by far the most serious social imbalance in the services performed by local governments. The F.B.I. comes much more easily by funds than the city police force. The Department of Agriculture can more easily keep its pest control abreast of expanding agricultural output than the average city health service can keep up with the needs of an expanding industrial population. One consequence is that the federal government remains under constant pressure to use its superior revenue position to help redress the balance at the lower levels of government.

Finally, social imbalance is the natural offspring of persistent inflation. Inflation by its nature strikes different individuals and groups with highly discriminatory effect. The most nearly unrelieved victims, apart from those living on pensions or other fixed provision for personal security, are those who work for the state. In the private economy the firm which sells goods has, in general, an immediate accommodation to the inflationary movement. Its price increases are the inflation. The incomes of its owners and proprietors are automatically accommodated to the upward movement. To the extent that wage increases are part of the inflationary process, this is also true of organized industrial workers. Even unorganized white-collar workers are in a milieu where prices and incomes are moving up. The adaption of their incomes, if less rapid than that of the industrial workers, is still reasonably prompt.

The position of the public employee is at the other extreme. His pay scales are highly formalized, and traditionally they have been subject to revision only at lengthy intervals. In states and localities inflation does not automatically bring added revenues to pay higher salaries and incomes. Pay revision for all public workers is subject to the temptation to wait and see if the inflation isn't coming to an end. There will be some fear—this seems to have been more of a factor in England than in the United States—that advances in public wages will set a bad example for private employers and unions.

Inflation means that employment is pressing on the labor supply and that private wage and salary incomes are rising. Thus the opportunities for moving from public to private employment are especially favorable. Public employment, moreover, once had as a principal attraction a high measure of social security. Industrial workers were subject to the formidable threat of unemployment during depression. Public employees were comparatively secure, and this security was worth an adverse salary differential. But with improving economic security in general this advantage has diminished. Private employment thus has come to provide better protection against inflation and little worse protection against other hazards. Though the dedicated may stay in public posts, the alert go.

The deterioration of the public services in the years of inflation has not gone unremarked. However, there has been a strong tendency to regard it as an adventitious misfortune—something which, like a nasty shower at a picnic, happened to blight a generally good time. Salaries were allowed to lag, which was a pity. This is a very inadequate view. Discrimination against the public services is an organic feature of inflation. Nothing so weakens government as persistent inflation. The public administration of France for many years, of Italy until recent times, and of other European and numerous South American countries have been deeply sapped and eroded by the effects of long-continued inflation. Social imbalance reflects itself in inability to enforce laws, including significantly those which protect and advance basic social justice, and in failure to maintain and improve essential services. One outgrowth of the resulting inbalance has been frustration and pervasive discontent. Over much of the world there is a rough and not entirely accidental correlation between the strength of indigenous communist parties or the frequency of revolutions and the persistence of inflation.

A feature of the years immediately following World War II was a remarkable attack on the notion of expanding and improving public services. During the depression years such services had been elaborated and improved partly in order to fill some small part of the vacuum left by the shrinkage of private production. During the war years the role of government was vastly expanded. After that came the reaction. Much of it, unquestionably, was motivated by a desire to rehabilitate the prestige of private production and therewith of producers. No doubt some who joined the attack hoped, at least tacitly, that it might be possible to sidestep the truce on taxation vis-à-vis equality by having less taxation of all kinds. For a time the notion that our public services had somehow become inflated and excessive was all but axiomatic. Even liberal politicians did not seriously protest. They found it necessary to aver that they were in favor of public economy too.

In this discussion a certain mystique was attributed to the satisfaction of privately supplied wants. A community decision to have a new school means that the individual surrenders the necessary amount, willy-nilly, in his taxes. But if he is left with that income, he is a free man. He can decide between a better car or a television set. This was advanced with some solemnity as an argument for the TV set. The difficulty is that this argument leaves the community with no way of preferring the school. All private wants, where the individual can choose, are inherently superior to all public desires which must be paid for by taxation and with an inevitable component of compulsion.

The cost of public services was also held to be a desolating burden on private production, although this was at a time when the private production was burgeoning. Urgent warnings were issued of the unfavorable effects of taxation on investment—"I don't know of a surer way of killing off the incentive to invest than by imposing taxes which are regarded by people as punitive."[3] This was at a time when the inflationary effect of a very high level of investment was causing concern. The same individuals who were warning about the inimical effects of taxes were strongly advocating a monetary policy designed to reduce investment. However, an understanding of our economic discourse requires an appreciation of one of its basic rules: men of high position are allowed, by a special act of grace, to accommodate their reasoning to the answer they need. Logic is only required in those of lesser rank.

Finally it was argued, with no little vigor, that expanding government posed a grave threat to individual liberties. "Where distinction and rank is achieved almost exclusively by becoming a civil servant of the state . . . it is too much to expect that many will long prefer freedom to security."[4]

With time this attack on public services has somewhat subsided. The disorder associated with social imbalance has become visible

[3] Arthur F. Burns, Chairman of the President's Council of Economic Advisers, *U. S. News & World Report,* May 6, 1955.
[4] F. A. Hayek, *The Road to Serfdom* (London: George Routledge & Sons, 1944), p. 98.

even if the need for balance between private and public services is still imperfectly appreciated.

Freedom also seemed to be surviving. Perhaps it was realized that all organized activity requires concessions by the individual to the group. This is true of the policeman who joins the police force, the teacher who gets a job at the high school, and the executive who makes his way up the hierarchy of Du Pont. If there are differences between public and private organization, they are of kind rather than of degree. As this is written the pendulum has in fact swung back. Our liberties are now menaced by the conformity exacted by the large corporation and its impulse to create, for its own purposes, the organization man. This danger we may also survive.

Nonetheless, the postwar onslaught on the public services left a lasting imprint. To suggest that we canvass our public wants to see where happiness can be improved by more and better services has a sharply radical tone. Even public services to avoid disorder must be defended. By contrast the man who devises a nostrum for a nonexistent need and then successfully promotes both remains one of nature's noblemen.

The Twisted Spirit

MICHAEL HARRINGTON

> We shall probably discover that the poor are even less ready to part with their neuroses than the rich, because the hard life that awaits them when they recover has no attraction, and illness in them gives them more claim to the help of others.
>
> —Sigmund Freud

THERE ARE FEW people in the United States who accept Rousseau's image of the "noble savage," of primitive, untutored man as being more natural than, and superior to, his civilized descendants. Such an idea could hardly survive in a society that has made technological progress one of its most central values. There are occasional daydreams about "getting away from it all," of going to an idyllic countryside, but these are usually passing fancies.

Yet, there is a really important remnant of Rousseau's myth. It is the conviction that, as far as emotional disturbance and mental disease go, the poor are noble savages and the rich are the prime victims of tension and conflict.

There are the literature of the harried executive, the tales of suburban neurosis, the theme of the danger of wealth and leisure. It is not so much that anyone says that the poor are healthy in spirit because they are deprived of material things. Rather, the poor are just forgotten, as usual. The novels and the popular sociology are written by the middle class about the middle class, and

---

Michael Harrington's book on poverty in the United States, *The Other America* (New York: The Macmillan Company, 1962), won a 1962 Hillman Prize Award. This chapter describes the emotional and psychological aspects of poverty.

there is more than a little strain of self-pity. The result is an image in which personal maladjustment flourishes at the top of society, the price the well-off pay for their power. As you go down the income scale, this theory implies, life becomes more tedious and humdrum, if less upset. (However, it should be noted that the white-collar strata have the chonicler of their quiet desperation in Paddy Chayevsky.)

The truth is almost exactly opposite to the myth. The poor are subject to more mental illness than anyone else in the society, and their disturbances tend to be more serious than those of any other class. This conclusion has emerged from a series of studies made over the past few decades. There is still considerable controversy and disagreement with regard to the reasons behind this situation. But the fact itself would seem to be beyond dispute.

Indeed, if there is any point in American society where one can see poverty as a culture, as a way of life, it is here. There is, in a sense, a personality of poverty, a type of human being produced by the grinding, wearing life of the slums. The other Americans feel differently than the rest of the nation. They tend to be hopeless and passive, yet prone to bursts of violence; they are lonely and iso-lated, often rigid and hostile. To be poor is not simply to be deprived of the material things of this world. It is to enter a fatal, futile universe, an America within America with a twisted spirit.

Perhaps the most classic (but still controversial) study of this subject is the book *Social Class and Mental Illness* by August B. Hollingshead and F. C. Redlich. Published in 1958, it summarizes a careful research project in New Haven, Connecticut. It is an academic, scholarly work, yet its statistics are the description of an abyss.

Hollingshead and Redlich divided New Haven into five social classes. At the top (Class I) were the rich, usually aristocrats of family as well as of money. Next came the executives and profes-sionals more newly arrived to prestige and power. Then, the mid-dle class, and beneath them, the workers with decent paying jobs. Class V, the bottom class, was made up of the poor. About half of its members were semiskilled, about half unskilled. The men had less than six years of education, the women less than eight.

As it turned out, this five-level breakdown was more revealing than the usual three-class image of American society (upper, middle, and lower). For it showed a sharp break between Class V at the bottom and Class IV just above it. In a dramatic psychological sense, the skilled unionized worker lived much, much closer to the middle class than he did to the world of the poor. Between Class IV and Class V, Hollingshead and Redlich found a chasm. This represents the gulf between working America, which may be up against it from time to time but which has a certain sense of security and dignity, and the other America of the poor.

Perhaps the most shocking and decisive statistic that Hollingshead and Redlich found was the one that tabulated the rate of treated psychiatric illness per 100,000 people in New Haven. These are their results:

Classes I and II	556 per 100,000
Class III	538
Class IV	642
Class V	1,659

From the top of society down to the organized workers, there are differences, but relatively small ones. But suddenly, when one crosses the line from Class IV to Class V, there is a huge leap, with the poor showing a rate of treated psychiatric illness of almost three times the magnitude of any other class.

But the mental suffering of the poor in these figures is not simply expressed in gross numbers. It is a matter of quality as well. In Classes I and II, 65 per cent of the treated psychiatric illness is for neurotic problems, and only 35 per cent for the much graver disturbances of psychoses. But at the bottom, in Class V, 90 per cent of the treated illness is for psychosis, and only 10 per cent for neurosis. In short, not only the rate but also the intensity of mental illness is much greater for the poor.

One of the standard professional criticisms of Hollingshead and Redlich is that their figures are for treated illness (those who actually got to a doctor or clinic) and do not indicate the "true prevalence" of mental illness in the population. Whatever merits this argument has in relation to other parts of the study, it points up that these particular figures are an understatement of the problem. The higher up the class scale one is, the more likely that there will be recognition of mental illness as a problem and that help will be sought. At the bottom of society, referral to psychiatric treatment usually comes from the courts. Thus, if anything, there is even more mental illness among the poor than the figures of Hollingshead and Redlich indicate.

The one place where this criticism might have some validity is with regard to the intensity of emotional disturbance. Only 10 per cent of the poor who received treatment are neurotics, yet the poor neurotic is the least likely person in the society to show up for treatment. He can function, if only in an impaired and maimed way. If there were something done about this situation, it is quite possible that one would find more neurosis in the other America at the same time as one discovered more mental illness generally.

However, it is not necessary to juggle with statistics and explanations in order to corroborate the main drift of the New Haven figures. During the fifties the Cornell University Department of Psychiatry undertook an ambitious study of "Midtown," a residential area in New York City. The research dealt with a population of 170,000 from every social class, 99 per cent of them white. (By leaving out the Negroes, there probably was a tendency to underestimate the problem of poverty generally, and the particular disabilities of a discriminated minority in particular.) The goal of the study was to discover "true prevalence," and there was interviewing in depth.

The Cornell scholars developed a measure of "mental health risk." They used a model of three classes, and consequently their figures are not so dramatic as those tabulated in New Haven. Yet they bear out the essential point: the lowest class had a mental health risk almost 40 per cent greater than the highest class. Once again the world of poverty was given definition as a spiritual and emotional reality.

The huge brute fact of emotional illness in the other America is fairly well substantiated. The reasons behind the fact are the subject of considerable controversy. There is no neat and simple summary that can be given at the present time, yet some of the analyses are provocative for an understanding of the culture of poverty even if they must be taken tentatively.

One of the most interesting speculations came from the Cornell study of "Midtown" in New York City. The researchers developed a series of "stress factors" that might be related to an individual's mental health risk. In childhood, these were poor mental health on the part of the parents, poor physical health for the parents, economic deprivation, broken homes, a negative attitude on the part of the child toward his parents, a quarrelsome home, and sharp disagreements with parents during adolescence. In adult life, the stress factors were poor health, work worries, money worries, a lack of neighbors and friends, marital worries, and parental worries.

The Cornell team then tested to see if there was any relationship between these factors and mental health. They discovered a marked correlation. The person who had been subjected to thirteen of these stress factors was three times more likely to be mentally disturbed than the person who had felt none of them. Indeed, the researchers were led to conclude that the sheer number of stress factors was more important than the quality of stresses. Those who had experienced any three factors were of a higher mental risk than those who had experienced two.

If the Cornell conclusions are validated in further research, they will constitute an important revision of some widely held ideas about mental health. The Freudian theory has emphasized the earliest years and the decisive trauma in the development of mental illness (for example, the death of a parent). This new theory would suggest a more cumulative conception of mental illness: as stress piles upon stress over a period of time, there is a greater tendency toward disturbance. It would be an important supplement to the Freudian ideas.

But if this theory is right, there is a fairly obvious reason for the emotional torment of the other America. The stress factors listed by the Cornell study are the very stuff of the life of the poor: physical illness, broken homes, worries about work and money, and all the rest. The slum, with its vibrant, dense life hammers away at the individual. And because of the sheer, grinding, dirty experience of being poor, the personality, the spirit, is impaired. It is as if human beings dilapidate along with the tenements in which they live.

However, some scholars have attempted to often the grimness of this picture with a theory about "drift." The poor, they argue, have a high percentage of disturbed people, not because of the conditions of life in the urban and rural slums, but because this is the group that gets all the outcasts of society from the rest of the classes. If this thesis were true, then one would expect to find failures from the higher classes as a significant group in the culture of the poor.

Hollingshead and Redlich tested this theory in New Haven and did not find any confirmation for it. The mentally impaired poor had been, for the most part, born poor. Their sickness was a product of poverty, instead of their poverty being a product of sickness. Similarly, in the Midtown study, no evidence was turned up to indicate that the disturbed poor were the rejects from other classes. There are some exceptions to this rule: alcoholics, as noted before, often tend to fall from a high position into the bitterest poverty. Still, current research points to a direct relationship between the experience of poverty and emotional disturbance.

And yet, an ironic point turned up in the Midtown research. It was discovered that a certain kind of neurosis was useful to a minority of poor people. The obsessive-compulsive neurotic often got ahead: his very sickness was a means of advancement out of the other America and into the great world. And yet, this might only prepare for a later crisis. On the lower and middle rungs of business society, hard work, attention to detail, and the like are enough to guarantee individual progress. But if such a person moves across the line, and is placed in a position where he must make decisions, there is the very real possibility of breakdown.

Someone in trouble, someone in sorrow, a fight between neighbors, a coffin carried from a house, were things that coloured their lives and shook down fiery blossoms where they walked.

SEAN O'CASEY

The feelings, the emotions, the attitudes of the poor are different. But different from what? In this question there is an important problem of dealing with the chaotic in the world of poverty.

The definition makers, the social scientists, and the moralists come from the middle class. Their values do not include "a fight between neighbors" as a "fiery blossom." Yet that is the fact in the other America. (O'Casey was talking about Ireland; he might as well have been describing any slum in the United States.) Before going on and exploring the emotional torment of the poor, it would be well to understand this point.

Take the gangs. They are violent, and by middle-class standards they are antisocial and disturbed. But within a slum, violence and disturbance are often norms, everyday facts of life. From the inside of the other America, joining a "bopping" gang may well not seem like deviant behavior. It could be a necessity for dealing with a hostile world. (Once, in a slum school in St. Louis, a teacher stopped a fight between two little girls. "Nice girls don't fight," she told them. "Yeah," one of them replied, "you should have seen my old lady at the tavern last night.")

Indeed, one of the most depressing pieces of research I have ever read touches on this point. H. Warren Dunham carefully studied forty catatonic schizophrenics in Chicago in the early forties. He found that none of them had belonged to gangs or had engaged in the kind of activity the middle class regards as abnormal. They had, as a matter of fact, tried to live up to the standards of the larger society, rather than conforming to the values of the slum. "The catatonic young man can be described as a good boy and one who has all the desirable traits which all the social agencies would like to inculcate in the young man of the community."

The middle class does not understand the narrowness of its judgments. And worse, it acts upon them as if they were universal and accepted by everyone. In New Haven, Hollingshead and Redlich found two girls with an almost identical problem. Both of them were extremely promiscuous, so much so that they eventually had a run-in with the police. When the girl from Class I was arrested, she was provided with bail at once, newspaper stories were quashed, and she was taken care of through private psychotherapy. The girl from Class V was sentenced to reform school. She was paroled in two years, but was soon arrested again and sent to the state reformatory.

James Baldwin made a brilliant and perceptive application of this point to the problem of the Negro in a speech I heard not long ago. The white, he said, cannot imagine what it is like to be Negro: the danger, the lack of horizon, the necessity of always being on guard and watching. For that matter, Baldwin went on, the Negro problem is really the white problem. It is not the Negro who sets dark skin and kinky hair aside as something fearful, but the white. And the resolution of the racial agony in America requires a deep introspection on the part of the whites. They must discover themselves even more than the Negro.

This is true of all the juvenile delinquents, all the disturbed people, in the other America. One can put it baldly: their sickness is often a means of relating to a diseased environment. Until this is understood, the emotionally disturbed poor person will probably go on hurting himself until he becomes a police case. When he is finally given treatment, it will be at public expense, and it will be inferior to that given the rich. (In New Haven, according to Hollingshead and Redlich, the poor are five times more likely to get organic therapy—including shock treatment—rather than protracted, individual professional care.)

For that matter, some of the researchers in the field believe that sheer ignorance is one of the main causes of the high rate of disturbance among the poor. In the slum, conduct that would shock a middle-class neighborhood and lead to treatment is often considered normal. Even if someone is constantly and violently drunk, or beats his wife brutally, people will say of such a person, "Well, he's a little odd." Higher up on the class scale an individual with such a problem would probably realize that something was wrong (or his family would). He will have the knowledge and the money to get help.

One of the researchers in the field who puts great stress on the "basic universals" of the Freudian pattern (mother figure, father figure, siblings) looks upon this factor of ignorance as crucial. He is Dr. Lawrence Kubie. For Dr. Kubie, the fundamental determinants of mental health and illness are the same in every social class. But culture and income and education account for whether the individual will handle his problem, whether he understands himself as sick, whether he seeks help, and so on. This theory leaves the basic assumptions of traditional psychoanalysis intact, but, like any attempt to deal with the poor, it recognizes that something is different.

For the rich, then, and perhaps even for the better-paid worker, breakdowns, neurosis, and psychosis appear as illness and are increasingly treated as such. But the poor do not simply suffer these disturbances; they suffer them blindly. To them it does not appear that they are mentally sick; to them it appears that they are trapped in a fate.

Much of this can be made specific if one looks at the grim winter of 1960-1961. This was a time of unemployment, of lagging production, of general eccnomic downturn. The statistics of the Gross National Product in this period were familiar to every newspaper reader in the nation. But behind them was a correlation between social tragedy and emotional disturbance.

During this time the National Federation of Settlements and Neighborhood Centers collected data from its agencies across the United States. Some of them were reporting on the inhabitants of the other America; others were describing the impact of a recession on organized workers who had made a good wage before the bottom dropped out of the economy. But in every case there is a sense of the way in which a social fact has its impact upon the delicate structure of a human personality, upon marriage and hope itself:

Rochester, New York: We are especially concerned about the effect [of the recession] on family life. Unemployment often leads to marital discord and desertions of families by the father, increased welfare dependency, increased crime, especially robberies, burglaries and muggings, and alcoholism among both teens and adults.

. . . The "A" family—father, mother, and six children. The father separated but provided $35 per week support until recently unemployed. Mother received Aid to Dependent Children, applied for additional assistance and was informed that oldest boy, senior in high school, not eligible because of age. Assistance arranged but mother passes stresses and strains on to son who feels he should quit school and get a job. (Not a realistic possibility.) Settlement must support son to stay in school without guilt feelings, help mother not to take anxieties out on son. Boy does well scholastically, is outstanding athlete and has excellent chances to go to college, which he wanted to do until current economic crisis occurred. But now questions this.

Chicago, Illinois: There has been a 30% increase in unemployment since September, 1960. . . .

This is creating criminal elements not before known to the community. Some are seeking some form of public assistance, thus overloading the rolls when found eligible. Loss of dignity because they are no longer able to support their family.

A 33-year-old man known to our agency was found hanged in his apartment just seven hours ago. He was apparently despondent over not being able to find a job, and unemployment compensation had been exhausted. His wife and four children had left him and had returned to Mississippi where they had immigrated from seven years ago. The family had been several months arrears in rent, and there was not proper food and clothing for the family during the harsh Chicago winter months.

Schenectady, New York: Among children and youth, resistance to paying fees, lack of pocket money for candy and pop, attendance at few movies. Concern about cost for social dances, general appearance, talk about enlisting in military service.

Young adults, lessening of aggressiveness in job-hunting pursuits, little conversation about the future, much conversation about getting out of town, greater lethargy about belonging, and doing more pocketing—"Ghettoizing" provincialism, small cliques who band together with beer, cards, and TV.

Cleveland, Ohio: Garnishments, overbuying on credit, increased dependency, crime.

Lorain, Ohio: Rising tide of appeals to private and public agencies. Family frustrations, sharp upcurve in children's illness and mental illness among the adults. Families are afraid to call the doctor because of lack of money to pay him and for medicine. One child almost died of pneumonia and family was charged with neglect. Fathers feel obliged to abandon families so that they will receive help more quickly.

Chicago, Illinois: The situation is serious here, probably as serious as in any other part of Chicago. The problem is complicated by the type of people in this area. They are, for the most part, unskilled laborers with little education, a language handicap and limited work experience. This means that they can do one type of work. When that job is not available they are unlikely to be transferred to another job or promoted.

Worried men and women, neglected health needs such as glasses, medical care and medicine, evictions, desertion of wage earner, creditors repossessing furniture and cars because payment cannot be met, and inadequate diets.

The group of work staff reports that children have no money for bus fares; the girls in sewing class have no money for sewing material; children less warmly dressed; and the need of haircuts . . .

Detroit, Michigan: Junior club members have been unable to pay the fifty cents annual membership fee. At Christmas children mentioned that they did not expect to receive any toys or new clothes. Adults sit home and when visited by settlement staff look helpless, depressed and not interested in participating in neighborhood life. "What's the use?" they ask. We have observed increased drunkenness among men and women to pass the time. Some neighbors are drinking Hadacol, a patent medicine.

In family camp last July, leaders observed that children who came to the program without breakfast ate and drank the milk with great relish. The mothers of the hungry children tried to cover up the reason for not serving breakfast at home. One mother with a large family told of going home to prepare a main meal of bread and spaghetti without meat. Another time this mother brought a poor-looking cake with peculiar icing for her contribution to the refreshments of a family life meeting. Her white and Negro neighbors who specialized in cake decorating rejected the cake, and the staff members were the only ones who ate it at the meeting.

Chicago, Illinois: With unemployment and the fear of it come an increase in tensions within the home, a tendency toward more rebellion and deviant behavior on the part of pre-teens and teens, etc. Practically every family situation is a multi-problem one.

Seattle, Washington: Personal depression and loss of personal value. One man in a housing project told us: "I have been out of work for nine months. I feel like half a man."

Some of these people, it is clear, are the inhabitants of the other America. But some of them are workers who are being pushed down, and the social chaos which these reports convey is another aspect of the attack upon the living standard of the middle third who gained through the rise of trade unionism. Moreover, these observations chronicle only the effects of a recession. But then these conditions are permanent in the culture of poverty; they persist in good times as well as in bad. The broken marriages, the drunkenness, the crime that comes to a neighborhood which once had known prosperity is a regular, daily aspect of life in the other America.

In this context, one might well take the word "depression" in a double sense, as applying to the human spirit as well as to the national economy. The people who are put down like this, who feel their social existence as if it were a futile fate imposed on them from above and without—these are the ones who swell the statistics of the mental health researchers in New Haven and Midtown, New York.

Out of all this, the research more and more suggests, there emerges the personality of poverty, the "typical citizen" of the other America.

This is how the Midtown researchers described the "low social economic status individual": they are "rigid, suspicious and have a fatalistic outlook on life. They do not plan ahead, a characteristic associated with their fatalism. They are prone to depression, have feelings of futility, lack of belongingness, friendliness, and a lack of trust in others." Translated into the statistics of the Midtown study, this means that the bottom of the society is three times more emotionally depressed than the top (36.2 per cent for the low, 11.1 per cent for the high).

A small point: America has a self-image of itself as a nation of joiners and doers. There are social clubs, charities, community drives, and the like. Churches have always played an important social role, often marking off the status of individuals. And yet this entire structure is a phenomenon of the middle class. Some time ago, a study in Franklin, Indiana, reported that the percentage of people in the bottom class who were without affiliations of any kind was eight times as great as the percentage in the high-income class.

Paradoxically, one of the factors that intensifies the social isolation of the poor is that America thinks of itself as a nation without social classes. As a result, there are few social or civic organizations that are separated on the basis of income and class. The "working-class culture" that sociologists have described in a country like England does not exist here, or at least it is much less of a reality. The poor person who might want to join an organization is afraid. Because he or she will have less education, less money, less competence to articulate ideas than anyone else in the group, they stay away.

Thus, studies of civilian-defense organizations during World War II showed that almost all the members were white-collar people. Indeed, though one might think that the poor would have more friends because they are packed densely together, there are studies that indicate that they are deprived in this regard, too. In one report, 47 per cent of the lower-class women said that they had no friend or no intimate friend.

Such a life is lonely; it is also insecure. In New Haven, Hollingshead and Redlich could find only 19 per cent of the people in the bottom class who thought that their jobs were safe. The Yale group described 45 per cent of the poor as "inured," and found that their motto was "We take what the tide brings in."

This fatalism is not, however, confined to personal experience alone, to expectations about job and family. It literally permeates every aspect of an individual's life; it is a way of seeing reality. In a poll the Gallup organization did for *Look* magazine in 1959 (a projection of what people anticipated in the sixties), the relationship between the social class and political pessimism was striking. The bottom group was much more likely to think that World War III was coming, that a recession was around the corner, that they would not take a vacation in the coming year. As one went up the income scale, the opinion of the world tended to brighten.

This pessimism is involved in a basic attitude of the poor: the fact that they do not postpone satisfactions, that they do not save. When pleasure is available, they tend to take it immediately. The smug theorist of the middle class would probably deplore this as showing a lack of traditional American virtues. Actually, it is the logical and natural pattern of behavior for one living in a part of American life without a future. It is, sad to say, a piece of realism, not of vice.

Related to this pattern of immediate gratification is a tendency on the part of the poor to "act out," to be less inhibited, and sometimes violent. There are some superficial observers who give this aspect of slum life a Rousseauistic twist. They find it a proof of the vitality, of the naturalness of the poor who are not constrained by the conventions of polite society. It would be hard to imagine a more wrongheaded impression. In the first place, this violence is the creature of that most artificial environment, the slum. It is a product of human density and misery. And far from being an aspect of personality that is symptomatic of health, it is one more way in which the poor are driven to hurt themselves.

If one turns to the family life of the other America, there is an almost summary case of the dislocation and strains at the bottom of society.

In New Haven, for instance, Hollingshead and Redlich found that in Class V (the poor) some 41 per cent of the children under seventeen lived in homes that had been disrupted by death, desertion, separation, or divorce. This, of course, has profound consequences for the personalities of the young people involved. (This would be an instance in which the traditional Freudian account of mental illness would be relevant to the other America. An unstable family structure, with a father or mother figure absent, would predict devastating personal consequences.)

Then, the types of family structure the Yale researchers found among the poor are important. Some 44 per cent of the children lived in "nuclear families," which unite father, mother, and children. But 23 per cent grew up in a "generation stem family," where different generations are thrown together, usually with a broken marriage or two. Under such circumstances there is the possibility of endless domestic conflict between the different generations (and this is exacerbated when the old people are immigrants with a foreign code). Another 18 per cent came from broken homes where one or the other parent was absent. And 11 per cent had experienced the death of a parent.

Another aspect of this family pattern is sexual. In New Haven the researchers found that it was fairly common for young girls in the slums to be pregnant before they were married. I saw a similar pattern in St. Louis. There, children had a sort of sophisticated ignorance about sexual matters at an early age. Jammed together in miserable housing, they knew the facts of sex from firsthand observation (though often what they saw was a brutalized and drunken form of sex). In this sense, they were much more sophisticated than the children in middle-class neighborhoods.

But the poor are never that really well informed. As noted before, along with a cynical version of the facts of life there went an enormous amount of misinformation. For instance, young girls were given systematic miseducation on the menstrual period. They were often frightened and guilt-ridden about sex at the same time that they were sophisticated.

And finally, the family of the poor lives cheek and jowl with other families of the poor. The sounds of all the quarreling and fights of every other family are always present if there happens to be a moment of peace in one household. The radio and the television choices of the rest of the block are regularly in evidence. Life is lived in common, but not in community.

So it is that the adolescents roam the streets. For the young, there is no reason to stay around the house. The street is a moment of relief, relaxation, and excitement. The family, which should be a bulwark against the sheer physical misery of the poor, is overwhelmed by the environment.

In this context, some of the rhetorical pieties of this society take on an unwitting irony. For example, here is Mayor Wagner of New York discussing the role of the promiscuous, addicted, violent girls in the gang wars of his city: "Of course," he continued, "the ultimate prevention of delinquency must begin in the home. Nothing the Government or the community can do," he said, "will substitute for the reassertion of parental control."

The only trouble with this familiar formula is that delinquency begins in the home and that these girls are, in all probability, fleeing a domestic shambles. To wait around until parental authority reasserts itself under the present conditions is to wait forever. The Government and the community must first make it possible for there to be a "home" in the deepest sense of the word. But that, of course, means massive action against the culture of poverty in the other America.

Poverty is expensive to maintain.

The tensions, the chaos, the dislocations described are a major item in the budget of every municipality. In some cities a quarter of the annual funds are devoted to taking care of the special fire, police, and health problems created by the slums. The cost of keeping these people at the bottom year in and year out (rather than making an investment in real change once for all) is considerable.

Another aspect of the high cost of poverty was computed a few years ago by Ernest M. Gruenberg and Seymour S. Ballin. They estimated that there were 9,000,000 people in the United States "suffering from a wide range of diagnosible disorders." (The disorders referred to were emotional and mental.) Of these, 1,500,-000 were hospital cases (but only half that number were in hospitals at a given time). These figures did not include the 1,500,000 who were mentally retarded.

In these statistics, one out of every sixteen persons in the United States was living an impaired life because of emotional disturbances. Gruenberg and Ballin suggest that mental illness of this magnitude causes the loss of a billion dollars in wages every year.

And they compute the Government expenditures in dealing with the problem at a little over a billion dollars. (This does not count the money spent by private agencies.) Thus, the immediate cost of these illnesses is over two billion dollars.

A major component of this enormous loss is provided by the other America. And, as noted before, their torment is a form of realism.

The emotional turmoil of the poor is, as Freud intimates in the quotation prefacing this chapter, a form of protection against the turmoil of the society, a way of getting some attention and care in an uncaring world. Given this kind of "defense," it requires an enormous effort for these people to cross over into the great society.

Indeed, emotional upset is one of the main forms of the vicious circle of impoverishment. The structure of the society is hostile to these people: they do not have the right education or the right jobs, or perhaps there are no jobs to be had at all. Because of this, in a realistic adaptation to a socially perverse situation, the poor tend to become pessimistic and depressed; they seek immediate gratification instead of saving; they act out.

Once this mood, this unarticulated philosophy, becomes a fact, society can change, the recession can end, and yet there is no motive for movement. The depression has become internalized. The middle class looks upon this process and sees "lazy" people who "just don't want to get ahead." People who are much too sensitive to demand of cripples that they run races ask of the poor that they get up and act just like everyone else in the society.

The poor are not like everyone else. They are a different kind of people. They think and feel differently; they look upon a different America than the middle class looks upon. They, and not the quietly desperate clerk or the harried executive, are the main victims of this society's tension and conflict.

Our Invisible Poor

DWIGHT MACDONALD

IN HIS SIGNIFICANTLY titled *The Affluent Society* (1958) Professor J. K. Galbraith states that poverty in this country is no longer "a massive affliction [but] more nearly an afterthought." Dr. Galbraith is a humane critic of the American capitalist system, and he is generously indignant about the continued existence of even this nonmassive and afterthoughtish poverty. But the interesting thing about his pronouncement, aside from the fact that it is inaccurate, is that it was generally accepted as obvious. For a long time now, almost everybody has assumed that, because of the New Deal's social legislation and—more important—the prosperity we have enjoyed since 1940, mass poverty no longer exists in this country.

Dr. Galbraith states that our poor have dwindled to two hardcore categories. One is the "insular poverty" of those who live in the rural South or in depressed areas like West Virginia. The other category is "case poverty," which he says is "commonly and properly related to [such] characteristics of the individuals so afflicted [as] mental deficiency, bad health, inability to adapt to the discipline of modern economic life, excessive procreation, alcohol, insufficient education." He reasons that such poverty must be due to individual defects, since "nearly everyone else has mastered his environment; this proves that it is not intractable." Without press-

---

In 1963 Dwight Macdonald reviewed *The Other America* in *The New Yorker*. His article, which was instrumental in bringing that book to the public's attention, was adapted for use as a Sidney Hillman Reprint.

ing the similarity of this concept to the "Social Darwinism" whose fallacies Dr. Galbraith easily disposes of elsewhere in his book, one may observe that most of these characteristics are as much the result of poverty as its cause.

Dr. Galbraith's error is understandable, and common. Last April the newspapers reported some exhilarating statistics in a Department of Commerce study: the average family income increased from $2,340 in 1929 to $7,020 in 1961. (These figures are calculated in current dollars, as are all the others I shall cite.) But the papers did not report the fine type, so to speak, which showed that almost all the recent gain was made by families with incomes of over $7,500, and that the rate at which poverty is being eliminated has slowed down alarmingly since 1953. Only the specialists and the statisticians read the fine type, which is why illusions continue to exist about American poverty.

Now Michael Harrington, an alumnus of the *Catholic Worker* and the Fund for the Republic who is at present a contributing editor of *Dissent* and the chief editor of the Socialist Party biweekly, *New America,* has written *The Other America: Poverty in the United States* (Macmillan). In the admirably short space of under two hundred pages, he outlines the problem, describes in imaginative detail what it means to be poor in this country today, summarizes the findings of recent studies by economists and sociologists, and analyzes the reasons for the persistence of mass poverty in the midst of general prosperity.

In the last year we seem to have suddenly awakened, rubbing our eyes like Rip van Winkle, to the fact that mass poverty persists, and that it is one of our two gravest social problems. (The other is related: While only eleven per cent of our population is non-white, twenty-five per cent of our poor are.) What is "poverty"? It is a historically relative concept, first of all. "There are new definitions [in America] of what man can achieve, of what a human standard of life should be," Mr. Harrington writes. "Those who suffer levels of life well below those that are possible, even though they live better than medieval knights or Asian peasants, are poor. . . . Poverty should be defined in terms of those who are denied the minimal levels of health, housing, food, and education that our present stage of scientific knowledge specifies for life as it is now lived in the United States." His dividing line follows that proposed in recent studies by the United States Bureau of Labor Statistics: $4,000 a year for a family of four and $2,000 for an individual living alone. (All kinds of income are included, such as food grown and consumed on farms.) This is the cutoff line generally drawn today.

Mr. Harrington estimates that between forty and fifty million Americans, or about a fourth of the population, are now living in poverty. Not just below the level of comfortable living, but real poverty, in the old-fashioned sense of the word—that they are hard put to it to get the mere necessities, beginning with enough to eat. This is difficult to believe in the United States of 1963, but one has to make the effort, and it is now being made. The extent of our poverty has suddenly become visible. The same thing has happened in England, where working-class gains as a result of the Labour Party's post-1945 welfare state blinded almost everybody to the continued existence of mass poverty. It was not until Professor Richard M. Titmuss, of the London School of Economics, published a series of articles in the *New Statesman* last fall, based on his new book, *Income Distribution and Social Change* (Allen & Unwin), that even the liberal public in England became aware that the problem still persists on a scale that is "statistically significant," as the economists put it.

Statistics on poverty are even trickier than most. For example, age and geography make a difference. There is a distinction, which cannot be rendered arithmetically, between poverty and low income. A childless young couple with $3,000 a year is not poor in the way an elderly couple might be with the same income. The young couple's statistical poverty may be temporary inconvenience; if the husband is a graduate student or a skilled worker, there are prospects of later affluence or at least comfort. But the old couple can look forward only to diminishing earnings and increasing medical expenses. So also geographically: A family of four in a small town with $4,000 a year may be better off than a like family in a city—lower rent, no bus fares to get to work, fewer occasions (or temptations) to spend money. Even more so with a rural family. Although allowance is made for the value of the vegetables they may raise to feed themselves, it is impossible to calculate how much money they *don't* spend on clothes, say, or furniture, because they don't have to keep up with the Joneses. Lurking in the crevices of a city, like piranha fish in a Brazilian stream, are numerous tempting opportunities for expenditure, small but voracious, which can strip a budget to its bones in a surprisingly short time.

It is not, therefore, surprising to find that there is some disagreement about just how many millions of Americans are poor. The point is that all recent studies[1] agree that American poverty is still a mass phenomenon.

Thus the Commerce Department's April report estimates there are 17,500,000 families *and* "unattached individuals" with incomes of less than $4,000. How many of the latter are there? "Poverty and Deprivation" (see note below) puts the number of single persons with under $2,000 at 4,000,000. Let us say that in the 17,500,000 under $4,000 there are 6,500 single persons —the proportion of unattached individuals tends to go down as income rises. This homemade estimate gives us 11,000,000 families with incomes of under $4,000. Figuring the average American family at three and a half persons—which it is—this makes 38,500,000 individuals in families, or a grand total, if we add in the 4,000,000 "unattached individuals" with under $2,000 a year, of 42,500 Americans now living in poverty, which is close to a fourth of the total population.

The reason Dr. Galbraith was able to see poverty as no longer "a massive affliction" is that he used a cutoff of $1,000, which even in 1949, when it was adopted in a Congressional study, was probably too low (the C.I.O. argued for $2,000) and in 1958, when *The Affluent Society* appeared, was simply fantastic.

The model postwar budgets drawn up in 1951 by the Bureau of Labor Statistics to "maintain a level of adequate living" give a concrete idea of what poverty means in this country—or would mean if poor families lived within their income ánd spent it wisely, which they don't. Dr. Kolko summarizes the kind of living these budgets provide:

Three members of the family see a movie once every three weeks, and one member sees a movie once every two weeks. There is no

[1] The studies, all of which are referred to by the author, include, Dr. Gabriel Kolko, *Wealth & Poverty in America* (Praeger); Dr. James N. Morgan, et al., *Income and Welfare in the United States* (McGraw-Hill); "Poverty and Deprivation" (pamphlet), Conference on Economic Progress, Leon H. Keyserling and others.

telephone in the house, but the family makes three pay calls a week. They buy one book a year and write one letter a week.

The father buys one heavy wool suit every two years and a light wool suit every three years; the wife, one suit every ten years or one skirt every five years. Every three of four years, depending on the distance and time involved, the family takes a vacation outside their own city. In 1950, the family spent a total of $80 to $90 on all types of home furnishings, electrical appliances, and laundry equipment. . . . The family eats cheaper cuts of meat several times a week, but has more expensive cuts on holidays. The entire family consumes a total of two five cent ice cream cones, one five-cent candy bar, two bottles of soda, and one bottle of beer a week. The family owes no money, but has no savings except for a small insurance policy.

One other item is included in the B.L.S. "maintenance" budget: a new car every twelve to eighteen years.

This is an ideal picture, drawn up by social workers, of how a poor family *should* spend its money. But the poor are much less provident—installment debts take up a lot of their cash, and only a statistician could expect an actual live woman, however poor, to buy new clothes at intervals of five or ten years. Also, one suspects that a lot more movies are seen and ice-cream cones and bottles of beer are consumed than in the Spartan ideal. But these necessary luxuries are had only at the cost of displacing other items—necessary, so to speak—in the B.L.S. budget.

The Conference on Economic Progress's "Poverty and Deprivation" deals not only with the poor but also with another large section of the "underprivileged," which is an American euphemism almost as good as "senior citizen;" namely, the 37,000,000 persons whose family income is between $4,000 and $5,999 and the 2,000,000 singles who have from $2,000 to $2,999. The authors define "deprivation" as "above poverty but short of minimum requirements for a modestly comfortable level of living." They claim that 77,000,000 Americans, or *almost half the population,* live in poverty or deprivation. One recalls the furor Roosevelt aroused with his "one-third of a nation—ill-housed, ill-clad, ill-nourished." But the political climate was different then.

The distinction between a family income of $3,500 ("poverty") and $4,500 ("deprivation") is not vivid to those who run things— the 31 per cent whose incomes are between $7,500 and $14,999 and the 7 per cent of the top-most top dogs, who get $15,000 or more. These two minorities, sizable enough to feel they *are* the nation, have been as unaware of the continued existence of mass poverty as this reviewer was until he read Mr. Harrington's book. They are businessmen, congressmen, judges, government officials, politicians, lawyers, doctors, engineers, scientists, editors, journalists, and administrators in colleges, churches, and foundations. Since their education, income, and social status are superior, they, if anybody, might be expected to accept responsibility for what the Constitution calls "the general welfare." They have not done so in the case of the poor. And they have a good excuse. It is becoming harder and harder simply to *see* the one-fourth of our fellow-citizens who live below the poverty line.

The poor are increasingly slipping out of the very experience and consciousness of the nation [Mr. Harrington writes]. If the middle class never did like ugliness and poverty, it was at least aware of them. "Across the tracks" was not a very long way to go. . . . Now the American city has been transformed. The poor still inhabit the miserable housing in the central area, but they are increasingly isolated from contact with, or sight of, anybody else. . . . Living out in the suburbs, it is easy to assume that ours is, indeed, an affluent society. . . .

Clothes make the poor invisible too: America has the best-dressed poverty the world has ever known. . . . It is much easier in the United States to be decently dressed than it is to be decently housed, fed, or doctored. . . .

Many of the poor are the wrong age to be seen. A good number of them are sixty-five years of age or better; an even larger number are under eighteen. . . .

And finally, the poor are politically invisible. . . . They are without lobbies of their own; they put forward no legislative program. As a group, they are atomized. They have no face; they have no voice. . . . Only the social agencies have a really direct involvement with the other America, and they are without any great political power. . . .
Forty to fifty million people are becoming increasingly invisible.

These invisible people fall mostly into the following categories, some of them overlapping: poor farmers, who operate 40 per cent of the farms and get 7 per cent of the farm cash income; migratory farm workers; unskilled, unorganized workers in offices, hotels, restaurants, hospitals, laundries, and other service jobs; inhabit-

ants of areas where poverty is either endemic ("peculiar to a people or district"), as in the rural South, or epidemic ("prevalent
among a community at a special time and produced by some special causes"), as in West Virginia, where the special cause was the
closing of coal mines and steel plants; Negroes and Puerto Ricans,
who are a fourth of the total poor; the alcoholic derelicts in the big-
city skid rows; the hillbillies from Kentucky, Tennessee, and Okla-
homa who have migrated to Midwestern cities in search of better
jobs. And, finally, almost half our "senior citizens."

The most obvious citizens of the Other America are those whose
skins are the wrong color. The folk slogans are realistic: "Last to
be hired, first to be fired" and "If you're black, stay back." There
has been some progress. In 1939, the non-white worker's wage
averaged 41.4 per cent of the white worker's; by 1958 it had
climbed to 58 per cent. A famous victory, but the non-whites still
average only slightly more than half as much as the whites. Even
this modest gain was due not to any Rooseveltian or Trumanian
social reform but merely to the fact that for some years there was a
war on and workers were in demand, whether black, white, or
violet. By 1947, the non-whites had achieved most of their
advance—to 54 per cent of white earnings, which means they have
gained, in the last fifteen years, just 4 per cent.

The least obvious poverty affects our "senior citizens"—those
over sixty-five. Mr. Harrington estimates that half of them—
8,000,000—live in poverty, and he thinks they are even more
atomized and politically helpless than the rest of the Other America. He estimates that one-fourth of the "unrelated individuals"
among them, or a million persons, have less than $580 a year,
which is about what is allotted *for food alone* in the Department of
Agriculture's minimum-subsistence budget. (The average American family now spends only 20 per cent of its income for food—an
indication of the remarkable prosperity we are all enjoying, except
for one-quarter of us.) One can imagine, or perhaps one can't,
what it would be like to live on $580 a year, or $11 a week. It is
only fair to note that most of our senior citizens do better: The
average per capita income of those over sixty-five is now estimated
to be slightly over $20 a week. That is, $1,000 a year.

The aged poor have two sources of income beside their earnings
or savings. One is contributions by relatives. A 1961 White House

Conference Report put this at 10 per cent of income, which works out to $8 a week for an income of $4,000—and the 8,000,000 aged poor all have less than that. The other is Social Security, whose benefits in 1959 averaged $18 a week. Even this modest sum is more than any of the under-$4,000 got, since payments are proportionate to earnings and the poor, of course, earned less than the rest. A quarter of them, and those in general the neediest, are not covered by Social Security. The last resort is relief, and Mr. Harrington describes most vividly the humiliations the poor often have to put up with to get that.

The whole problem of poverty and the aged is especially serious today because Americans are living longer. In the first half of this century, life expectancy increased 17.6 years for men and 20.3 years for women. And between 1950 and 1960 the over-sixty-five group increased twice as fast as the population as a whole.

The worst part of being old and poor in this country is the loneliness. Mr. Harrington notes that we have not only racial ghettos but geriatric ones, in the cheap rooming-house districts of large cities. He gives one peculiarly disturbing statistic: "One-third of the aged in the United States, some 5,000,000 or more human beings, have no phone in their place of residence. They are literally cut off from the rest of America."

Ernest Hemingway's celebrated deflation of Scott Fitzgerald's romantic notion that the rich are "different" somehow—"Yes, they have money"—doesn't apply to the poor. They are different in more important ways than their lack of money, as Mr. Harrington demonstrates:

. . . Emotional upset is one of the main forms of the vicious circle of impoverishment. The structure of the society is hostile to these people. . . . The poor tend to become pessimistic and depressed; they seek immediate gratification instead of saving; they act out.

Once this mood, this unarticulated philosophy, becomes a fact, society can change, the recession can end, and yet there is no motive for movement. The depression has become internalized. The middle class looks upon this process and sees "lazy" people who "just don't want to get ahead." People who are much too sensitive to demand of cripples that they run races ask of the poor that they get up and act just like everyone else in the society.

The poor are not like everyone else. . . . They think and feel differently; they look upon a different America than the middle class looks upon.

The poor are also different in a physical sense: they are much less healthy. According to "Poverty and Deprivation," the proportion of those "disabled or limited in their major activity by chronic ill health" rises sharply as income sinks. In reasonably well-off families ($7,000 and up), 4.3 per cent are so disabled; in reasonably poor families ($2,000 to $3,999), the proportion doubles, to 8 per cent; and in unreasonably poor families (under $2,000), it doubles again, to 16.5 per cent. An obvious cause, among others, for the very poor being four times as much disabled by "chronic ill health" as the well-to-do is that they have much less money to spend for medical care—in fact, almost nothing. This weighs with special heaviness on the aged poor. During the fifties, Mr. Harrington notes, "all costs on the Consumer Price Index went up by 12 per cent. But medical costs, that terrible staple of the aged, went up by 36 per cent, hospitalization rose by 65 per cent, and group hospitalization costs (Blue Cross premiums) were up by 83 per cent."

This last figure is particularly interesting, since Blue Cross and such plans are the A.M.A.'s alternative to socialized medicine, or, rather to the timid fumblings toward it that even our most liberal politicians have dared to propose. Such figures throw an unpleasant light on the Senate's rejection of Medicare. The defeat was all the more bitter because, in the usual effort to appease the conservatives (with the usual lack of success—only five Republicans and only four Southern Democrats voted pro), the bill was watered down in advance. Not until he had spent $90 of his own money—which is 10 per cent of the annual income of some 3,000,000 aged poor—would a patient have been eligible. And the original program included only people already covered by Social Security or Railroad Retirement pensions and excluded the neediest of all—the 2,500,000 aged poor who are left out of both these systems.

Mental as well as physical illness is much greater among the poor, even though our complacent cliché is that nervous breakdowns are a prerogative of the rich because the poor "can't afford them." (They can't, but they have them anyway.) This bit of middle-class folklore should be laid to rest by a study made in

New Haven: *Social Class and Mental Illness,* by August B. Hollingshead and Frederick C. Redlich (Wiley). They found that the rate of "treated psychiatric illness" is about the same from the rich down through decently paid workers—an everage of 573 per 100,000. But in the bottom fifth it shoots up to 1,659 per 100,000. There is an even more striking difference in the *kind* of mental illness. Of those in the four top income groups who had undergone psychiatric treatment, 65 per cent had been treated for neurotic problems and 35 per cent for psychotic disturbances. In the bottom fifth, the treated illnesses were almost all psychotic (90 per cent). This shows there is something to the notion that the poor "can't afford" nervous breakdowns—the milder kind, that is—since the reason the proportion of *treated* neuroses among the poor is only 10 per cent is that a neurotic can keep going, after a fashion. But the argument cuts deeper the other way. The poor go to a psychiatrist (or, more commonly, are committed to a mental institution) only when they are completely unable to function because of psychotic symptoms. Therefore, even that nearly three-fold increase in mental disorders among the poor is probably an underestimate.

The main reason the American poor have become invisible is that since 1936 their numbers have been reduced by two-thirds. Astounding as it may seem, the fact is that President Roosevelt's "one-third of a nation" was a considerable understatement; over two-thirds of us then lived below the poverty line, as is shown by the tables that follow. But today the poor are a minority, and minorities can be ignored if they are so heterogeneous that they cannot be organized. When the poor were a majority, they simply could not be overlooked. Poverty is also hard to see today because the middle class ($6,000 to $14,999) has vastly increased—from 13 per cent of all families in 1936 to a near-majority (47 per cent) today. That mass poverty can persist despite this rise to affluence is hard to believe, or see, especially if one is among those who have risen.

Two tables in "Poverty and Deprivation" summarize what has been happening in the last thirty years. They cover only multiple-person families; all figures are converted to 1960 dollars; and the income is before taxes. I have omitted, for clarity, all fractions.

The first table is the percentage of families with a given income:

	1935-6	1947	1953	1960
Under $ 4,000	68%	37%	28%	23%
$4,000 to $ 5,999	17	29	28	23
$6,000 to $ 7,499	6	12	17	16
$7,500 to $14,999	7	17	23	31
Over $15,000	2	4	5	7

The second table is the share each group had in the family income of the nation:

	1935-6	1947	1953	1960
Under $ 4,000	35%	16%	11%	7%
$4,000 to $ 5,999	21	24	21	15
$6,000 to $ 7,499	10	14	17	14
$7,500 to $14,999	16	28	33	40
Over $15,000	18	18	19	24

Several interesting conclusions can be drawn from these tables:

(1) The New Deal didn't do anything about poverty: The under-$4,000 families in 1936 were 68 per cent of the total population, which was slightly *more* than the 1929 figure of 65 per cent.

(2) The war economy (hot and cold) did do something about poverty: Between 1936 and 1960 the proportion of all families who were poor was reduced from 68 per cent to 23 per cent.

(3) If the percentage of under-$4,000 families decreased by two-thirds between 1936 and 1960, their share of the national income dropped a great deal more—from 35 per cent to 7 per cent.

(4) The well-to-do ($7,500 to $14,999) have enormously increased, from 7 per cent of all families in 1936 to 31 per cent today. The rich ($15,000 and over) have also multiplied—from 2 to 7 per cent. But it should be noted that the very rich, according to another new study, "The Share of Top Wealth-Holders in National Wealth, 1822-1956," by Robert J. Lampman (Princeton), have experienced a decline. He finds that the top 1 per cent of wealth-holders owned 38 per cent of the national wealth in 1929 and own only 28 per cent today.

(5) The reduction of poverty has slowed down. In the six years 1947-53, the number of poor families declined 9 per cent, but in the following seven years only 5 per cent. The economic stasis that

set in with Eisenhower and that still persists under Kennedy was responsible. (This stagnation, however, did not affect the over-$7,500 families, who increased from 28 per cent to 38 per cent between 1953 and 1960.) In *The New York Times Magazine* for last November 11th, Herman P. Miller, of the Bureau of the Census, wrote, "During the forties, the lower-paid occupations made the greatest relative gains in average income. Laborers and service workers . . . had increases of about 180% . . . and professional and managerial workers, the highest paid workers of all, had the lowest relative gains—96%." But in the last decade the trend has been reversed; laborers and service workers have gained 39% while professional-managerial workers have gained 68%. This is because in the wartime forties the unskilled were in great demand, while now they are being replaced by machines. Automation is today the same kind of menace to the unskilled—that is, the poor —that the enclosure movement was to the British agricultural population centuries ago. "The facts show that our 'social revolution' ended nearly twenty years ago," Mr. Miller concludes, "yet important segments of the American public, many of them highly placed Government officials and prominent educators, think and act as though it were a continuing process."

The post-1940 decrease in poverty was not due to the policies or actions of those who are not poor, those in positions of power and responsibility. The war economy needed workers, wages went up, and the poor became less poor. When economic stasis set in, the rate of decrease in poverty slowed down proportionately, and it is still slow. Kennedy's efforts to "get the country moving again" have been unsuccessful, possibly because he has, despite the suggestions of many of his economic advisers, not yet advocated the one big step that might push the economy off dead center: a massive increase in government spending. This would be politically courageous, perhaps even dangerous, because of the superstitious fear of "deficit spending" and an "unbalanced" federal budget. American folklore insists that a government's budget must be arranged like a private family's. Walter Lippmann wrote, after the collapse of the stock market last spring:

There is mounting evidence that those economists were right who told the Administration last winter that it was making the mistake of trying to balance the budget too soon. It will be said that the budget is

not balanced: it shows a deficit in fiscal 1962 of $7 billion. . . . But . . .
the budget that matters is the Department of Commerce's income and
product accounts budget. Nobody looks at it except the economists
[but] while the Administrative budget is necessary for administration
and is like a man's checkbook, the income budget tells the real
story. . . .

[It] shows that at the end of 1962 the outgo and ingo accounts will
be virtually in balance, with a deficit of only about half a billion
dollars. Thus, in reality, the Kennedy administration is no longer stim-
ulating the economy, and the economy is stagnating for lack of stimulation. We have one of the lowest rates of growth among the advanced
industrial nations of the world.

One shouldn't be hard on the President. Franklin Roosevelt, a
more daring and experimental politician, at least in his domestic
policy, listened to the American disciples of J. M. Keynes in the
early New Deal years and unbalanced his budgets, with splendid
results. But by 1936 he had lost his nerve. He cut back government spending and there ensued the 1937 recession, from which
the economy recovered only when war orders began to make up
for the deficiency in domestic buying power. "Poverty and Deprivation" estimates that between 1953 and 1961 the annual growth
rate of our economy was "only 2.5 per cent per annum contrasted
with an estimated 4.2 per cent required to maintain utilization of
manpower and other productive resources." The poor, who always
experience the worst the first, understand quite personally the
meaning of that dry statistic, as they understand Kipling's "The
toad beneath the harrow knows/Exactly where each tooth-point
goes." They are also most intimately acquainted with another set
of statistics: the steady postwar rise in the unemployment rate,
from 3.1 per cent in 1949 to 4.3 per cent in 1954 to 5.1 per cent
in 1958 to over 7 per cent in 1961. (The Tory Government is
worried because British unemployment is now at its highest point
for the last three years. This point is 2.1 per cent, which is less
than our lowest rate in the last fifteen years.)

It's not that Public Opinion doesn't become Aroused every now
and then. But the arousement never leads to much. It was aroused
twenty-four years ago when John Steinbeck published *The Grapes
of Wrath,* but Mr. Harrington reports that things in the Imperial Valley are still much the same: low wages, bad housing,

no effective union. Public Opinion is too public—that is, too general; of its very nature, it can have no sustained interest in California agriculture. The only groups with such a continuing interest are the workers and the farmers who hire them. Once Public Opinion ceased to be Aroused, the battle was again between the two antagonists with a real, personal stake in the outcome, and there was no question about which was stronger. So with the rural poor in general. In the late fifties, the average annual wage for white male American farm workers was slightly over $1,000; women, children, Negroes, and Mexicans got less. One recalls Edward R. Murrow's celebrated television program about these people, "Harvest of Shame." Once more everybody was shocked, but the harvest is still shameful. One also recalls that Mr. Murrow, after President Kennedy had appointed him head of the United States Information Agency, tried to persuade the B.B.C. not to show "Harvest of Shame." His argument was that it would give an undesirable "image" of America to foreign audiences.

There is a monotony about the injustices suffered by the poor that perhaps accounts for the lack of interest the rest of society shows in them. Everything seems to go wrong with them. They never win. It's just boring.

Public housing turns out not to be for them. The 1949 Housing Act authorized 810,000 new units of low-cost housing in the following four years. Twelve years later, in 1961, the AFL-C.I.O. proposed 400,000 units to complete the lagging 1949 program. The Kennedy administration ventured to recommend 100,000 to Congress. Thus, instead of 810,000 low-cost units by 1953, the poor will get, if they are lucky, 500,000 by 1963. And they are more likely to be injured than helped by slum clearance, since the new projects usually have higher rents than the displaced slum-dwellers can afford. (There has been no dearth of government-financed *middle*-income housing since 1949.) These refugees from the bulldozers for the most part simply emigrate to other slums. They also become invisible; Mr. Harrington notes that half of them are recorded as "address unknown." Several years ago, Charles Abrams, who was New York State Rent Administrator under Harriman and who is now president of the National Committee Against Discrimination in Housing, summed up what he had learned in two decades in public housing: "Once social reforms have won tonal appeal in the public mind, their slogans and goal-symbols may degenerate into tools of the dominant class for beleaguering the minority and often for defeating the very aims which the original sponsors had intended for their reforms."

And this is not the end of tribulation. The poor, who can least afford to lose pay because of ill health, lose the most. A National Health Survey, made a few years ago, found that workers earning under $2,000 a year had twice as many "restricted-activity days" as those earning over $4,000.

Although they are the most in need of hospital insurance, the poor have the least, since they can't afford the premiums; only 40 per cent of poor families have it, as against 63 per cent of all families. (It should be noted, however, that poor who are war veterans can get free treatment, at government expense, in Veterans Administration Hospitals.)

The poor actually pay more taxes, in proportion to their income, than the rich. A recent study by the Tax Foundation estimates that 28 per cent of incomes under $2,000 goes for taxes, as against 24 per cent of the incomes of families earning five to seven times as much. Sales and other excise taxes are largely responsible for this curious statistic. It is true that such taxes fall impartially on all, like the blessed rain from heaven, but it is a form of egalitarianism that perhaps only Senator Goldwater can fully appreciate.

The final irony is that the Welfare State, which Roosevelt erected and which Eisenhower, no matter how strongly he felt about it, didn't attempt to pull down, is not for the poor, either. Agricultural workers are not covered by Social Security, nor are many of the desperately poor among the aged, such as "unrelated individuals" with incomes of less than $1,000, of whom only 37 per cent are covered, which is just half the percentage of coverage among the aged in general. Of the Welfare State, Mr. Harrington says, "Its creation had been stimulated by mass impoverishment and misery, yet it helped the poor least of all. Laws like unemployment compensation, the Wagner Act, the various farm programs, all these were designed for the middle third in the cities, for the organized workers, and for the . . . big market farmers. . . . [It] benefits those least who need help most." The industrial workers, led by John L. Lewis, mobilized enough political force to put through Section 7 (a) of the National Industrial Recovery Act, which, with the Wagner Act, made the C.I.O. possible. The big farmers put enough pressure on Henry Wallace, Roosevelt's first Secretary of Agriculture—who talked a good fight for liberal principles but was a Hamlet when it came to action—to establish the two basic propositions of Welfare State agriculture: subsidies that now cost $3 billion a year and that chiefly benefit the big farmers; and the exclusion of sharecroppers, tenant farmers, and migratory workers from the protection of minimum-wage and Social Security laws.

No doubt the Kennedy administration would like to do more for the poor than it has, but it is hampered by the cabal of Republicans and Southern Democrats in Congress. The 1961 revision of the Fair Labor Standards Act, which raised the national minimum wage to the not exorbitant figure of $1.15 an hour, was a slight improvement over the previous act. For instance, it increased coverage of retail-trade workers from 3 per cent to 33 per cent. (But one-fourth of the retail workers still excluded earn less than $1 an hour.) There was also a considerable amount of shadow-boxing involved: Of the 3,600,000 workers newly covered, only 663,000 were making less than $1 an hour. And there was the exclusion of a particularly ill-paid group of workers. Nobody had anything against the laundry workers *personally*. It was just that they were weak, unorganized, and politically expendable. To appease the conservatives in Congress, whose votes were needed to get the revision through, they were therefore expended. The result is that of the 500,000 workers in the laundry, dry-cleaning, and dyeing industries, just 17,000 are now protected by the Fair Labor Standards Act.

It seems likely that mass poverty will continue in this country for a long time. The more it is reduced, the harder it is to keep on reducing it. The poor, having dwindled from two-thirds of the population in 1936 to one-quarter today, no longer are a significant political force, as is shown by the Senate's rejection of Medicare and by the Democrats' dropping it as an issue in the elections last year. Also, as poverty decreases, those left behind tend more and more to be the ones who have for so long accepted poverty as their destiny that they need outside help to climb out of it. This new minority mass poverty, so much more isolated and hopeless than the old majority poverty, shows signs of becoming chronic. "The permanence of low incomes is inferred from a variety of findings," write the authors of the Morgan survey. "In many poor families the head has never earned enough to cover the family's present needs."

For most families, however, the problem of chronic poverty is serious. One such family is headed by a thirty-two-year-old man who is employed as a dishwasher. Though he works steadily and more than full time, he earned over $2,000 in 1959. His wife earned $300 more, but their combined incomes are not enough to support themselves and their three children. Although the head of the family is only thirty-two, he feels that he has no chance of advancement partly because he finished only seven grades of school. . . . The possibility of such families leaving the ranks of the poor is not high.

Children born into poor families today have less chance of "improving themselves" than the children of the pre-1940 poor. Rags to riches is now more likely to be rags to rags. "Indeed," the Morgan book concludes, "it appears that a number of the heads of poor families have moved into less skilled jobs than their fathers had." Over a third of the children of the poor, according to the survey, don't go beyond the eighth grade and "will probably perpetuate the poverty of their parents." There are a great many of these children. In an important study of poverty, made for a Congressional committee in 1959, Dr. Robert J. Lampman estimated that eleven million of the poor were under eighteen. "A considerable number of younger persons are starting life in a condition of 'inherited poverty,' " he observed. To which Mr. Harrington adds, "The character of poverty has changed, and it has become more deadly for the young. It is no longer associated with immigrant groups with high aspirations; it is now identified with those whose social existence makes it more and more difficult to break out into the larger society." Even when children from poor families show intellectual promise, there is nothing in the values of their friends or families to encourage them to make use of it. Of the top 16 per cent of high-school students—those scoring 120 and over in I.Q. tests—only half go on to college. The explanation for this amazing —and alarming—situation is as much cultural as economic. The children of the poor now tend to lack what the sociologists call "motivation." At least one foundation is working on the problem of why so many bright children from poor families don't ever try to go beyond high school.

Mr. Raymond M. Hilliard, at present director of the Cook County (i.e., Chicago) Department of Public Aid and formerly Commissioner of Welfare for New York City, recently directed a "representative-sample" investigation, which showed that more than half of the 225,000 able-bodied Cook County residents who were on relief were "functionally illiterate." One reason Cook County has to spend $16,500,000 a month on relief is "the lack of basic educational skills of relief recipients which are essential to compete in our modern society." An interesting footnote, apropos of recent happenings at "Ole Miss," is that the illiteracy rate of the relief recipients who were educated in Chicago is 33 per cent, while among those who were educated in Mississippi and later moved to Chicago it is 77 per cent.

The problem of educating the poor has changed since 1900. Then it was the language and cultural difficulties of immigrants from foreign countries; now it is the subtler but more intractable problems of internal migration from backward regions, mostly in the South. The old immigrants wanted to Better Themselves and to Get Ahead. The new migrants are less ambitious, and they come into a less ambitious atmosphere. "When they arrive in the city," wrote Christopher Jencks in an excellent two-part survey, "Slums and Schools," in the *New Republic* last fall, "they join others equally unprepared for urban life in the slums—a milieu which is in many ways utterly dissociated from the rest of America. Often this milieu is self-perpetuating. I have been unable to find any statistics on how many of these migrants' children and grandchildren have become middle-class, but it is probably not too inaccurate to estimate that about 30,000,000 people live in urban slums, and that about half are second-generation residents." The immigrants of 1890-1910 also arrived in a milieu that was "in many ways utterly dissociated from the rest of America," yet they had a vision—a rather materialistic one, but still a vision—of what life in America could be if they worked hard enough; and they did work, and they did aspire to something more than they had; and they did get out of the slums. The disturbing thing about the poor today is that so many of them seem to lack any such vision. Mr. Jencks remarks:

While the economy is changing in a way which makes the eventual liquidation of the slums at least conceivable, young people are not seizing the opportunities this change presents. Too many are dropping out of school before graduation (more than half in many slums); too few are going to college. . . . As a result there are serious shortages of teachers, nurses, doctors, technicians and scientifically trained executives, but 4,500,000 unemployables.

The federal government is the only purposeful force—I assume wars are not purposeful—that can reduce the numbers of the poor and make their lives more bearable. The effect of government policy on poverty has two quite distinct aspects. One is the indirect effect of the stimulation of the economy by federal spending. Such stimulation—though by war-time demands rather than government policy—has in the past produced a prosperity that did cut down American poverty by almost two-thirds. But I am inclined to agree with Dr. Galbraith that it would not have a comparable effect on present-day poverty:

It is assumed that with increasing output poverty must disappear [he writes]. Increased output eliminated the general poverty of all who worked. Accordingly it must, sooner or later, eliminate the special poverty that still remains. . . . Yet just as the arithmetic of modern politics makes it tempting to overlook the very poor, so the supposition that increasing output will remedy their case has made it easy to do so too.

He underestimates the massiveness of American poverty, but he is right when he says there is now a hard core of the specially disadvantaged—because of age, race, environment, physical or mental defects, etc.—that would not be significantly reduced by general prosperity. (Although I think the majority of our present poor *would* benefit, if only by a reduction in the present high rate of unemployment.)

To do something about this hard core, a second line of government policy would be required; namely, direct intervention to help the poor. We have had this since the New Deal, but it has always been grudging and miserly, and we have never accepted the principle that every citizen should be provided, at state expense, with a reasonable minimum standard of living regardless of any other considerations. It should not depend on earnings, as does Social Security, which continues the inequalities and inequities and so tends to keep the poor forever poor. Nor should it exclude millions of our poorest citizens because they lack the political pressure to force their way into the Welfare State. The governmental obligation to provide, out of taxes, such a minimum living standard for all who need it should be taken as much for granted as free public schools have always been in our history.

It may be objected that the economy cannot bear the cost, and certainly costs must be calculated. But the point is not the calculation but the principle. Statistics—and especially statistical forecasts—can be pushed one way or the other. Who can determine in advance to what extent the extra expense of giving our 40,000,000 poor enough income to rise above the poverty line would be offset by the lift to the economy from their increased purchasing power? We really don't know. Nor did we know what the budgetary effects would be when we established the principle of free public education. The rationale then was that all citizens should have an equal chance of competing for a better status. The rationale now is different: that every citizen has a right to become or remain part of our society because if this right is denied, as it is in the case of at least one-fourth of our citizens, it impoverishes us all. Since 1932, "the government"—local, state, and federal—has recognized a responsibility to provide its citizens with a subsistence living. Apples will never again be sold on the street by jobless accountants, it seems safe to predict, nor will any serious political leader ever again suggest that share-the-work and local charity can solve the problem of unemployment. "Nobody starves" in this country any more, but, like every social statistic, this is a tricky business. Nobody starves, but who can measure the starvation, not to be calculated by daily intake of proteins and calories, that reduces life for many of our poor to a long vestibule to death? Nobody starves, but every fourth citizen rubs along on a standard of living that is below what Mr. Harrington defines as "the minimal levels of health, housing, food, and education that our present stage of scientific knowledge specifies as necessary for life as it is now lived in the United States." Nobody starves, but a fourth of us are excluded from the common social existence. Not to be able to afford a movie or a glass of beer is a kind of starvation—if everybody else can.

The problem is obvious: the persistence of mass poverty in a prosperous country. The solution is also obvious: to provide, out of taxes, the kind of subsidies that have always been given to the public schools (not to mention the police and fire departments and the post office)—subsidies that would raise incomes above the poverty level, so that every citizen could feel he is indeed such. *"Civis Romanus sum!"* cried St. Paul when he was threatened with flogging—and he was not flogged. Until our poor can be proud to say *"Civis Americanus sum!,"* until the act of justice that would make this possible has been performed by the three-quarters of Americans who are not poor—until then the shame of the Other America will continue.

The Challenge of Automation

W. WILLARD WIRTZ

I PROPOSE TO use the word "automation" as describing all of those developments, most of them technological, which have the result of permitting work to be done in less time than it could be done before. We are surrounded today by machines which can do all manner of things which before we thought only men could do.

I suggest that we have no alternative except to accept automation as a fact, as an inexorable force, and a force for good as far as the development of civilization is concerned.

The alternative to automation is stagnation in our economy. The only way we can possibly maintain the standard of living we have in this country is by doing the most highly efficient job that can conceivably be done. That is the only way we can maintain the standard of living which is one of our hallmarks.

Now, in some people's minds, this is all there is to be said about automation, that it is inexorable, that it is necessary, and that it can work out for the better.

I suggest that automation will be successful only as we attend to its *human* as well as its economic consequences, and that beyond that it will work most effectively, in purely economic terms, if we take care of the human implications and the human concerns which it creates.

I assert the necessity, if we are to serve our principles and our purposes, of putting to use all of the people whom we have in this

---

In 1963 Secretary of Labor W. Willard Wirtz gave a lecture sponsored by the Hillman Foundation at the University of Rochester. His major points are included in these excerpts.

country. There is a common assertion, an assumption, on which a good many of us have been brought up, that we don't need to worry about this because machines create as many new jobs as they replace.

I suggest to you that the present accumulating evidence is directly to the contrary in respect to this proposition. We have enjoyed during the past fifteen years an extraordinary increase in productivity per man hour in this country, about 60 percent, but during the past fifteen years this has not happened to the rate of job growth in this country.

For the next eight or ten years at least, the work force is going to be growing by one million people a year. But jobs have increased in the private sector of the economy only at the rate of 175,000 a year for the last five years. This is the story of what automation is presently doing to jobs in the economy, and the problem we face today is how we are going to take care of a work force which is expanding at the rate of a million a year, when the increase of jobs in the private sector of the economy is only 175,000 a year.

Even if automation does supply as many jobs as it displaces, they are going to be different jobs from the ones which were there before. They will be jobs requiring different skills. They will probably be jobs in different places, and they will be different in a number of other respects.

If you take all of the goods-producing industries in the country —including, particularly, agriculture, mining, what we call contract construction, and manufacturing—in the last fifteen years there has been a drop of a million and a half jobs in that sector of our economy. While the work force has been going up, there has been a drop in these areas in absolute numbers of a million and a half—and over half of that has come in the last five years. In respect to geographical areas, thirty days from today about 400,-000 people will be working in this country in a different geographical area from the one in which they are working today. Thirty days from today 800,000 people will be doing jobs different from the ones they are doing today, involving a major difference as far as their skills are concerned.

We grew up on the idea a job is something a man does all of his life, and now all of a sudden that isn't true, and the implications of it are very broad in their significance. Perhaps the most specific, identifiable effect of automation is this one that I have mentioned, that is, reducing so substantially the proportion of unskilled jobs in the economy.

Let me make this point in terms of a problem with which most of us think we are familiar. I refer to what we call the dropout problem. Most people in this country think the dropout problem is getting worse. Exactly the contrary is true. The dropout rate in 1960 was exactly half what it was in 1925, thirty-five years before. But that's not the rub. The situation used to be that if someone dropped out of school, almost by definition untrained, there was an unskilled job for him; now there is not an unskilled job.

There will be about a million and a half people finishing high school this year or dropping out this year without any real know-how as far as making a living is concerned, people who will not be going on to college, who will be moving directly into a world of work with no skills and in a situation in which there is virtually no unskilled work left to be done. The unemployment figure for boys and girls sixteen to twenty-one who are looking for work is 13 percent, and the unemployment figure for all members of non-white groups in this country is also 13 percent, and the unemployment figure for non-white boys between the ages of sixteen and twenty-one is 21 percent, because it is among the minority groups and among the younger workers where there is the least skill.

On the other hand, what automation is doing of course is to create an extraordinarily larger number of demands for skilled, professional, semi-professional, scientific and sub-scientific personnel. And here again we have a paradox, that where you've got a surplus, now, of unskilled workers in this country, you've also got real shortages in some of these other areas.

The meeting of this problem of what to do about the impact of technology on the needs of the work force in this country today is both a public and a private job.

We are right now training what we hope will be about 50,000 people in a combination federal and state training program in this country. Everybody recognizes that the cost of retraining those who have been attached to the work force cannot be borne by the private establishment in a good many cases and has to be picked up under the auspices of the state and the federal governments. That program will develop.

But this is only a small part of the answer. Most of the answer to the problem has got to be worked out in the school systems. It means, in my judgment, more vocational education for those who would otherwise be unskilled workers. That problem has to be met, and so does the problem of training for the higher skills and the professional competence which is also called for.

I would say to you with all of the conviction that I can summon that every single dollar which is spent today to educate or to train a worker, particularly a young worker, will come back many times over. We too often fail to realize that the alternative is to carry these people the rest of their lives, and that means a cost in terms of public aid, of unemployment insurance benefits, of institutional costs, of drains upon family and friends and private organizations of one kind or another, a cost infinitely larger than the cost of training them now to make them productive members of the society. Not only productive members of the society, but consumers; and perhaps more significantly in connection with the point of costs, taxpayers too. When I hear this talk about not passing debts on to the next generation, I can only cringe at the realization that the worst possible debt we could pass on to the next generation would be that they would not be trained to know how to make a living. This isn't somebody else's debt; it's a debt of this generation, and it's one to pay.

Another area in which this problem will have to be met is in the area of collective bargaining. Most of the national emergency disputes with which this country has been faced recently have resulted from the developing pace of automation. Almost all of the disputes have involved the question of whether men are to step aside when the machines come in and, if so, on what terms they are to step aside. Featherbedding is sheer waste, but don't think of featherbedding as something which reflects men's desires not to work; it reflects their desires—very strong desires—*to* work and their concern about getting another job if the one they have disappears. This is a completely understandable concern.

Last year we lost in strikes in this country about nineteen million man days of potential production—that's waste, that's a serious, unexcusable loss. But that figure doesn't mean a thing until you compare it with some other figures. Nineteen million man days lost last year from strikes; forty million man days lost last year from on-the-job accidents; and lost from unemployment, nine hundred million man days of potential production—forty-two times as much as we lost from strikes.

If we could get that figure of lost potential production from unemployment down, then these problems that arise in connection with collective bargaining would be infinitely less difficult than they are today. We can meet these problems if we will put the economy back onto a basis where there is a demand for all of the services of people who are available.

In the long run the only answer to unemployment, the only answer to the use of both machines and men, is to put this economy onto a basis where it is doing all of the things we want so much to do, and which we *can* do, to fill the unmet needs which we still have.

I suspect that the most serious portent of the future today is not by any means that robots will take over man's work, or that this suddenly exploding population of ours will prove that after all Malthus was right. I think rather that the most serious portent of the future is that the geometrical accumulation of scientific knowledge that the world is now experiencing in effect dooms the great majority of us to live in ignorance of the forces which will control our lives.

There was a very great safety factor in man's being subject to what used to be accepted as the laws of nature, laws which most of us could by reasonable application understand. But now the world's scientists have pressed on to a point where these laws are their playthings and where we, living now and forevermore just one spark away from destruction, cannot understand those forces or even communicate meaningfully with those who do. It seems to me no overstatement at all to suggest that the continuance of the free society as we know it probably depends on narrowing the present gap between the knowledge of a very few about what can be done with the newly harnessed forces and the abysmal ignorance of a great many who have to make the decisions as to what should be done with those forces. I think the future depends —in a free, democratic, decentralized decision-making society— on having a working majority of people in this country who are equipped to cope with the question of those possibilities.

Nothing we face demands of us anything we do not have or cannot produce. But I realize, and it concerns me, that we are more timid today in the field of the social and political sciences than we are in the field of the physical sciences, where we are very bold indeed. We are very concerned about heresy today in the political and social sciences, and I sometimes wonder what has happened since that period in earlier history when it was the political inventors who were the exalted men of their times, and it was the scientific inventors who were condemned for heresy. The whole thing seems some way to have turned around and we are at the point today where we have to establish the same boldness, the same ingenuity, in the area of learning how to control these forces that we have in the area of learning how to develop them.

I would say only that the need in both areas seems to me to be for an attitude toward change, an attitude which views change as something not to be opposed, and not just to be met, but to be seized upon with enthusiasm, an attitude which views change as the essential quality of growth, which thinks of growth as the essential meaning of life, and which thinks that the future is a good idea, which I do.

The American City—
Mirror to Man

PAUL YLVISAKER

MEN MAY FIND God in nature, but when they look at cities they are viewing themselves. And what Americans see mirrored in their cities these days is not very flattering. To any of the awakened senses, urban America can be a depressing experience.

Walk the dilapidating streets of Boston's Roxbury section, North Philadelphia, New York's Harlem and Lower East Side, East St. Louis, West Dallas, the poverty-scarred sections of Phoenix, the San Francisco Bay area's West Oakland and North Richmond.

Travel such corroding arteries as Route 1 through New England, the Baltimore Pike in Delaware County, University Avenue from Minneapolis into St. Paul, Figueroa Street south through Los Angeles to Long Beach.

Look out over the maze of boxes that have been merchandised as suburbs all the way from the Florida coast to Puget Sound.

Inhale the stench of the Jersey "meadowlands" with their oil refineries and open dumps, the steel complex of Gary-Hammond, the smelting towns of West Virginia. Follow—if you have the lungs and stomach to do so—the open-air sewers that clog over Los Angeles and drift as a giant's bad breath all the way from St.

Currently New Jersey's Commissioner of Community Affairs, Paul Ylvisaker was previously Director of the Ford Foundation Public Affairs Program. This article, which appeared in *Life* in 1966, was reprinted in the Hillman Reprint Series.

Louis to New York. Watch as the great streams and lakes of this nation—the Hudson, the Potomac, the Mississippi, Lake Erie, Lake Tahoe—become the drainage ditches and cesspools of a society flooding in the wastes of uncontained growth.

Scan the spectral web of utility poles and wires that haunt a skyline once graced by trees. Search for a park and fountain in downtown Troy; a pleasant place to stroll at Kennedy Airport; a path for cycling in Detroit.

Trace the city's growing edge: the shack and shanty towns of the outer rim; labor camps converting into year-round slum communities; towns of poverty jerry-built and gerrymandered out of the utility and voting boundaries of neighboring municipalities; trailers packed in Everytown's ghetto of "just outside"; catch-as-catch-can housing along every available strip of exurban roadway; barns and fences pasted over with the garish advertisements of the urban culture soon to follow. And then contemplate some of the latter-day samples of this emerging urban esthetic, among them the soaring brick piles that promise the city dweller "total living"—if only he can find a place to park.

Admittedly, urban America isn't all that bleak. Here and there are clearings in the urban jungle where the eye finds delight, or at least is not offended; that is, given the presence of wealth, or a sensitive builder, or an exacting client, or an advantaged university, or a moment of architectural and civic greatness, an engineering triumph, or some natural feature that overpowers even the mediocrity around it. Beacon Hill and the Boston Common, the planned community of Radburn, New Jersey; Westchester County parkways in New York; much of Washington, D.C.; Chapel Hill, North Carolina; Savannah, Georgia; Boulder, Colorado; remnants of San Francisco.

Sometimes even the gargantuan whole of urban America can be a thing of beauty. By air, and especially by night, our cities are as much a feast to the eyes as any settlement of history. And they are so *because* of their supposed faults, not in spite of them. Gaudy neon lights become flashing gems set against the velvet of darkness. With the flow of headlights along streets and highway they help trace the anatomy of a metropolis in which even the bulldozed monotony of nondescript developments acquires grace and meaning.

The rub is, of course, that only one in five Americans has ever seen his city by air, and the few who do soon return to contend with the grubbier realities below.

Must these urban realities of America be so grubby? Led by the White House, the nation is at last beginning seriously to ask that question. But it is a question that is far easier to ask than answer —and a problem much easier to wring one's hands over than solve. There are many concerns but two stand above all others.

One cuts straight to the heart of our democratic philosophy: Can we develop standards of order and beauty which amount to something more than the foisting of one man's tastes and self-interests upon another?

The other challenges our political skill and technical ingenuity: Can we get that extraordinarily free-wheeling and irascible figure, the American citizen-entrepreneur, to accept restraints on his ability to build as he wishes and make money as he can? And can we couple those controls with incentives powerful enough to prod and excite Americans into creating the more attractive urban environment which they obviously have the talent and means to achieve?

The Romans, who were no slouches at building cities of their own, were painfully aware of the first problem, and in one of their favorite maxims indicated it was too tough a nut to crack. "When it comes to tastes," they said, "there's not much point arguing."

The pragmatic, I'm-as-good-as-you-are American has tended to agree. Much can be said in his defense. For one man's taste is almost certain to be another's displeasure. The higher critics are still debating whether such monumental works as Lincoln Center in New York, or Philadelphia's Penn Center, or Pittsburgh's Golden Triangle are masterly or just mediocre. At a humbler level, the Tennessee mountaineer who moved to Akron, Ohio, may have half-a-dozen cannibalized cars rusting in his shantied backyard, but mixed among them twice that many birdhouses set with poetic concern and tender loving care.

When tastes and attachments can be that diverse, the average voter is bound to be skeptical of any effort at administered beauty. Who's to say what's attractive and what is not? And by an instinct which is something more than vulgar, the American has sensed a logic to governed esthetics that is not to his democratic liking. Beauty is related to order, regularity, consistency. Urban beauty—

at least as historical examples are cited to us—has been linked to concentrations of power and wealth seemingly necessary to produce it. Leningrad is Peter the Great, ordering the city into existence over the heads of his subjects and with the best European architects working as his hired hands. Paris is Louis Napoleon, by whose authority Baron Georges Haussmann could translate design into fact.

An autocrat's wish—and a city of splendor. But the American wonders whether the City Beautiful can also be a city of, for and by the people. To say the least, he's dubious. He becomes even more the doubting Thomas when he sees the sometimes nonsense, caprice, confusion and malice that can slip in under the banner of urban betterment.

How many times have a community's basic faults and problems been swept under a carpet of beautification? Consider the clean-up, fix-up campaigns which put brushes in the hands of slum dwellers but not mortgages, paint cans but not paychecks, brooms but not better municipal services. Or the downtown renewal and slum clearance projects which amassed scarce resources under an appeal to the general interest but wound up benefitting a predictable few. Or the reservation of green belts which turned out, in Charles Abrams' wryly satiric definition, to be "those belts which separate white belts from black belts." Or "zoning for orderly development," which has been used by many a municipality to exclude most anyone not already living there. The "Pointe System," by which an exclusive neighborhood rates the suitability of candidates for residence. The creation of parks, but only for the use of those communities lucky enough to have the sites and tax resources available. The adoption of health and building codes, with such standards and enforcement that the poorer family is squeezed from the community.

The first problem of urban esthetics, then, *is* a problem of philosophy—and not merely one of definition but of values, purpose and motive. It will avail America nothing if it gains the City Beautiful but by means and intent which destroy its own soul.

Still, it is one thing to be aware of a philosophical problem, and another to be paralyzed by it. The classic puzzler—whether you can ever reach a certain destination when each step takes you only half the remaining distance—is solved not by eternal reflection but by deciding whether or not you want to get there; and if you do, to start and keep moving at a steady pace.

Beauty, order, grace—these are admittedly elusive as the civic objectives but no more so than the Liberty and Pursuit of Happiness or the Declaration of Independence, or the General Welfare and Due Process of the Constitution.

It is a question of how badly they are wanted. At that point, the politician takes over from the philosopher, asking, as he always must, "How many are willing to fight whom to get what?"

The democratic battles which Americans like most to remember are those in which "the people" are pitted as suffering heroes against an entrenched, rapacious few. But in the struggle for more attractive cities, the American people are pitted against themselves, which makes it damnably difficult for any leader who enters the political fray to muster his troops and sustain an attack. He will also have a problem pinpointing "the enemy." The sign and billboard people probably qualify as well as any. They really do mess up the landscape—and in public opinion polls they're rejected by 2 to 1. But their numbers are legion and their faces indistinct—they range from the biggest of business to the smallest of men with the sign reading EAT AT JOE'S.

Therefore, the enemy must be referred to with raised eyebrows but in lower case: "the fast-buck developer," "greedy commercial interests," "the highway lobby," "slum landlords."

There is no doubt that these fuzzy captions match up with some real people who on many known—and heaven only knows how many less known—occasions have proved themselves to be an esthetic menace. But the categories they cover, the interests they include and, more basically, the human traits they describe, sooner or later implicate just about every American.

Which property-owner hasn't had at least one speculative eye open for the highest bidder, some mixed feelings about zoning regulations which stand in the way of re-use or development at maximum possible gain?

Which taxpayer hasn't boggled at the thought of spending those extra sums to add an architect and some amenities to public housing projects, or balked at giving up color television so that his community could acquire some green acres?

Which of us, having just attended a public hearing to stop a road from coming through our neighborhood, hasn't already rejoined the automobile lobby when snarling our way home over congested thoroughfares? And if the title search is pressed far enough, which major American institution—church, university, bank, insurance company—hasn't been found the owner of slum properties? Which investor hasn't expected the managers of his portfolio and the corporate executives to fetch the largest possible return, even if it means cutting local tax and civic contributions of branch offices or polluting the streams of exurban sanctuaries which offered low taxes and a relaxed approach to planning?

These are the untidy qualities found in all of us which help mess up our cities. Sometimes they break out into flagrant cases of moral, legal and esthetic indecency; mostly they remain at the endemic level of individual shrewdness and civic indifference, live-and-let-live, get-what-you-can and yell-when-you're-hurt.

The city, after all, is a mirror to man. And isn't this the human image one finds, say, in the transition of country road to city street? Trace the familiar process through:

Farmer Smith, who owns half the roadside acreage, needs some extra cash to support his son through trade school. Small-townsman Jones, the eldest son of the corner grocer, is getting married, wants a place of his own, can't find anything in town. His father buys a half-acre lot from Smith and gives it to his son for a wedding present. Young Jones buys a shell house on contract, finishes it after working hours, puts in a septic tank and digs a well. Life gets lonely for his wife—she persuades two other young couples to settle next to them. One more shell house, a trailer, two more septic tanks, two more wells, three cinder driveways and a dozen utility poles. Farmer Smith's son comes back from school, gets a permit to convert one of the farm buildings into a machine shop, puts up a six-foot, hand-painted sign, builds on an addition to the old farmhouse with picture window, brick veneer, a television aerial and aluminum trim. (His wife is very happy.) A buddy of his says, "Let's go partners on a filling station across the road." Then their wives, looking for some extra household money, open up a roadside stand and diner.

Soon Farmer Smith, with agricultural prices dropping and his years advancing, starts reading those ads about retiring in Florida, lets it be known he's willing to talk to a developer. The town taxpayers hear about it, calculate the number of schoolchildren the development will bring and the cost of educating them, get all stirred up by rumored versions of the odd ones and barbarians who are moving in, and decide it's time for planning and zoning for the orderly growth of the community. Differences are forgotten long enough to get a federal "701" planning grant. Then, while an itinerant expert puzzles out the jigsaw of a master plan (substituting prefabricated parts for the missing local pieces), they enact a one-acre zoning ordinance requiring paved roads, curbs, gutters, storm sewers, sidewalks and water connections. With costs raised, the developer isn't interested any more, at least not at the land prices Smith is now quoting.

Farmer Smith starts grumbling. So do those whose second thought is that they might get all that extra work and business which comes with town growth and still manage to keep the taxes down. More farmers are reading the Florida ads. While the town debates, Farmer Clark—down the road from Smith and in another township—sells his land to the original developer. A few days later Smith and cohorts start a campaign to amend the zoning ordinance from one acre to half an acre, with reduced road and sidewalk requirements. Pandemonium at the next meeting of the zoning board! The chairman gets mad and quits, his replacement votes for the amendment and eventually it's adopted. Smith sells his acreage and moves to California.

Now you can play this sequence through with or without bribery, corruption and wicked intent. Farmer Smith may well have been a skinflint. He may have persuaded a few of his old cronies on the zoning board by plying them with favors. He, the developer, and a conniving real estate agent might have promised the town engineer or attorney a percentage of the sale price. On the other hand, the entire cast of characters could have been earnest, God-fearing citizens whose only faults were their limited incomes, choice and sensitivity.

In either case the esthetic results would be essentially the same —and identical with what has happened to the mass of urban America. Call it by any name—chaos, unplanned growth, ribbon development, social anarchy, slurbs, the decline of American civilization, the resurgence of *laissez-faire*. But recognize it for what it is—a people's *laissez-faire*, which sinks its roots down past any rotting level of corrupt and cynical behavior by the few into a subsoil of widespread popular support and an abiding tradition of private property, individual freedom and "every-man's-home's-his-castle."

The search for urban policy thus begins with the public's conflicting replies to the philosopher's unrelenting question: What kind of city are you looking for, what kind of beauty, what kind of order?

Merely whisper the question these days and 57 varieties of answers will be thrust upon you by anxious hands. The one ingredient most have in common is the assumption that other things must change and everyone else conform to the tastes and advantage of the one who is doing the proposing. This one ingredient almost unfailingly poisons the solution. *In a democracy the city to strive for is one in which diverse human beings can live freely together, respect each other's varying tastes and share the immense power of their differences.*

It is relatively simple to achieve beauty and order, at least of a sort, by building something less than this open city. The ready-mix formula is usually some combination of wealth, homogeneity and exclusion. Our urban landscape is fast growing with examples of choice suburbs where a more fortunate few manage to find sanctuary from the sorrier conditions of the many. The names of some of these retreats have become hallmarks of American character: Gross Pointe, Mich., Winnetka, Ill., Tuxedo Park, N.Y., to mention a few.

It is also relatively simple to say what urban policy should be if you are bent on perfecting only that kind or piece of a city you have a special interest in. If you want the automobiled, shopping-center city, go on subsidizing highways, parking and single-family homes on large-sized lots. If you want the sort of European city American tourists love to visit and downtown merchants want to keep, subsidize mass transit, zone for apartments, and allow taxpayers to deduct rent as well as mortgage-interest payments on their federal income tax returns.

If you are the mayor of Central City, charge suburbanites for their use of your facilities and use the proceeds to modernize your public services. If you are the mayor of Suburbia tell the mayor of Central City to go to blazes and use the money to buy your own water and sewer system. If you are the citizen of Exurbia, tell both mayors to go to blazes, because it is already costing you a bundle to pay for your own well and septic tank. If you are the denizen of Downtown Slum, tell them all to go to hell, join the next rent strike and march on Washington.

If you want a city which is tidy and symmetrical, urge the establishment of an architectural review board. If you like your cities a little on the messy side and full of visual surprises, vote "no" on that proposal. And if you like your cities totally spontaneous, cast another ballot against any form of zoning or planning whatsoever. Houston, without either, seems to have boomed, sprawled and skyscraped as well—or as badly—as any other American city. On the other hand, you might also want to consider the civic damage done to Staten Island during its recent years of free-for-all development.

To repeat, it is relatively easy to decide what policy should be when you have factored America's conflicting tastes and interests into homogeneous pieces of the city—particularly when you can keep the other pieces from voting in your jurisdiction.

But what do you do when, as President or as thoughtful citizen, you have to deal with the whole of the divided American metropolis—and simultaneously with all the diversities of that Great American City which our nation is fast turning into?

Part of the answer, a fundamental and healthy part, is this division of the whole into more manageable sections. If our system did not allow for some compartmentalization of political, social and esthetic differences, creativity would be stifled and conflict would become so massive as to be possibly unresolvable.

Another part of the answer is to avoid becoming too solemn and inflexible. A good deal of urban beauty comes, as the beauty in a coral reef, from generations of accumulating individuality and seemingly random growth. And half of the art of urban planning is to recognize when to control and when to let alone.

But make no mistake about it—these pieces of urban America, particularly when they are based on the principle of I've-got-mine-now-you-get-yours, do not automatically add up to an environment in which the nation can feel great pride or satisfaction. There is, of course, a need for broader vision and direction.

If you doubt this, ask the zoning board of a township which

succeeds in keeping its stretch of road and river uncluttered, only to see its neighboring township spew forth everything from junkyards to raw sewage. Or the city planners who are constantly being asked to crowd a region's economy into the one municipality they are hired by. Or the health officer—paralyzed by the thought of "taking on" the industry that gives his community its jobs and taxes—who quietly prays for the day when state or nation will crack down on those who contaminate the city's air and water. Or that sensitive property owner, forced by straitened circumstances to sell his historic mansion and wooded estate to the highest bidder with lowest standards, who cries out for a national declaration that *there are some things private money cannot buy but the public must be willing to pay for.*

Nothing short of a nation's concern and deliberate policy will build a better environment. Until that concern and policy emerge, individual choices and local decisions will go on missing and sputtering. When they do emerge, the decentralized, spontaneous energies of America will finally have their chance of being harnessed into creating beauty rather than chaos.

This is not an argument for central domination of local affairs. Quite the contrary. It is a call for elevating problems of our city to a place on the nation's public agenda—on a par with employment, rocketry and national defense—and for giving mayors and others who deal with these problems the attention, dignity and resources they deserve.

Urban policy of this sort will undoubtedly contain stronger elements of control than we have known, and some limitation of choice. There is no longer good reason to leave the trenching of utility lines, or the control of air and water pollution, or the junking of automobiles, or the regulation of highway billboards, or the guarantee of open occupancy, to individual and local determination.

But for a diverse and free society, urban policy will have to be far more sophisticated than mere regulation and control. Controls are too hard to come by and too easy to get around. They usually are enacted too late and are too often used for purposes other than what they were created for. And at best they represent the common denominator of what we are against, rather than the measures of excellence and public appeal of the cities we hope to create.

When developing urban policy in this society, we will have to rely more on the carrot than on the stick—creating incentives which are far-reaching enough to express a nation's concern, and powerful enough to exert a national influence.

One form of incentive too easily overlooked lies in the reshaping of existing controls which now keep local authorities and private citizens from acting flexibly and imaginatively. Antiquated building codes are a prime example. The work now being done with zoning regulations to allow both the municipality and the developer more than one way of satisfying minimum requirements is a welcome instance of how creativity can be encouraged rather than stifled by controls.

Tax incentives are even more promising because they go to the jugular vein of private decisions and have the combined effect of both carrot and stick. There is a long list of possible uses. Both the local property tax and the federal income tax can be adapted so as to reward the man who maintains his property rather than the slumlord who exploits it and the slothful owner who lets it go. Taxes can also be revised to give a break to those willing to add some esthetic extras to the cost of construction. As the laws stand now, concern for beauty will only increase your tax assessment. Another tax break should go to those willing to donate open land, or development rights, to their communities for public use. Stiff taxes might be imposed on those who pollute air, land or water—with all or part of these same taxes remitted if the offender agrees to spend equivalent sums to prevent further pollution.

Another line of tax reform should start channelling more of our national revenues to our beleaguered municipalities, especially our central cities. Even allowing for that elusive margin of increased efficiency and trimmed services, the financial requirements for keeping American cities going—let alone improving them—have long ago outstripped the capacity of the fiscal system we have grown up with. As a nation, we have dangerously under-invested in our urban plant. We have skimped on maintenance and what little we have done to establish a reserve for depreciation and renewal would have any private accountant tearing his hair out. Recently, there has been talk of a major redistribution of the nation's tax resources, one proposal being the "Heller Plan" for turning back part of any federal tax surplus to the states. This plan badly needs amending to make certain that urban communities become the prime beneficiaries.

In addition to tax incentives, the nation can also expand its present repertory of grants-in-aid. Such assistance might go to communities willing to invite expert criticism and outside competition in the design of local subdivisions and public facilities. Also, grants could be made available to cities willing to preserve precious land and landmarks from too-eager bulldozers. Grants could be made to states ready to experiment with new forms of municipal acquisition and disposition of land, and also willing to risk the political hazards of moving with help and controls into the vacuum of farmland and metropolitan fringe before these are filled by haphazard development; to universities prepared to train urban experts who are also politically knowledgeable, and then to evaluate performance in words the public can understand; to schools finally ready to expose their pupils to the rudiments of urban esthetics and city planning.

Incentives should also go to the private sector, extending financial, legal, technical and moral support to those who are pioneering imaginative new settlements on America's urban frontier. Men like Robert Simon, the builder of Reston, Va.; and James Rouse, the developer of Columbia, Md. They and growing numbers of others like them are advancing beyond what the public presently demands or is content to buy. They could move out further, especially in providing lower-income housing and better public facilities, if given more help than is presently available. These men are representative of the new breed of private enterprisers dedicated to the public interest. They might do even better if prodded themselves by some public competition. There has already been talk of "Oakland East," "Minneapolis South," and "Chicago West"— suburbs built by the Mother City, much as the communities of Ancient Greece, when they reached a certain size, spawned urban offspring of their own. We presently have working for our cities mayors and public enterpreneurs clearly capable of such massive endeavors, should the public one day decide to let them capitalize on their experience and try building a few new towns of their own.

And what might be the happy result if governmental agencies like the Post Office were stimulated to try something more than branch architecture, and to start matching the elegance—or at least enlightenment—of national industries in the design and layout of local offices and working facilities?

Such "competition in the public interest" could be extended into other areas. American cities are now the by-product of other purposes, the residual of countless decisions made with some other intent than an improved environment for the urban population. Their technology is the leavings from industrial and military research; their officials and personnel the second-class citizens of America's executive establishment. But why should an America which has applied its ingenuity with such system and success to lesser objectives fail to provide an equivalent base of research and development for the largest and most important enterprise of all—the building of its cities?

There is no budget for urban research worthy of the name—though we still appropriate nearly $100 million a year for farm research; no Bureau of Standards dedicated to the needs of America's municipalities; no "Bell Laboratory" for urban planning; no Rand Corporation for urban transportation; no Brookhaven with resources enough to score breakthroughs in the control of pollution and contamination; no Bauhaus to spur building research and community design; no staff college to dignify and continuously stretch the minds and competence of municipal officials. No single one of these facilities would be enough. The scale of urban development in the U.S. is so immense, and our ignorance of cause and solution so vast, that we will surely need the simultaneous and often competitive probing of many minds in many institutions—public and private, profit and nonprofit—to catch up with the problem and some day move ahead.

There is obviously a long way to go and much to do. But much has already been done and a number of signs augur well.

We do, after all, have prototypes—and criticisms of these prototypes—on which to consolidate much broader programs of urban renewal, restoration, regional and social planning, new town development, interracial housing, open-space procurement, and even underground wiring. We also have a growing cadre of extraordinarily capable urban planners, managers, technicians and researchers.

We have begun—through civil-rights legislation and the poverty program—to face up to the moral and human requirements of building better cities, making up much of what has been lacking in earlier efforts at physical and economic planning. Prodded by the poor and by social critics, we have become increasingly sophisticated as consumers of public services—creating new mechanisms for civic complaint and waxing ever more eloquent in expressing our urban needs and dissatisfactions.

We have finally recognized, at least symbolically, the importance of urban problems by elevating the federal Housing and Home Finance Agency to Cabinet rank and broadening its title to something worthy of its task: the Department of Housing and Urban Development.

American business has turned increasingly to urban betterment—no longer as a polite slogan but aggressively and competitively as a major new market.

Slowly and not yet surely enough, we are facing up to the harsh realities and deadly hazards of urban neglect. The handwriting on the wall is there to read: the riots in Watts; the long, dark night of the Northeastern blackout; the water shortage in the New York metropolitan region; the rising crime rate; the ominously increased morbidity from contaminated air. And if the recent spate of urban literature and legislation is any indication, the American public has finally put on its glasses and looked to see what the handwriting has long been saying.

The most encouraging of all our urban developments is the fact that the preservation of nature's beauty and man's perfection of his own cities have become presidential themes. This is a certain sign that the nation has become concerned enough for its political leaders to calculate the odds and conclude that there is more to be lost than gained by avoiding the issue, and more to be won than lost by advancing the cause. The President could not risk this commitment until a heroic procession of local leaders had explored the political terrain before him. Especially mayors.

When the record of a more livable America is written, future school-children should be reading the names of Clark and Dilworth in Philadelphia: Lee in New Haven; Collins in Boston; Tucker in St. Louis; Cavanagh in Detroit; Hartsfield and Allen in Atlanta; Daley in Chicago; Lawrence in Pittsburgh; Briley in Nashville—to list some of those mayors deserving of special tribute.

Now that the presidency is finally allied with City Hall the pace of urban progress is bound to quicken. Not only because the White House can command far greater resources and talent, and a far better press, but because the nation at last feels certain that the subject is worth arguing about and that something major is likely to be done.

The argument and the action now can and will begin—in earnest and increasingly with results. The modest proposals placed before Congress this past session, and the lesser legislation that emerged from the usual round of political compromise, will go through the inevitable process of amendment and escalation.

Or should one qualify the word "inevitable"? Remember the verbal games we have played before: the "long levers of great action" that have turned out to be but small bars of self-interest joined to drooping promises and limp excuses; architectural pyrotechnics that ended in large contracts and minor improvements; local action defeated by national apathy?

The answer remains a matter of faith—and perseverance.

Yet, somehow, I believe the American public won't let this new subject of better cities go without a struggle, or let their politicians rest—which means the public will in turn be led and prodded.

Once Americans start seeing examples rather than promises, and are given visions rather than alibis, what is to keep them from working and paying for better cities with all the restless energy they have been spending on faster cars and easier kitchens? A family argument about who gets what, how to do it, and who's to pay? I doubt it. In our history so far, it never has.

PART FOUR

Foreign Affairs

The postwar period began with a search for universal order, a search made more pressing by the specter of nuclear destruction. Herblock summed it up with a few lines, which became a symbol of the age. At the same time the United States hastily discarded a century and a half of peacetime isolation and entered into the world community with an intensity rivaling the empires of antiquity. Theodore H. White gave an early report on the nation as it plunged into its new role.

But making democracy secure soon developed into a more complicated task than we had imagined, and voices of caution began to be heard—that our goal could not be achieved through a blind anti-communist passion, or by imposing our economic system on others. The distinguished student and practitioner of foreign affairs, George F. Kennan, was one of the early cautioners; Norman Cousins and Stuart Chase added their viewpoints in later years.

Meanwhile the pressures of new nations with rising expectations and of old antagonisms never resolved were stretching the capabilities of the U.N. almost beyond the breaking point, but even though it never fulfilled our early expectations there seemed to be no other path to international order. Adlai Stevenson, one of the U.N.'s most articulate exponents, defended it in general terms, while David Morse discussed some specific goals in the economic arena.

Finally all the hopes of world peace and international justice came crashing against the rock of Vietnam, which seemed to signal a 180 degree swing in U.S. policy, from isolation to intervention, in two decades. Henry Steele Commager, from the viewpoint of history and common sense, analyzed our current posture and offered some guidelines for the future.

Decision at Washington

THEODORE H. WHITE

ONE DAY IN Paris the scholarly Ambassador of a very minor power told me a story.

He had collected the White Papers, Blue Books, Yellow Books, Orange Books and all the published notes and dispatches of the diplomacy that had led to the First German War in the summer of 1914. He had wanted to trace, day by day, the negotiations of the last six weeks before that great accident. For the First World War, he insisted, was an accident that might have been avoided, while all the horrors that have since followed have flowed inevitably from that accident as flame from fire. The Ambassador had been, there-fore, naturally disappointed in studying the clocked and dated cables that went Vienna-Belgrade, Belgrade-St. Petersburg, Berlin-Vienna, Vienna-Paris, Paris-London, London-Berlin to find that, even with a generaton of hindsight, he could not pick out the man or the decision or any precise moment-of-no-return when the war might have been stopped before it was triggered off.

But he found something equally exciting. It was an omission. For, if his researches were correct, said he, in all the published cables of foreign ministers, sovereigns, ambassadors and chancel-lors not a single European diplomat had mentioned the United States, speculated on its strength, or wondered about its attitude. Not only that—none of the published records of those last

Fire In The Ashes (New York: William Morrow and Company, Inc., 1953) was written by Theodore H. White, famed correspondent, fol-lowing a five-year study of Europe's postwar needs and the Marshall Plan. This is the concluding chapter of the book, which won a 1953 Hillman Prize Award.

twilight weeks recorded the intervention, remonstrance, or initiative of any American emissary in the six great capitals to assert the will of America in the century which she was to dominate.

The Ambassador told this story in a moment of exasperation, adding, "But that was only thirty-five years ago! And now—now we cannot plan, we cannot think, we cannot breathe without asking first, before anything else, what will America do? What does America want? What can we do about them?"

The Ambassador was not unfriendly. He represented, indeed, one of those nations on whose automatic support America instinctively counts. What exasperated him was that he and his country were no longer fundamentally independent. They had been dragged by this century's events into an association that made them, willy-nilly, members of a community from which they dared not break and in which leadership was irrevocably American.

It is with similar exasperation that Americans sometimes look out on the world. They are annoyed like the Ambassador because they can no longer act independently and dare not break from the community they lead. They are upset because they cannot face, alone, a world of ever larger social-and-power agglomerations. Powerful as America is, she cannot ignore the fact that decisions are no longer made by single nations; decisions are made by a diplomacy of communities of nations, in action and in contest with other communities.

Let us look at these communities.

The two major blocs of power in the world are the Atlantic and Russian-satellite blocs. But beyond these are other sharply defined communities—the Moslem Community of nations with particular problems and aspirations of its own, the Latin-American Community, the Africans, only now emerging into an awareness of their own kinship, the community of peoples called India, called Southeast Asia, the Japanese, and the Chinese.

At this writing, America is no longer at war with the Chinese but is still greatly threatened by the Russians. It can count on the support only of the Atlantic Community and the Latin-American Community. All other civilizations and communities hang in the balance, in various degrees of disturbance and ferment, between ourselves and the adversary.

The simple listing of community names suggests the strategy imposed on the Atlantic world.

Defensively, it is to preserve and strengthen the unity of our community and defend it from Russia's effort of disruption.

Offensively, it is to swing the communities-in-between firmly to our side and then, ultimately, go on to divide the adversary's community from within and leave him isolated.

For Americans, in this strategy, Europe is the key.

It is the defense key because it gives us a line of resistance that starts 3,500 miles east of Staten Island and multiplies our military strength with powerful allies.

It is the offensive key because Europe is an association of powers who still wield far greater influence than ourselves in the changing civilizations of Africa, Southeast Asia and the Middle East, whom we hope to swing to our side.

The defense approach to strategy requires, above all, that Europe be kept content within the Atlantic Community, immune to the seduction and intrigue of Russian diplomacy. This brings us, therefore, to the two current problems of Europe which press like twin nightmares on the day-to-day operation of American diplomacy across the Atlantic.

The first of these is the recurrent economic stagnation of Western Europe; the second is the German problem.

The first complication—Europe's economic stagnation—is the most inviting area of vulnerability to Russian attack. Nothing is more eloquent of Russian thinking than the stability of their garrison strength in Central Europe since the war. It is questionable, looking back, that the Red Army's garrison divisions were ever deployed for attack at a preconceived date. It is more likely that they represented an insurance policy, a guarantee in the Russian mind that if an accident happened they would be able to strike swiftly and mop up easily, or, at any rate, jump off with an advantage while their home reserves rolled in for a second and finishing blow.

The NATO effort to purchase a counterinsurance policy was as necessary in our counterstrategy as was the Russian garrison in theirs. But this effort has been so costly and the emotion needed to force it on the taxpayer so intense that it has diverted the United

States from the original interrupted purpose of American intervention in Europe in 1947, which was the Marshall Plan whose goal was originally set as the reorganization of European economic life. It is usually forgotten that the Marshall Plan expired in quiet,

FROM *The Herblock Book* (Beacon Press, 1952)

halfway through, as we have seen, without ever having finished its tasks.

Western Europe thus lies vulnerable today not so much to Russian military aggression as to Russian political-economic aggression. At this writing, the Organization of European Economic Cooperation reports that production in Western Europe, after rising ten per cent a year from 1948 through 1951, has been stationary since the beginning of 1952 and is sustained chiefly by the American boom and the domestic arms effort which is so unpopular politically.

Although the full political impact of a rising standard of living in Russia may be twenty years away—or even further—Russia's growth has given her powers of economic disruption which are immediate. Though Russia's masters may be unable to give their growing population for many years much more than their present meager pantry supplies, they may find it quite profitable politically to dump wheat on the world market, selling it cheaply to England, Germany or the other major European importers, at once, to cut them away from America. Though millions of ordinary Russians do not even dream of driving their own automobiles, Russia's masters may well buy up oil they do not need. They may find it profitable to take Persian oil at the Persian Gulf in their own tankers, swapping it for cheap textiles or capital equipment, in order to break the Anglo-American petroleum control of the Middle East. Other raids in the world market are equally possible. They would be disturbing in any situation, but in a Europe that marks time, socially and economically, as it does today, these raids could be devastating.

The second problem within Europe—Germany—is diplomatically even more perplexing than economic stagnation.

Since 1947, all American diplomacy in Europe has been erected on the assumption that Germany was permanently split and that Western Germany could thus be brought to mesh its strength in a greater dynamic West European Union. The rigid counterdiplomacy of Joseph Stalin made this assumption valid and permitted us what success we have so far won. But it now lies in the power of Stalin's successors to undo our diplomacy by undoing his. Should they offer to give up Eastern Germany on condition that Western Germany repudiate association with the West through European Union, they might be able to undo all our work overnight.

This prospect of a Russian offer on Eastern Germany haunts our statesmen. But what is usually ignored is how deeply intertwined this problem is with the problems of Europe's economic health. The Germans, whether split or united, will probably swing to the power bloc that offers them the greatest opportunity to thrive and earn a living. Germany's amazing recovery has taken place in the post-Korean boom, when both devastated Germany and the entire world clamored for hard goods. But the Germans have not yet been forced to face a buyer's market, or meet the competition of the more efficient heavy industries of England and the United States. The slight downturn of 1949 in world trade found the Ruhr eager and avid to sell and trade its goods with the Russian world; a major depression might twist all German commercial aspirations in that direction. The Germans are a people not yet naturally and traditionally convinced of democratic values; while many Germans cherish freedom, many would willingly sacrifice it for other benefits. Behind the dignified façade of the Bonn government these contrary impulses clash. The problem of the division of Germany is technically manageable as long as the Western world is booming, for Germany reunited, no matter what compact is signed on paper, will gravitate to the most inviting and most vigorous of the rival blocs. In a depressed Europe and a depressed world, however, Germany, even staked down by our half-million troops, will be tugged politically and emotionally away from us.

If these twin problems—Germany and economic stagnation—are intertwined, certain strategic measures are obviously necessary to meet them at once.

The first is so necessary even from a domestic point of view that it needs no laboring. It is that our economy be so managed, at whatever cost, that no nineteen-thirty-style depression recur. A depression of this depth is the only thing absolutely certain to rip apart the entire structure of resistance to a Communist-dominated world.

The next is the encouragement of a system of trade which lets Europeans both trade in our markets and share in the resources of the trading world which at the moment is dominated by America. It is impossible to keep Western European industries from exchanging what they produce with the Soviet world if they cannot squeeze through the tariff barriers of the United States to earn the dollars they need to buy our goods.

Yet, again, a third measure is the support of the movement toward European Union. This movement is important not so much because the German troops it promises may be useful militarily, but because it is the only authentic structural change yet proposed that may rock West Europe off dead center.

European Union, it should be stressed, is not an iron-clad guarantee of dynamic forward motion; it is only the opportunity. The use Europeans make of the opportunity depends mostly on them.

But the United States can help. It can help, technically, by underwriting on the American capital market the investment loans of the Schuman Plan already adequately underwritten by its High

Authority, or it can help by tax concessions to American investors in such foreign bonds as are deemed in the national interest. It can help, even now, with money. Though the first enthusiasm for the Marshall Plan is over, the United States will be appropriating billions for foreign aid for years to come. At the moment, this aid is rigidly linked to military purpose. Yet if Congress would permit, once more, a flexible approach so that the sum might be used either for military or civilian aid, we might be able with far less money to do more good. For now, with the experience of the Marshall Plan behind us, we know where the bottlenecks are which must be smashed, where the Communist political strongholds are, what the argument is about, and we could earmark our grants, politically, not for relief, or for budget-balancing, but for specific social and structural reforms.

If these are the burdens on American policy, burdens equally grave lie upon Europe. For the Europeans are as responsible for the present peak of strain in the Atlantic Community as are the Americans.

Europeans have a tendency all too human to blame all their ills and failures on American leadership, as if the perils and problems which America crudely forces them to grapple with were of American confection, not the ugly face of reality. Sometimes their petulance has the same ring as that of a sensitive adolescent forced by a coarse parent to do his ugly, unpleasant, but necessary homework.

Much can be overlooked—even the European attitude toward the Korean War. Though nothing in postwar history, except the Marshall Plan, more swiftly raised American prestige in European eyes than our defense of Korea, no other American action was more swiftly transformed into a source of emotional criticism of America. Many Europeans look on the American effort in Korea as a twentieth-century reproduction of the Northwest Frontier between India and Afghanistan—a far-off frontier, held on a skirmish line between civilization and barbarism, which can be manned for decades with adventure-seeking regular officers and the sodden outcasts of industrial unemployment. For them, MIG Alley is the equivalent of the Khyber Pass. Although European soldiers fought on the front lines in Korea, no European appreciates the extent of American involvement, nor does he grasp

the fact that thousands of Americans, drafted from the age of
eighteen, fought daily in defense of a land which was not theirs,
that the United States was strained emotionally and physically by a
major war, and the dead returned with each ship from the Orient.
Europeans focus generally, in their thinking, on the ugly phenomena the Korean War produced in American domestic politics, or on the exaggerated military burdens which American
emotion demanded of them.

American diplomacy can—and must—overlook this attitude if
the Community is to survive; it must overlook many other European failings and faults.

What American diplomacy cannot overlook, what it must hold
Europeans primarily responsible for, is to provide the initiative
and will to make of their own resources a new life. If the chief
burden of America's diplomacy in Europe is to aid Europe toward the expanding, fluid society, the chief duty of the Europeans
in this strategy is to make themselves healthy, to tear down what
is ancient, or has become useless with age, and go forward to make
opportunity for each of their individuals.

This is the essential drama of Europe, for there is fire in the
ashes of the old civilization. America can fan it to flame or smother
it, but the flame cannot be fed from America, it must blaze from
its own sources.

The offensive approach to world strategy begins in Europe, too.

The offensive approach must start with what is held—the Atlantic Community and the Latin-American Community—and go
on to acquire the friendship and support of the other communities
that lie between ourselves and the Russians.

In most of these in-between communities, the Atlantic Community relies for immediate negotiation and bargaining on French-
men, Britons and Belgians, who are or have been established
abroad in positions of power, or are about to withdraw from them.

Neither we nor the Europeans have ever as foreigners thoroughly understood these in-between civilizations.

These neutral blocs are usually included in the phrase "Free
World" which is both misleading and dangerous. Almost all the
people in these other blocs, steeped in poverty, hunger and disease, deprived of education and decision, are incapable of thinking
informedly about the twentieth-century world, or of choosing

their own governments. Anyone who thinks that world problems (which baffle even the educated West) can be wisely decided by the free vote of illiterate and superstitious peasants whose horizons reach no farther than the village well is the victim of self-delusion. Governments are imposed on these people and they persist and succeed, perish and disappear only as they draw loyalty and give opportunity to the ambitious few with the acquiescence of the hungry many. To millions in these countries, communism masquerades as true progress. The people of these countries seek chiefly that the governments imposed on them appear to be governments of their own, not governments of alien white men, and that these governments bring some tiny visible advantages to their daily life. Among such people, communism can take hold—but only if we, by ignoring reality, permit it.

Much of Western political thinking is irrelevant for the in-between countries. Freedom, as it developed in the West, was a unique growth that went hand in hand for two centuries with the development of science and industry. Most of the peoples of the backward world in their lust to create a modern technology are willing to skip freedom, in order more quickly to have the technologies that freedom fostered. Freedom may develop among them later, as it works down from the top to an increasingly educated, increasingly well-fed citizenry. But for this generation, freedom, as we conceive it, does not weigh too heavily in their choice. What they want is to be governed efficiently by men of their own tongue and training and led, however slowly, toward some of the wonders of modern civilization of which village gossip whispers.

The problem in the in-between communities is, therefore, one of transfer of power, a transfer of power from the hands of Atlantic government to the hands of efficient native leadership, followed by such astute maneuvering as will make these native leaders see that there is more to be gained by friendship with the Atlantic world than friendship with Russia. Such a transfer has taken place effectively in both India and Japan. It is being bungled in the Middle East and large regions of Africa.

Basic strategy must be to keep India and Japan with us, to soothe and smooth the transfer in the Middle East, Africa and Southeast Asia, and then, finally, come to grips with China in a political-economic effort to magnetize her away from Russia where her national interests diverge from those of Moscow.

This strategy, imposed on us by the world, must shape the tactical approach to each concrete problem.

To begin with, there are two wars in Asia to be settled, of which one, the Korean, now that the truce has been signed, approaches at this writing the stage of final negotiation.

The second, in Indo-China, will be far more difficult to settle. Examined coldly, it must be at once apparent that a healthy France in Europe is of far greater importance to the Atlantic Community than a sickly, sullen France bled white by war in Asia. If, then, France desires, as the majority of the French Assembly seems now to desire, to negotiate directly with the Communists in Indo-China, or if it means that Indo-China must be split in two as most countries on the Communist border are, then it is to our interest that this be done. For what we may lose territorially in Indo-China, we will gain in Europe by creating a France better able to lead the drive to European Union she launched.

Moreover, an Indo-China settlement permits us to move closer to another strategic objective in Asia. It not only liquidates a colonial domain repulsive to the Southeast Asian communities but brings about a general peace. And only peace in that area will permit the natural strains between China and Russia—encouraged by us—to reassert themselves.

Nor, if we know what we are doing, is the German problem, though the most difficult in Europe, entirely bleak.

Our interest in Germany is first to encourage her internal democracy over a period of years, and next to incorporate her strength in a European Union which she cannot dominate by brute force.

But, while it is still necessary that German social and industrial strength be geared into a broad, expanding European Union, it is, in our present position of military strength, no longer immediately urgent that German troops be armed and put on the line at once. We have advanced swiftly toward both objectives of German rearmament and European Union in the past years. We are therefore in an enormously powerful position to wring Russian consent to the more important goal, European Union, at the expense of the latter, German arms.

Moreover, the entire context of international affairs strengthens our bargaining hand. For the Russians, it is clear, are under greater strain internally and in their fermenting satellites than we might have hoped for several years ago. Never since the war have the Russians expressed such eagerness to sit down and talk with the West as in this year of tidal decision, 1953. It was to wring this respect and attitude from the Russians that all American diplomacy in Europe was so ably conceived five years ago.

So thoroughly have the Russians lost in Central Europe that it now appears they are willing to offer settlement on a basis which is almost as great a gamble for them as for us—the neutralization of a reunited Germany as a buffer between the East and West. Such a settlement, however, achieves none of the vital purposes of American diplomacy, for it again opens the opportunity for Germans and Russians to connive and concert together as they have done so often in the past. Our diplomacy has won a position in Europe strong enough to repudiate such a settlement, while simultaneously trading little for much in the interlocking of interests between East and West.

What appears to worry the Russians, fundamentally, is the specter of an armed Germany as spearhead of an Atlantic coalition. By postponing the arming of Germans, or yielding on it altogether, we can exact an enormous price. We can exact, in the first instance, the reunification of Germany by free elections which is necessary to bring the Germans wholeheartedly into European Union. We can advance, and possibly ultimately get, the next proposal on our program which is the promise of free elections in Czechoslovakia, the only people of democratic tradition in Communist grip.

The yielding on the rearmament of Germany may to many Americans seem a huge concession. It does, indeed, require the most skillful adjustment of our diplomacy so that the Constitution of Europe and the other organs of European Union do not falter or collapse because the European Army is allowed to lapse. But a reunited Germany, bound in social and industrial union with the rest of West Europe, under the surveillance of England and America, is a far more valuable quantity than a split Germany, with twelve divisions, trying to bargain her way out of our embrace by a separate understanding with the Russians.

There are tactical and interim solutions to almost every problem on the map of Europe. But only provided we realize that this struggle is to be a long one; that peace is not to be had by one climactic settlement but rather by a myriad of small ones, made

"Don't Mind Me—Just Go Right On Talking"

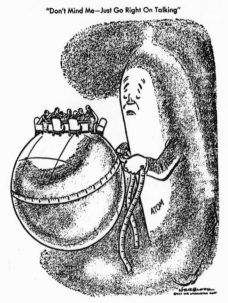

FROM *The Herblock Book* (Beacon Press, 1952)

and revised from year to year; and that no rigid military posture or investment in arms is adequate in itself.

American diplomacy comes to the world's stirring politics bearing two traditions that have confused and contradicted each other from the beginning of our country's history.

One is the tradition of the crusade, and the other the tradition of the deal.

It is the crusade we usually learn about in our history books— the brave words of "Unconditional Surrender," of "Fifty-four Forty or Fight," of "Freedom of the Seas," "Millions for Defense, Not One Cent for Tribute." The deals are less often honored. Yet it was a deal with a ruthless dictator that added the Mississippi

Valley to the original revolutionary states, even as that dictator prepared to wipe out liberty in Europe. It was a deal that stretched the northern border of our country to the Pacific along the forty-ninth parallel although the nation had screamed "Fifty-four Forty or Fight." It was a deal which settled the most unfortunate war in our history, in 1815, when three of the best poker-players of Congress sat down to undo the war the "War Hawks of Congress" had screamed into being. Only after the death of Abraham Lincoln and the seizure of power by the Congressional zealots of Reconstruction did victory, total and unchallenged, complete and uncompromising, become the major attitude of American diplomacy in the world. And only the ever-swelling power of America in a world that could not stay her made this attitude possible.

Today, America stands more perilously poised than ever between the alternatives of the crusade and the deal, at a time when our power is, for the first time in a century, limited by powerful enemies. The alternatives of crusade and deal reach deep into American domestic politics, too, for they aggravate the sputtering institutional rivalry between our Congress and our Presidential leadership. Since, in the emotional language of American politics, "crusade" is a far more appealing word than "deal," by corollary, the Congress of the United States has always been in favor of the crusade, while the President and his Executive officers have been forced, whatever their profession of faith, over and over again into the deal.

Of the crusade as a foreign policy little need be said. Its strategy is clear. It means war with Russia at the earliest opportunity. But its implications are obscure. All crusades, from the first adventures that bore that name, have begun at home, venting their wrath on victims closest at hand who may be real, fancied or completely innocent objects of suspicion. The crusade must then prepare the instruments of attack at a cost incalculably higher than the present huge burdens of defense and seek the opportunity to strike. It must strike not knowing whether it will carry allies with it on the strike or not. Under whatever name the crusade masquerades, "Roll-back," "Liberation" or "preventive attack," it cannot be had cheaply. We might eventually win, but our cities would, in the process, become rubble heaps, our children die and our entire economic life collapse.

The alternative, the deal, seems superficially to carry immortal shame—the tolerance of the evil of communism.

Yet the deal need not smell. It is only shameful if it is approached naively, or in the spirit of friendship to be pledged with the enemy. If it is sought, however, on the only terms that the adversary might consider—as an interim solution in a long-range struggle until a new relation of force-dominance gives one or the other of us permanent advantage—it can be both shrewd and advantageous. For the Russians believe, by their inflexible mythology, that we are a world doomed to rot from within, while we know we are not. For them, in their thinking, time, relaxation and stagnation are certain to erode us into impotence. Yet we, by our thinking, know that the power not only to survive but to thrive and build a better world lies in our hands. By their thinking, the other communities that lie between the Atlantic and themselves must eventually fall, by their laws of history, into the world of communism. But, if we are wise enough, we can make this dogma as false as their dogma of the classless society. Their rigid laws of history and politics see no vigor left in our philosophy of liberty—which makes them that much more vulnerable, at every contact, to penetration by the acids of our free culture and thought. Our philosophy even when engaged in crusade must brook the constant internal penetration of their ideas and their faith. Their philosophy cannot be penetrated by our ideas and faith except by prolonged contact and the education of negotiation. The deal—made of the myriad little deals—is the easiest way of exposing them to the seepage of questions and perplexing alternatives which ultimately, we hope, will erode their system of politics, at home and abroad, into impotence.

Starting off from these assumptions, each adversary believing he will outwit the other, we can make slow adjustments, wisely, carefully, successfully, provided we do so under certain conditions of thinking and practice.

The first should be the realization that at no given date will it be ever possible to arrive at any one settlement of all the issues between ourselves and communism in Russia. What separates us is so vast, so many-sided, so difficult even to phrase in common terms that never can there be, in the future, a great peace conference after which all is sweetness and light. The deals to be made are little deals, separate, individual adjustments at points of greatest mutual irritation. The last time a war of conflicting faiths rolled over Europe in the seventeenth century it took thirty years of a butchery which reduced Central Europe in places to cannibalism before men arrived at a tolerance of what they felt were each other's abominations. Only then, without ever having settled the issues on which they went to war, did the antagonists abandon their crusading and resign themselves to adjustments on a day-to-day basis, permitting each ruler domestically to impose his religion on his own people in his own way. The issues of faith between ourselves and the Russians can never be settled; only external irritations can be adjusted. But they are important.

The second condition is that a program of arms be continuously maintained throughout the long process of bargaining, a program that does not jerk from impotent slackness to intolerable economic burden imposed by emergencies. Without such a base in arms, the adversary might find victory so cheap and tempting as to make impossible any reasonable adjustment.

Yet another condition is that America accept the fact that the chief vulnerability of the Atlantic Community now lies within —socially, politically, economically. To armor this vulnerability our allies must be urged and helped to change as we have changed in this half-century. Not all these changes will be in America's image, and many will be the subject of bitterest controversy both where they occur and within our Congress. Yet our allies must change if they are to go forward. The corollary of this approach is that if the burden of arms becomes too heavy for them to bear, we must not force them to carry so much that the burdens will crush the necessary social changes we seek.

A fourth condition is that American leadership, acting within the broad purposes laid down by Congress, be free to do so without impossible daily congressional interference. For what the Executive must do is not only to think clearly and vigorously; it must adjust this thinking to match the maneuvers of the adversary, of the communities-in-between and of the allies we already hold within our community. It cannot make these adjustments if, at the same time, it must conduct an equally burdensome strategy of compromise and foreign relations with its own Congress.

There is a last requisite which is the most important. It is that

America remain, or recapture, the image of freedom and the promise of prosperity. For, whenever the edges of liberty are nibbled in America, or whenever Americans fumble at home in their progress to a better and more vigorous life, millions of people trembling between rival attractions are shaken loose into Russian hands. No maneuver of the enemy in the long period of negotiations that may now be likely could hurt America in the outside world as much as political squalor or economic chaos in the homeland.

Which is why, now, for the first time in fifteen years the story of American's security lies chiefly at home. And why this correspondent, after fifteen years of following that story abroad, is coming home.

The Illusion of Total Security

GEORGE F. KENNAN

OUR TIME, THIS MORNING, is brief: the occasion pleasant. I have racked my brain to think of something to say to the members of this graduating class at such a moment, that would not involve those bitter questions of foreign and domestic policy that have been debated at such length and at the cost of so much unpleasantness in these recent months. One alternative, of course, would be to speak of personal life. But some two decades of parenthood have finally taught me something of the reality of the gap in the generations, and of my limitations as a dispenser of wisdom and advice to younger people in personal matters. That thrusts us back on the field of public affairs, where the choice is not great.

A distinguished American recently observed that "one of the most curious and persistent myths of democratic society is that political figures have anything important or interesting to say, especially when they are out of office."

The same, goodness knows, could be said with equal aptness of retired government officials. We are, I fear, a gloomy race. Our faith in our country is there, and undiminished, but it lies deeply imbedded within us, in troubled depths. We do not fail to greet with immense inner satisfaction those things that do seem to us to be constructive and hopeful; but by and large we follow the course of public events with a sort of anxious and paternal apprehension,

In 1954 former Ambassador to the Soviet Union George F. Kennan addressed the Radcliffe College commencement. A condensation of that address appeared in the Hillman Reprint Series.

like a sailor who watches a strange crew sailing his craft; and if you prod us into a reaction—as anyone does who asks us to speak at Commencement ceremonies—what you get are our anxieties, for they are so much more explicit and so much closer to our tongues than our hopes.

So this morning, at the risk of speaking of matters that have perhaps been too much spoken of already, I am going to tell of one or two things that cause me anxiety and then of a common conclusion I derive from them that might usefully be borne in mind by people just entering the status of adult citizenship.

The first of these anxieties relates to foreign affairs. As many of you may know, I have never taken an alarmist view, and do not take one now, of the nature of our conflict with Soviet power. I have never felt, and do not feel today, that another great war could possibly serve as a useful instrument for promoting the interests of either side in this unhappy conflict. In a number of reflections about the nature of our world; in the fact that war has become so obviously self-defeating and suicidal; in the tendency of time to change all things and to erode all militant faiths—in these things I have found reason for hope and good cheer, and have spent much of my time and energy in these recent years trying to persuade others to approach what we call the East-West conflict in a similar spirit.

Yet I am bound to say that in recent weeks and months I have witnessed with increasing dismay what has seemed to me to be the progressive neglect or rejection, or disappearance for one reason or another, of the more hopeful possibilities for making progress in this problem by peaceful means. Above all, I have watched with a sinking of the heart the way in which many people in our country have, as it seems to me, been pressed relentlessly into states of mind where they can see no solution to these difficulties at all, and even no end to them, except in the horrors of atomic war. This has happened in some instances because people have been impatient of partial solutions and unable to contemplate continued uncertainty. In other cases, I suspect people have been carried by the deceiving compulsions of the weapons race into conclusions that neglect all the ulterior considerations, and particularly the imponderables. In still other cases, people may have been the victims of their own brave and rash slogans. But in any event, those longer and more subtle and less obvious paths by which we might reasonably hope to make progress in this situation are ones that a great many people in our country, for one reason or another, either reject or fail to understand; and with this rejection or failure of understanding, I fear I see a deterioration in the prospects for our continuing to muddle through these difficulties in the direction of a more hopeful future.

I do not mean to blame ourselves in any exclusive way for the present trend—we do live in a world where there have been released great forces of hatred and violence and vindictiveness, and we have been confronted with a great deal more in the way of provocation than we have given, over the course of these past two decades. And I do not mean to blame any party or administration among us. But I must emphasize that today it is precisely these subjective factors—factors relating to the state of mind of many of our own people—rather than the external circumstances, that seem to constitute the most alarming component of our situation. It is such things as the lack of flexibility in outlook, the stubborn complacency about ourselves and our society, the frequent compulsion to extremism, the persistent demand for absolute solutions, the unwillingness to accept the normal long-term hazards and inconveniences of great power—it is these things in the American character that give added gravity to a situation which would in any case be grave enough, and cause me for the first time to question seriously whether we are really going to be able, with our present outlooks and approaches, to avoid the complication of our international situation to a most dangerous degree.

The second of the anxieties I wish to mention relates to our internal situation. It is equally well-worn and equally unstartling; but it must be mentioned nevertheless.

There has been much in our domestic life of these recent months that I am sure we should all like to forget; and I hope that we shall soon be permitted to forget a great deal of it. But there are certain overriding facts that ought not to pass too quickly out of our memories. We ought not to forget that we have witnessed in these recent months the spectacle of many millions of Americans unable to put in its place and to assess with any degree of balance and equanimity the time-honored and unexceptional phenomenon of foreign political activity, intrigue, and espionage in our midst—a phenomenon which no great power has ever been spared throughout the course of human history, and from which surely no other great power is immune today. Millions of our people have been unable to accept this normal burden of international leadership at its true worth—have been uncertain as to the value to be assigned to it, uncertain as to what weight to give it in comparison with other problems of our national life. And this uncertainty has given them a peculiar vulnerability—a vulnerability to being taken advantage of, to having their fears exploited, and to being stampeded into panicky, ridiculous, and dangerous attitudes, unworthy of their own national tradition, unworthy of themselves.

Under the sign of this weakness we have seen things that cannot fail to bring deepest concern to any thinking American. We have seen our public life debauched; the faith of our people in great and distinguished fellow citizens systematically undermined; useful and deserving men hounded thanklessly out of honorable careers of public service; the most subtle sort of damage done to our intellectual life; our scholars encouraged to be cautious and unimaginative in order to escape being "controversial," a pall of anxiety and discouragement thrown over our entire scientific community, our libraries and forums of knowledge placed on the defensive before the inroads of self-appointed snoopers and censors, a portion of our youth encouraged to fear ideas on the pretext of being defended from them.

We have seen the reputations of our great private philanthropic foundations, with their immense and unique records of contribution to the national life, recklessly attacked; ingratitude flung in the face of the entire institution of private benevolence. We have seen our people taught to distrust one another, to spy, to bear tales, to behave in a manner which is in sharpest conflict with the American tradition. We have seen our friends in other countries frustrated in their efforts to help and support us, reduced to an embarrassed and troubled silence before the calumnies of our enemies upon us, for they were no longer sure whether these calumnies did not contain some measure of truth. And all of this in the name of our protection from Communist subversion, and yet every bit of it agreeable to Communist purposes as almost nothing else could be; and all of it supported by people who then have the effrontery to come before us and to say, "Show us one innocent man who has suffered."

Now it would not be hard to name such a man: but it would be possible to name something far more important; it would be possible to name a great people, no more innocent or less innocent than any of the other great peoples of this world, but nevertheless a people of an immense fundamental decency and good will and practical energy, a people in an unparalleled position to exercise a useful and hopeful influence in this tortured and threatened world community, a people to whom an historic opportunity had been given, to whom the hopes of the world had turned; it would be possible to name such a people and to show it now, at the moment of its greatest historic responsibility, disaffected and disoriented in some of the deepest sources of its national morale, injured in its capacity to react to the challenges history has laid upon it, reduced from its natural condition of confidence and buoyancy to a state of cynicism and fearfulness and disgust with the processes of its own public life—and all of this in the name of its protection from external subversion.

I do not mean to overrate these things. I have no doubt that in its superficial aspects all of this will pass—is probably already passing. The names, the idols, the scapegoats, the stereotypes, the abused words, and the perverted symbols—I have no doubt that these will all soon disappear, to join the records of the Know-Nothing movement and the chauvinistic hysteria of 1919 in the unhappier annals of our public life.

But I think we cannot comfort ourselves too much with this reflection. These things *have* happened. We *have* reacted this way, on this occasion. There must have been a reason for our doing so. Have we found that reason and learned from it? Are we going to be better armed to understand the next danger—to resist the next attempt by the unscrupulous to mobilize us against ourselves under the banner of our fears?

The causes of these phenomena have undoubtedly been many, and deep, and complex. One cannot attempt to recount them or to analyze them in the few brief moments we have at our disposal this morning. But among these possible causes there is one I should like particularly to mention as perhaps worth your attention at this time.

In the case of each of these disturbing situations I have spoken of, I wonder whether an appreciable portion of our difficulty has not been a certain philosophic error to which we twentieth-century Americans, for one reason or another, are prone. I am referring here to that peculiar form of American extremism which holds it possible that there should be such a thing as total security, and attaches overriding importance to the quest for it. A great deal of the impatience that underlies the growing despair in some quarters over the prospects for coping with world Communism by means short of large-scale violence seems to me to flow precisely from the illusion, no doubt bred by our nineteenth-century experience, that there could and should be such a thing as total military security for the United States, and that anything short of this is in the long run intolerable. And similarly, these frenzies many of us seem to have developed with respect to the problem of internal subversion—do they not reflect a belief that it should be possible for a great power to free itself completely from the entire problem of penetration and intrigue in its life by outside forces and, again, that it is intolerable that this should not be done; so intolerable in fact, that if it is *not* done, this must be attributed to some stubborn delinquency, if not treason, in the bowels of our public establishment?

If the evil of all this were limited to the fact that it does involve a certain philosophic error, that it causes people to bark up the wrong trees and occasions an inordinate and futile sort of effort, I would not bother to speak of it this morning. But the fact is that it bears dangers worse than any of these. Shakespeare described these dangers, in his inimitable way, in the following words:—

> Take but degree away, untune that string,
> And, hark! what discord follows; . . .
> Then everything includes itself in power,
> Power into will, will into appetite,
> And appetite, a universal wolf, . . .
> Must make perforce a universal prey,
> And last eat up himself.

There is something about this quest for absolute security that is self-defeating. It is an exercise which, like every form of perfectionism, undermines and destroys its own basic purpose. The French have their wonderful proverb: *Le mieux est l'ennemi du bien*—the absolute best is the enemy of the good. Nothing truer has ever been said. A foreign policy aimed at the achievement of total security is the one thing I can think of that is entirely capable of bringing this country to a point where it will have no security at all. And a ruthless, reckless insistence on attempting to stamp out everything that could conceivably constitute a reflection of improper foreign influence in our national life, regardless of the actual damage it is doing or the cost of eliminating it, in terms of other American values, is the one thing I can think of that could reduce us all to a point where the very independence we are seeking to defend would be meaningless, for we would be doing things to ourselves as vicious and tyrannical as any that might be brought to us from outside.

This sort of extremism seems to me to hold particular danger for a democracy, because it creates a curious area between what is *held* to be possible and what *is* really possible—an area within which government can always be plausibly shown to have been most dangerously delinquent in the performance of its tasks. And this area, where government is always deficient, provides the ideal field of opportunity for every sort of demagoguery and mischief-making. It constitutes a terrible breach in the dike of our national morale, through which forces of doubt and suspicion never cease to find entry. The heart of our problem, here, lies in our assessment of the relative importance of the various dangers among which we move; and until many of our people can be brought to understand that what we have to do is not to secure a total absence of danger but to balance peril against peril and to find the tolerable degree of each, we shall not wholly emerge from these confusions.

Perhaps I may be permitted, in conclusion, to observe that these reflections are not without their relevance to the problems of the human individual.

In this personal existence of ours, bounded as it is at both ends by suffering and uncertainty, and constantly attended by the possibility of illness and accident and tragedy, total security is likewise a myth. Here, too, an anxious perfectionism can operate to destroy those real underpinnings of existence, founded in faith, modesty, humor, and a sense of relativity, on which alone a tolerable human existence can be built. The first criterion of a healthy spirit is the ability to walk cheerfully and sensibly amid the congenital uncertainties of existence, to recognize as natural the inevitable precariousness of the human condition, to accept this without being disoriented by it, and to live effectively and usefully in its shadow.

In welcoming you, then—as it is my privilege this morning to do—into the fellowship and responsibility of maturity, let me express the hope that in each of your lives, as individuals and as citizens, *le bien* may be permitted to triumph over its ancient and implacable enemy *le mieux*. And if any of your friends come to you with the message that the problems of public life have become intolerable and require some immediate and total solution, I think you might do well to bear in mind the reply which a distinguished European statesman, Bismarck, once gave to certain of his more impatient and perfectionist contemporaries, who wanted him to solve all his country's problems right away, and entirely. "Let us leave just a few tasks," Bismarck suggested, "for our children to perform; they might be so bored in this world, if they had nothing to do."

We Need Not Lose Asia

NORMAN COUSINS

I DO NOT believe that anything we do or fail to do, by itself, can save Asia or win Asia. The Asian peoples themselves intend to write their own history. In fact, there seems to have been too much of a disposition in the United States to assume that we can reverse vast upheavals by some last-minute Act of Congress or muscle or both. Some of these upheavals have been in the making for a century or more.

When I say we need not lose Asia, I have one thing uppermost in mind.

We need not lose the power and influence that comes from having the good will and support of the Asian peoples. We need not lose by default to communism in the battle for the majority now looming in the world.

We may not be able to create a pat design or way of life for a billion or more people, but we can certainly put moral leadership to work in a way that does not alienate those people and that, quite possibly, can win their support.

Such moral leadership is neither complicated nor murky.

What it means, first of all, is that we have to convince the majority of the world's peoples that we are ready to join the human race. This means we have to furnish the dramatic and visible evidence that they have our respect as human beings, and that we will have no part of any attempt by any Western nation to regard them as inferiors, biologically or politically.

In 1956 the Hillman Foundation and the University of Rochester co-sponsored a conference on Eastern studies, in which Norman Cousins, editor of *Saturday Review,* was a participant. This is a summary of his remarks.

It means that we comprehend the significance of our own history. We were born in revolution. We knew what we wanted and what we didn't want when we decided to tear ourselves loose from outside rule. If we can't understand the same language, when used by other peoples today, we don't understand the language of the twentieth century.

The peoples of Asia and Africa are determined to achieve freedom from outside rule and to keep it. Nothing we do can keep that from happening. But if we do the wrong things, we can get in the way of it and be swept aside by it.

It is argued that if we identify ourselves with peoples in their struggle for freedom from outside rule we will only strengthen the communist forces inside those nations. It is argued that many of the Asian peoples are not ready for national freedom.

The answer, I believe, is that the surest way of strengthening communism in Asia and Africa is to enable the Communist to come before those peoples as their only champion. We don't retard world communism by giving it a clear field.

Next, the stability that Asia needs will have to take many forms —political stability, economic stability, international stability.

Anything that enables the peoples whose freedom is newly won to consolidate that freedom is to their advantage. Thus security against aggression becomes just as important as freedom itself.

It is in this respect that the interests of the Asian and American peoples coincide most strongly. And it is in this respect that our leadership inside the United Nations—leadership in the direction of a world safe and free from aggression—is both essential and effective.

A world free from aggression is a world ready for the great steps that can now be taken for liberating the human species from hunger, degradation, disease. For the same energies that can pulverize this planet can make of it a good earth.

Freedom from aggression means armaments control; it means enforceable world law; it means a United Nations strong enough to safeguard the cause of human life.

Such a United Nations may be a long time in coming. But the advocacy of that kind of United Nations by the United States—day-in-and-out advocacy as the central objective of our foreign policy—may in fact constitute our greatest source of security.

Past, Present, Future of the U.N.

ADLAI E. STEVENSON

In APRIL, 1945, near the end of humanity's most terrible war—but before any man had seen the atomic age—the architects of peace met in San Francisco to complete the design of a new dwelling house for the Family of Man, to be called the United Nations.

I was there during those golden weeks. And no one who was will ever forget them. It was a beginning—fresh with the hope of a new day.

Now, more than sixteen years later, what is the report? The house is crowded: 104 members; every room is full, and more are coming!

The house is battered. It resounds endlessly with family quarrels. Outside, the cold winds of war and danger, of hatred and fear from every quarter of the globe, rattle the doors and windows.

And, as is not uncommon in such cases, quite a few of the tenants are behind in the rent.

But the house is still standing. Through the cold war it has stood, and the Korean War; through the communizing of mainland China; through the revolutionary surges of colonial peoples toward national independence; through the terror of Hungary, the shock of Suez and the worse shock of the Congo; and through the perilous, infinitely frustrating tangle of the race in nuclear arms.

In 1961, while U.S. Ambassador to the United Nations, Adlai E. Stevenson wrote this article for *The New York Times Magazine*. It was subsequently used as a Hillman Reprint.

Troubles are a test of man's spirit—and none of us foresaw how the men who held the fate of the United Nations in their hands would respond in their time of testing. What could be done was done: the United Nations was built to last, and to withstand unknowable storms.

Then the record began to be written:

Soviet troops withdraw from Iran; and French and British from Syria and Lebanon; the Palestine armistice agreements; U.N. support to repel aggression in Korea.

Vexing colonial conflicts which disappeared from the U.N. agenda as new nations were born and became members: Indonesia, Libya, Morocco, Tunisia, Cyprus.

Other nations, once outside the U.N. world, restored to full standing in the community: Austria, Italy, Japan.

Territorial and minority disputes brought under some degree of restraint: Kashmir, Alto Adige and West New Guinea.

And a measure of security, at great cost and effort to the U.N., for areas under outside attack: Greece, Suez, Lebanon, Laos.

Such are some of the nations which, since 1946, have owed at least a part of their independence, or even their security against direct or indirect aggression, to the United Nations. As this is written our hopes are rising that another name may take its place on this list: the Congo. Here, in spite of errors and omissions going back many years, a new nation of immense possibilities is in the process of being rescued by the United Nations, without military involvement of any great power, from a multitude of mortal dangers: internal chaos, Balkanization, and a new imperial yoke far worse than the old. Because of the United Nations it is possible to do this without a direct military clash of the great powers. The price has been great, but so is the achievement—possibly one of the greatest and most decisive in all United Nations history. Indeed, one early measure of its greatness was Mr. Khrushchev's towering rage.

All these "political" actions, let us remember, are supported by U.N. economic and technical programs of great and growing value, and all aimed at the same major purpose: to enable the weaker and less developed nations to stand on their own feet in the modern world.

There are failures, too—or, at best, hopes deferred. A dozen

U.N. resolutions made the cause of the Hungarian Freedom Fighters world-famous, but they have not freed Hungary. A thicket of mistrust still chokes the hope for Arab-Israeli peace. A decade of U.N. protest has failed to mitigate apartheid in South Africa, or to free North Korea. Fifteen years have not been enough to dissipate the Soviet suspicions which have made the disarmament debates so sterile.

And the recent unhappy case of Goa showed that the writ of the United Nations does not always run even in the country whose heroic Gandhi taught nonviolence to the world.

It is painfully evident that pious platitudes do not keep the peace—nor does verbal respect for great principles nor does sterile debate. It is painfully evident that the rule of law and order requires the means for enforcing the law—that peaceful change and the settlement of disputes require machinery for effecting change and containing dispute.

And it is painfully evident that we have neither used as well as we might the existing procedures for peaceful settlements and the peace-keeping machinery of the United Nations, nor have we used them frequently enough; nor have we paid sufficient attention to the improvement and expansion of the machinery at hand—not just in connection with colonial questions but in connection with others as well.

But today the greatest drama of the United Nations—full of both promise and danger—lies not in one dispute or another but in the sudden, almost explosive growth of the membership.

In the United Nations of 1945, out of fifty-one members only eleven were from Africa or Asia. Today, of 104 members, fifty are from Africa or Asia. Of the twenty-two members today from sub-Sahara Africa, only two—Ethiopia and Liberia—were original members.

The authors of the Charter could hardly have anticipated the speed of this vast independence movement, or the turbulence and tragedy that would sometimes attend it. During the war President Roosevelt, whose views were decidedly anti-colonial, urged the example of the Philippines (then on the verge of independence) as "a pattern for the future of other small nations and peoples of the world."

But the Philippines had had over forty years of peaceful tutelage aimed at eventual independence—far more than any of the new nations of Africa. Nor did the Philippines have to cope with a large minority of colonists, such as has bedeviled the independence movement in so many countries since the war.

It is idle to ask whether this flood of colonial emancipation was wise or not. It is almost complete, and whatever the weaknesses and dangers it has this to commend it: it is overwhelmingly the will of the people concerned. Thus the agents of Moscow in most of Africa have lost their best grievance against the West, and the new United Nations members have entered in an atmosphere of comparative friendliness which cuts across racial lines.

When you think how eager the Soviets have been to act as grand marshal in the African freedom parade, it is no small thing that they have been denied such an opportunity in most of Africa. The British Government, and President de Gaulle's Government in France, deserve enormous credit for the statesmanship that made this possible.

Would that this were also true in the Portuguese colonies, and some other areas of Africa!

But the question persists—I hear it or read it every day: Aren't these new members irresponsible? Won't they side with the Russians and turn the United Nations against us? Hasn't the United States "lost control of the United Nations," and hadn't we better reduce our emphasis on it and rely on alliances like NATO instead?

I think the record of the General Assembly in 1961 gives us a fair test of these questions.

Irresponsible? In some situations I think the word is justified—but let him who is without sin cast the first stone!

The fever of all-out, "ultra" anti-colonialism, fed always by Soviet encouragement, produced some hot speeches and a few rash resolutions which were not entirely sound or in accord with the Charter and parliamentary due process. Such moves not only put a strain on the United Nations; they also put a strain on mutual confidence between the Afro-Asian nations and the industrial Western powers who are their natural friends and collaborators in the generation of development that lies ahead. And that, quite certainly, is why the Soviet Union always encourages such extremes.

There is no need to deny these difficulties; but neither is there any excuse for building them up into artificial monsters to frighten ourselves out of a true estimate of the United Nations. If the record of last fall's General Assembly is studied, it will be found that this allegedly feeble, irresponsible, Soviet-influenced body of 104 members did these things:

Put U Thant in office, and thereby assured that an independent and active Secretariat—so vital to the U.N.'s life—had not died with Dag Hammarskjold.

Met the issue of China head-on, and solidly defeated the attempt to replace the delegates of Taipei with the delegates of Peiping.

Provided for the financing of the Congo operation by an unprecedented $200 million bond issue.

Endorsed three major United States proposals—the U.N. Decade of Development, a new start in U.N. cooperation on outer space, and a new $100 million world food program.

Resolutely faced, once again, the issues of Communist injustice in Korea, Hungary and Tibet.

Endorsed our plea for the renewal of talks in Geneva for a *controlled* nuclear-test ban.

On this last point, however, the record should be kept straight by frankly acknowledging that there were also some rash votes on resolutions dealing with nuclear testing, which, in the opinion of the United States, ill-advisedly omitted any reference to inspection and control—and these at the very moment the Soviets were testing nuclear weapons!

The above is only a partial list, but the significance of it is that every decision listed was supported by—or even proposed by—the United States and most of them were strongly resisted by the Soviet Union. They could not have been adopted without the backing of most of the new Afro-Asian nations.

Cries that the United States has "lost control of the U.N." do not alarm me. I am reminded of the man who said: "Things are not like they used to be in the good old days—in fact, they never were." The United States never "controlled" the U.N. and never sought to. What is the use of holding debates with yourself?

I was a delegate to the first two sessions in 1946 and 1947, and I know how much persuasion, and how much careful listening, went into our job of leadership. It was a tough job then, and now in the doubled U.N. it is at least twice as tough—but qualitatively it is the same thing.

Must we, just because the going is hard, turn away from the United Nations to some supposed "alternative"? Are we now to drop the U.N. in favor of NATO, or a "concert of free nations," or a better foreign-information program to win "the war for the minds of men," or the Peace Corps and people-to-people exchanges, or the opening of Soviet society to outside influences, or religious faith, or higher ethical behavior here at home—or our military strength?

The fallacy is that these things are not alternatives at all. Every one of them has its essential place in our strategy of peace and freedom. And at the heart of that strategy is, and must remain, the United Nations.

The United Nations was built for trouble and thrives on it. It has gained its strength and authority not from the drafting of blueprints but from the hot breath of emergency: Korea, Suez, the Congo. The General Assembly has demonstrated its ability to act —with or without Soviet consent. The authority of the office of the Secretary General, steadily built up by Trygve Lie and Dag Hammarskjold and by "the felt necessities of the time," has been preserved—and is now being fully exercised by U Thant.

We hear the United Nations called weak and timid.

An organization which fully debates and judges injustice from Hungary to South Africa, despite loud cries of "intervention" from the accused powers, is not a timid organization—unless timidity consists in unwillingness to resort to war to correct what war cannot correct.

An organization which can put 20,000 troops into the field to prevent communism, or any other force, from reconquering or partitioning the Congo, is not a weak organization.

Indeed, I think those who call today's United Nations weak must have forgotten their history. The United Nations at its birth was hedged about with restrictions: there was the veto in the Security Council; the General Assembly was conceived as a body that would only debate and recommend; intervention in "internal" affairs of sovereign states was sternly forbidden; and the Secretary General was conceived as scarcely more than the chief clerk of the organization.

Circumscribed as it was, the United Nations of those early days seemed to hold out only limited promise. But now, apparently, all that is forgotten by those who dwell on the "impotence" of the U.N. of today—and who compare it unfavorably with an ideal institution of absolute powers which in fact never existed.

The failures and mistakes have been many, and there will be more. Only one way exists to avoid them—and that is for the U.N. to stand aside from all the really tough and tangled problems of the world. Then it would look good, like a well-pressed parade-ground soldier, undefeated in battle because he has never been in battle. Compared to him, Bill Mauldin's exhausted Willie and Joe make a sorry sight—but it is Willie and Joe who win the wars. And it is the weary but durable diplomats of the marathon conference who win the victories for peace.

What a lot of criticism (not to say calumny) the U.N. could have avoided by staying out of the Congo! But history would not have been kind to a U.N. which turned its back on a situation so fraught with danger to the peace of Africa and the world.

Fortunately, the U.N. has not stood aside.

For years it has been struggling in the arena of history, and by those struggles it has grown steadily in strength and authority. Every one of the main Charter restrictions has been loosened: the veto circumvented by the General Assembly; the right of free debate and recommendation used again and again despite loud cries of "intervention"; the executive capacity of the Secretary General strengthened beyond all early expectations.

I suspect that, if in 1945 there had been proposed such a world organization, endowed with all the actual authority and energy which the U.N. is showing today, the nations would never have agreed to it.

Yet today this vigorous U.N.—this Western device—has become indispensable not only to the West but to most of the nations of the world. It is our common ground. It is the center where the peoples of the Atlantic and of the Afro-Asian worlds, with so much of conflict and mutual hostility in their past relations, can build the harmony of interest and action so vital to them all.

Certainly it is hard work. Its hardness is one proof that we are dealing with real problems. And in this generation, as never before, our nation in its foreign affairs, and notably in its conduct as a leader of the United Nations, has the chance to develop qualities of maturity and endurance.

As long as there is trouble in the world there will be people selling "get-peace-quick" plans. Some consist of wishful utopianism; others suggest that we "fight fire with fire" and let the world burn up if it must. Both are the escapist fantasies of the impatient and the immature. The U.N.—the real U.N.—has no place for either one.

The real U.N. is an organization in which nations can—and, however imperfectly, do—combine their power and influence, and place it at the service of the Charter's aims: peaceful settlement of disputes; the independence and security of nations, including the small and weak; cooperation for economic and social progress and for the advancement of human rights; self-government and self-determination for dependent peoples; justice and respect for international law.

On these great premises, validated by particular U.N. actions through more than sixteen years, the great majority of members have striven across barriers of culture and race and tradition to achieve that golden mean, that mid-point between world anarchy and world conformity: a *community* of nations.

That word "community"—how little it is understood, even by us of the West among whom the idea arose! Yet this is the broad, inclusive, tolerant principle that can one day truly unite the nations, if anything can. This is the unity-in-diversity by which nations of all regions and cultures can outgrow old hatreds and old injuries and live in peace.

Community is not ideology. It is more flexible and more durable. When communism says to us: "Our ideology will bury yours," America—or any true member of the United Nations—could well make some such reply as this:

"Ideology? We have none and we don't want one, for no imposed ideology can comprehend the human spirit. But we are members of a world-wide *community*—its members diverse, tolerant and free. And one day, when your ideology has been eroded by experience, and you too have learned tolerance, the community will welcome you, too."

The United Nations is not dead. It is alive with the spirit of the age to come.

Will Communism Conquer the World?

A Balance Sheet

STUART CHASE

To most Americans, judging by letters to the newspapers and sidewalk polls, "Communism" seems to mean a kind of loathsome beast preparing to overrun and subjugate the world. The monster always lives in Moscow, though Peiping houses a related jackal. Tito's third species of "Communism," living in Yugoslavia, is seldom mentioned.

The popular picture of this ugly brute is strongly reminiscent of the pre-war image of "Fascism," which to most Americans was also a loathsome monster bent on world domination. I remember maps in the press showing Hitler's anticipated routes of conquest reaching into the Western Hemisphere like so many tentacles. Here, under the big arrow, the armored divisions would take off from Casablanca to the bulge of Brazil (dotted line), and thence up to Texas—with a fine disregard for the Amazon, the Orinoco, and the jungles of Panama. Similar arrows in the newspapers today show the possible path of "Communism" down through Southwest Asia.

To exorcise the Communist monster, both military and political weapons are advocated. They range from more guns to Laos and

Stuart Chase, long one of America's foremost social analysts, is the author of numerous books, the most recent of which is a preview of the future entitled *The Most Probable World*. This article, which first appeared in *The Progressive* in 1962, was a Sidney Hillman Reprint.

the landing of Marines in Cuba, to the witch hunts of the John Birch Society, and even include the demand for the impeachment of the Chief Justice as a Communist agent.

Erich Fromm, who is devoting his talents to a study of international affairs from the viewpoint of a psychiatrist, fears that many of us suffer from paranoid thinking. In a recent book, *May Man Prevail?*, Fromm wrote:

> Most Americans today think about Russia in a paranoid fashion; namely, they ask what is *possible* rather than what is *probable*. It is possible that Khrushchev wants to conquer us by force. It is possible that he makes peace proposals in order to make us unaware of the danger . . . If we think only of possibilities, then indeed there is no chance for realistic political action.
>
> Sane thinking means not only to think of possibilities, which in fact are always relatively easy to recognize, but to think also of probabilities. That means to examine the realistic situations, and to predict to some extent an opponent's probable action by means of an analysis of all the factors and motivations that influence his behavior.

On a probability basis there is good reason to believe that the West is confronted not with a tentacled monster, but with two dynamic nations, Russia and China. They use Marxian slogans and call themselves "Communist;" but most careful analysts agree that they are not following the course charted by Marx and Lenin. Russia in particular is off course. Her leaders, for instance, no longer envisage war with "capitalism" as inevitable, as did Marx. Soviet Premier Nikita Khrushchev has repeatedly said that Marx did not anticipate a nuclear war, and war in the nuclear age, he says, is more likely to result in mutual suicide than in victory.

There is good reason to believe on a probability basis that the threat from Moscow is not so much that of an ideological monster as that of a high-powered nationalism on the march; not so much Karl Marx as Peter the Great. Such a view removes the mysticism and translates the threat to something more realistic and familiar: the drive of empire, well-known and well-documented from Alexander the Great to Kaiser Wilhelm II.

We thus have, in semantic terms, the Marxian model of Communism, wherein the workers of the world, the "prisoners of starvation," arise, strike off their chains and overthrow the "capitalists;" and a quite different Communism, whereby two dynamic nations press for new spheres of influence, using Marxian slogans as an aid. This article is geared to the latter Communism, as more probable and so more realistic than the traditional portrait of Communism. Most of the time I shall label it "Russia-or-China" in the interest of clarity, letting the label "Communism" stand for the old Marxian ideology.

If pressed, Khrushchev might admit another unprecedented effect of the nuclear age: his enormous land armies no longer dare overrun Europe, as they might have done in 1946. This is not because of NATO, but because Russian cities behind his armies would probably be incinerated by a shower of hydrogen bombs within hours after he started to move. He can destroy the West with his own hydrogen bombs, but he cannot conquer it militarily.

Meanwhile the growth of affluence in the West has immunized most of its workers against the Marxian dialectic. There will be no uprisings of the proletariat so long as the West remains reasonably prosperous. This high probability has been inadequately appreciated. Agents of the Russian and Chinese empires can make strong appeals to the peoples of other nations whose allegiance and resources they covet. But these appeals are potent only in the so-called Hungry World. They fall on deaf ears in highly developed societies. What was true a hundred years ago when Marx wrote the *Communist Manifesto*—a savagely exploited industrial proletariat in the mines and mills of Western Europe—is no longer true.

The advent of the welfare state and the industrial evolution to a mixed economy have robbed Marxism of its attraction. Political groups dedicated to violent revolution, or even to the supremacy of manual workers via the ballot, are in retreat in the United States, Canada, Britain, Germany, Western Europe, Australia, and Japan. Manual workers in these areas care less for the class struggle than for vacation time and color television.

Russia and China, furthermore, are not attempting to foment revolutions in any of these areas. Stalin, indeed, had a fixed policy against doing so. The ring of "Communist" satellites around Russia from Poland to Bulgaria were not products of revolution, but captives of the Russian armies set up as barriers against another Hitler. Communist parties in the West have not been encouraged to revolt, but to act as agents for Russian foreign policy, including the use of espionage.

The reason is clear. "Communism" in any form is politically dead in the West, because workers are relatively so prosperous under the democratic system. On a recent trip to Russia, I returned via Vienna and London. Observing the goods in the shop windows, the clothing of the people on the streets, particularly their shoes, observing slums and housing developments, the traffic stream, parks and playgrounds, I would roughly rate Vienna fifty per cent, and London one hundred per cent higher in living standards than Moscow. New York, of course, is higher still. The manual worker's average annual wage is about $1,200 in Russia, but four times that in the United States. Russia may "catch up" in a decade or two, but it is doubtful if China ever can; there are not enough raw materials available on the planet.

However, the underdeveloped societies of the Hungry World—those in Asia, Africa, and Latin America with family incomes below $100 a year, and a literacy rate of less than fifty per cent—are wide open to the appeals of Russian and Chinese agents. According to Paul G. Hoffman, Director of the United Nations Special Fund, 1.3 billion people in the underdeveloped countries—not including the Chinese—are at economic rock bottom. Furthermore, they are aware of it, Hoffman says. "There is hardly a village anywhere that does not have its radio," he points out, "and hardly a villager who is not now convinced that a better life is possible for him and his children."

The first great appeal of Russia and China is the promise of that better life. The poor peasant hears on the village radio about the food, housing, and luxuries enjoyed by the workers of industrialized societies. When agents from Russia or China say that they will help his country industrialize and get these commodities too, he listens eagerly, even if the dialectics escape him. The agents at his door are riding the wave of the Twentieth Century technological revolution.

The second great appeal of Russian and Chinese salesmen is to local pride and patriotism. Your country, they say, will be rescued from colonialism and imperialism. It will have a flag, a national anthem, a 21-gun salute, and a seat at the United Nations. You are as good as anyone, whatever your color, or education, or previous condition of servitude. The urge to be free and independent is massive throughout the Hungry World, as the growing membership in the United Nations bears witness.

The third great appeal is psychological; it is the appeal to hatred. The restless villager is urged to hate the rich, the landlords, the usurers, the war lords, and the potentates, who have taken half or more of his crop since time out of mind. The rich are easy to hate. The shell of culture, which has held in check these timeless resentments and hatreds, is now cracking open. It would be cracking even if there were no agents from Russia or China. The poor peasant, prompted by the village radio, has had enough.

The agents of Russia and China can go far by manipulating these powerful appeals for a better life, a proud state, and hatred of overlords, domestic and foreign. Agents in Cuba are using all three very effectively at the present moment. Cuba will also provide, I suspect, an illuminating case history of the weaknesses of this approach, for reasons which I shall now try to make clear.

Attempts by Russia-or-China to dominate the peoples of the Hungry World collide with four stubborn economic barriers, one stubborn political barrier, and, perhaps most serious of all, the high improbability that two dynamic national empires, far apart in tradition and culture, can amicably cooperate to conquer the world. The question is bound to come, and some of us think it has already come in Moscow and Peiping: "Who's in charge around here?"

First, the economic barriers:

ONE—Neither the Russians nor the Chinese have reckoned adequately with the population explosion. I attended a conference with Russian intellectual leaders in the Crimea last year where the idea that population would soon outrun food supply on the Malthusian formula was branded by the Russians as "completely incorrect." All available statistical evidence, however, points to a gap which is fast widening. Only in Japan has the birth rate been held in check.

This raises a most interesting question. Assuming that Russia and China make considerable headway with their appeals as set forth above, how long can they supply the bread lines of their dependents—especially as both are having considerable trouble in their own bread departments? China is said to be in the midst of a major famine, and is buying wheat from Canada, while Khrushchev is obliged to rush frequently to the "virgin lands" in Siberia to find out what has gone wrong. Food surplus on the U.S. model are unthinkable for many years in China and Russia. Meanwhile, their proposed wards and allies in the Hungry World will grow hungrier year by year, unless the birth rate is reduced to less than thirty per thousand—a project to which neither empire has given adequate thought. Eugene R. Black of the International Bank of Development affirms that even large sacrifices by highly developed societies for greatly increased foreign aid will be unavailing "in the face of existing rates of population growth."

Russia and China are bound to collide with this barrier in the near future. It is axiomatic, I think, that their wards cannot be held firmly in line unless they are fed. Starving dependents do not make good sales talk.

TWO—When Russia-or-China have helped to engineer a local revolution they must then help organize a socialist economy, in which the government owns and operates the principal means of production. This is axiomatic too, but promises to be at best an uncertain business in the world of today. Perhaps the nation can coast along for a while by dividing up the lands and other assets of the expropriated rich, as Cuba is trying to do. But the only permanent solution—assuming the birth rate is held low enough—lies in scientific agriculture and industrialization, including ample supplies of inanimate energy. To provide the technical specialists, the supplies, and equipment for this socialist society is likely to make quite a hole in the resources of Russia and China—a good deal more, one suspects, than any raw materials which might be received as an offset. This service must go on for years, with every new socialist state increasing the drain. I would very much like to see the account in Moscow's ledger marked "Cuba, 1961."

It has taken Russia forty years to build her own industrial plant to a point where it is in competition with the West, while China has barely begun. Consider the cost in manpower and materials of equipping Africa, Asia, and Latin America with a modern industrial and agricultural establishment. Consider the colossal training programs. Most citizens of the Hungry World now possess neither mechanical nor administrative skills. Most of them—as in the Congo—cannot read a primer, let alone a blueprint.

THREE—The promises of socialism often backfire. Its promoters and propagandists always promise in advance, and most explicitly, that wages will be higher, housing better, working hours shorter, together with a complex program of medical care, education, and social security. "Relax, comrades, Utopia will be won!"

When I was investigating "Operation Bootstrap" in Puerto Rico, I found there had been a similar reaction at the beginning of the experiment in the late 1940s. Workers in the five new state factories believed that socialism had arrived, and took it easy. They were now the favored class, according to theory, and they expected favored treatment—high wages, short hours, fringe benefits of all kinds. But the factories soon lost so much money that they had to be sold to private owners, and the goal of socialism shifted to the mixed economy prevalent throughout the West, wherein the state undertakes only those essential functions which private enterprise will not, or cannot perform.

Russia and China, on the calculus of probability, will not be happy with the profit and loss accounts of most local enterprises financed by them in Africa, Asia, and Latin America—at least not under the kind of welfare system explicitly promised, and the one to which the peoples of the Hungry World aspire. So Russia-or-China will have to meet the operating deficits or lose an ally.

FOUR—The alternative to the above program of loans and advances for capital formation is the program Russia herself has followed: take the needed capital out of the annual production of the workers. By enforcing rigorous discipline, with long hours, low wages, neglected housing, no luxuries, and dreadful penalties for strikes and stoppages, enough has been produced to build an impressive industrial establishment, while keeping consumers alive, if not contented. I visited Russia in the late 1920's and observed the formula beginning to operate after the collapse of "war Communism."

If is safe to say that no open society would tolerate such a method of capital formation today—though some did in the Nineteenth Century. It is extremely doubtful if any society in the Hungry World will tolerate it—especially after hearing all the Utopian promises. If Russia and China use this method of forced savings in an emerging nation, they will have to abandon all Utopian promises, and reduce the country to virtual slavery. This will not make particularly good propaganda for a Communist program of world conquest. Also there may be a serious raw materials problem.

There are only two ways to industrialize—borrow or wangle capital from abroad, or save it out of current production at home. Russia used the latter; China is trying to do the same, aided, however, by some loans from Russia.

FIVE—The fifth barrier to the conquest of the world by Russia-or-China is more political than economic. Castro in Cuba will furnish an interesting test. It should be clearly apparent that there can be no "democracy" in our sense of the term in any country of the Hungry World. Political democracy, with free speech, free press, free investment and consumer choices, is unworkable without a high degree of literacy and a substantial middle class—assets which no nation in the Hungry World now possess. A military junta (as in South Korea) or a single strong man (as in Egypt) will break through any paper constitution, however eloquent, and take over.

Will the local power faction be amenable to serving as the tool of Russia or China? Will it meekly endure having its decrees written or over-ruled by Moscow or Peiping? The probabilities are strongly against it. Egypt's Nasser gives an illuminating answer. The West thought he had sold out to Russia at one time; Russia thought he was a pawn of the West at another time. Actually, as we now know, Nasser has skillfully played off one side against the other, receiving large handouts from both. He never had the slightest intention of being anybody's pawn. Dictators and military juntas are tough, or they would not be there, and they tend to be fiercely patriotic. Once they surrender power to Moscow or Peiping, the second great appeal collapses, the promise of a proud and independent state. Will a local strong man, just free of the colonialism, say, of Portugal, be willing to enter the colonial empire of China? The question answers itself.

SIX—The last and greatest barrier to world conquest is the inevitable competition for leadership between two dynamic empires. Russia and China are even now competing for that strategic land that lies between them, Outer Mongolia. This is only the beginning. Presently they will become involved in fierce altercations over which empire is to assume the obligations of their Hungry World dependents. They are already far apart ideologically, but this cleavage is a tiny crack compared to what may separate them when it comes to the division of large areas of the world.

On the assumption of two dynamic nationalisms, rather than

one ideological monster, "Communism" is less threatening. It becomes subject to realistic analysis in space and time rather than an exercise in demonology. A modern Machiavelli, studying the balance sheet, might go so far as to say, let Russia and China assume the liabilities of the Hungry World unimpeded. There is no better way to bankrupt them. But we are not Machiavelli, and we cannot be so cynical. We must help the people of the Hungry World because they need help, not just use them as pawns in the cold war. All formulas for help, however, should take account of the difficulties listed in the balance sheet, especially the burgeoning populations.

In summary, Russia and China now have no reliable class base with which to subvert and convert the gainfully employed in the affluent societies of the West. It is safe to say that they never will have such a base so long as the West is reasonably prosperous. They can make, and are making, three powerful appeals to the Hungry World: higher living standards for poor peasants, national independence, and encouragement of the class hatreds already endemic. To make these appeals good, however, Russia-or-China must be prepared to feed, organize, and equip the Hungry World at a cost in capital formation far beyond available resources, with population outrunning subsistence in Asia, Africa, and Latin America.

Furthermore, Russia and China are almost certain to have serious difficulty in converting local strong men into subservient stooges. Finally, the Communist nations are extremely liable to get into lethal disagreements about the responsibility of each in underwriting the operational deficits of three continents.

In short, on the basis of any realistic analysis, the case for "Communism" conquering the world is highly improbable.

Labor Policies and the Development of International Trade

DAVID A. MORSE

IT IS BECOMING increasingly clear that it is urgently necessary, for both economic and political reasons, not only to expand the volume of world trade, but also to enable the developing countries to benefit more fully from readier access to world markets. The consolidation of the votes of what were seventy-five and have since become seventy-seven developing countries at the 1964 United Nations Conference on Trade and Development has brought to the world's attention in a more concrete and dramatic form than ever before the aspirations of the two thirds of the world's population that live below standards we wish for ourselves. There are some very compelling reasons why the rich nations of the world should sympathetically consider the demands of the poor, and why they should go at least some way toward meeting their demands.

Not the least of these reasons is that, unless new trading arrangements can be devised to the benefit of the developing countries, their efforts at economic development will be checked, hampered, or even nullified by a shortage of foreign exchange. Statistics indicate that the underdeveloped countries of the world are

In 1966 David A. Morse, Director General of the International Labour Organization, was the Hillman lecturer at the University of Pittsburgh. These are excerpts from his lecture.

falling increasingly further behind the developed countries in terms of per capita income and economic growth. Among the factors that are contributing to the widening of this gap is the severe restraint which is being placed on the economic growth of the developing countries by the slow growth of their exports and the instability of world prices for raw materials, which today still constitutes the bulk of these exports. The resulting balance of payments difficulties have seriously curtailed their capacity to import the capital goods and equipment which are essential for their industrial development and consequently for developing new export potential.

In the face of these conditions the developing countries have no alternative but to look to increasing their trade in foreign markets. Indeed, this is essential if their newly acquired political independence is to be anything more than a façade concealing their real dependence on the donations of the richer nations of the world.

The real initiative now lies with the developed countries. It would be conceivably possible for them to isolate themselves in a small prosperous trading club, continuing to distribute charitable aid to the developing countries, but otherwise making no effort to improve these countries' trading position. To continue on this path would not only be fatal for the economic development of the third world; it would also, in the long run, exacerbate the tensions and frustrations which have already begun to manifest themselves among the poverty-stricken populations of the developing countries. If these tensions and frustrations cannot be relieved by concrete achievements in the field of economic and social development they are likely to result in outbreaks of violence and social upheaval leading to such widespread chaos that all nations, rich and poor, would be affected. I am firmly convinced that the economic and social backwardness of the developing countries constitutes by far the most dangerous threat to world peace, and that, in this sense at least, an expansion of world trade could prove to be a powerful weapon in favor of peace.

The ease with which an accelerated transition to new patterns of world trade can be made depends to a very large extent on whether developed and developing countries alike are able to devise labor and social policies to deal with the problems posed by radical change. For it is not enough merely to state that new patterns of trade are desirable; we must also seek reasonable ways of assisting this transition.

The problem facing the developing countries is essentially one of building up viable export industries. Before the developing countries can improve their trading position they need to produce, and at competitive prices, goods that are in demand on the world market. And they can only improve their competitive position by achieving an increase in productivity and a greater diversity of output—in a word through industrialization.

The success of the industrialization efforts of the developing countries, and consequently the improvement of their trading position, depends on their ability to develop social and labor policies which are consistent with, and which back up, such economic measures as they may take to promote industrialization. There have been examples of countries whose social policies have been too ambitious, too complex or too costly for their economies to support. At the same time, other countries have ignored the need for constructive policies of social promotion and adjustment, with disastrous consequences for their industrialization and economic development programs. But it is only recently that governments—and this applies to governments of advanced as well as developing countries—have begun to realize that a well-conceived social policy is not merely a luxury, not merely a burden on the economy; it can be, and should be seen as an investment in human capital, the returns of which are quite as valuable for the economy as investment in physical capital.

To be more explicit, I would say that there are, generally speaking, in the developing countries four main obstacles of a social nature to technological change and industrialization. One is the *ignorance* of the broad masses of the population, which makes them incapable of acquiring the new skills for work in industry or of applying new techniques in agriculture. The second is the lack of *social mobility,* which effectively prevents the emergence of entrepreneurs and other dynamic leaders of an industrial society. The third is the *failure to invest resources,* often concentrated in the hands of certain limited and privileged sections of the population, in the most productive fashion. And the fourth is the *inadequacy of institutions and procedures* for enabling all sections of the population to participate in the work of production and modernization.

The aim of a social policy in such countries should be to remove these very powerful brakes on economic and social development. It should aim at developing educational and training programs which will produce a labor force that is adequately skilled for the occupations which are most needed for the development of the country's industries, and, in particular, its export industries. It should aim to develop government services in the industrial and rural sectors, as well as institutions such as co-operatives, trade unions, peasants' associations, community development programs and so on which can gradually modify the traditional social structures and make the population as a whole more receptive to social and technological change. Finally, it should aim to devise wage and Social Security policies, regulations governing hours of work, and other labor policies, which, without burdening the economy with excessive labor costs, can contribute to a more rational distribution of income; which can provide adequate incentives for social mobility; and which can build up a stable, contented and productive labor force. In this process, cooperation between workers, employers and governmental authorities is crucial, as it is in already industrialized countries notwithstanding variations in institutional or political structure. One cannot expect labor relations in the developing countries to be exact reflections of procedures in the United States or Western Europe. But the collaboration of all concerned with industrialization is no less important to the extensive effort of developing export industries.

There is, as I see it, no immediate danger of world markets being swamped by a wide range of manufactured products from developing countries. The range of products which the developing countries will be able to export in any quantity and at competitive prices will for many years to come remain very narrow. Nevertheless, as their export industries develop, so will their demand for capital equipment and the products of more capital-intensive and "sophisticated" industries in which the developed countries have the advantage. Therefore, competition from low-wage countries does not pose a general threat to over-all employment or living standards in the high-wage countries. The problem is really one of the possible "disruptive effects" of competition in particular markets. In essence, sharp increases in imports, over a brief period of time and in a narrow range of commodities, may be very harmful to particular producers, both employers and workers, and may thus have serious economic and social repercussions in the importing countries. It is with these repercussions of structural change that those formulating policy in the industrialized countries should be concerned, rather than in perpetuating a protectionist position.

Whether the problem arises as a result of automation or of new trade patterns, the cardinal principle of labor policies to meet the problem must be that structural change should not take place at the expense of individuals who may lose their jobs or their businesses. The cost of any necessary adjustments to alleviate hardships and to maintain the buoyancy of the economy should be assumed by the community as a whole, and governments must be prepared to formulate and implement appropriate measures in order to help people to train for, to find, and, if necessary, to move to, new jobs.

So far I have focused my remarks on the types of labor and social policies which need to be taken at the national level to facilitate an expansion of international trade. I would like now to examine the need for, and the possible scope of, international action in the social field, which can contribute to this end. It is my view that, while governments have in the last twenty years been singularly resourceful in setting up machinery at the international level to negotiate new trading arrangements, the social component of international trade has all too often been left out of account in their negotiations. And while it is true that the development of social policy is, and must remain, the prerogative of the governments of sovereign states, there is nevertheless a need for coordinated action in the social field if trade agreements are to yield the results that are expected of them. Such coordinated action might conceivably take the form of a fund in which all nations would participate, based on a levy on production or national product, administered by an international organization and designed to mitigate hardship by facilitating the social adjustments resulting from trade expansion.

In short, I do not think that the expansion of international trade can be ensured merely by international tariff agreements or international agreements on the prices of raw materials. That is why I think international machinery for action in the social field needs to be used to the full, and to be brought into close collaboration with such bodies as GATT and UNCTAD and to complement such progressive instruments as the 1962 Long-Term Arrangement Regarding Trade in Cotton Textiles. This is why the International Labor Organization has an important supporting role to play in the development of international trade. It has for many years been attempting to develop a constructive approach to social policy in all countries, developed and developing. Moreover, it provides the only forum where the voices of workers and employers, the parties most directly affected by changes in world trade, as well as those of governments, can be heard at the international level.

International labor standards, that is, internationally agreed rules of good labor policy, represent one form of international action in the social field which has a bearing on international trade. Indeed many of the ILO's existing conventions on such questions as minimum wages, Social Security and general working conditions were originally conceived not only in order to set minimum standards of social protection and welfare but also to discourage "social dumping" in the form of exports produced by sweated labor. However, experience has shown that in effect the main value of such standards has been their influence on the distribution of the fruits of production, and thus their contribution to social harmony and stability, their influence on international trade has been, generally speaking, far less significant.

International action such as I have suggested can only point out possible solutions to certain problems; it can only propose a concerted international approach to these problems. But national authorities, in cooperation with national trade unions and national businessmen, alone are competent to devise the detailed policies and measures which will make new directions in trade possible.

How Not to Be a World Power

HENRY STEELE COMMAGER

THE WORD POWER is awkward and dangerous, for it is used in two ways which are fatally easy to confuse. It is clear that the United States has immense power anywhere on the globe it decides to use it. But it is by no means clear that the United States is, therefore, a world Power—with a capital P—nor does it follow that we should wish to be such a Power. If a nation has the strength, and does not care overmuch about consequences, it is easy enough to exercise power, but to be a Power is a very different thing, and it is a very difficult thing.

I do not think the United States is prepared to be a Power everywhere—in the Western Hemisphere, in Europe, in Asia—nor do I think we should wish to exercise power everywhere. In the long course of history, there have been many nations that regarded themselves, always with some justification, as world Powers; but there has never been a nation that could, in fact, exercise power everywhere on the globe, not one whose word—to use Secretary of State Richard Olney's phrase—was fiat everywhere.

What impresses me most about material power—I am not talking here about intellectual and moral power—is the limitation on the effective use which those who possess power can make of it. All of us, for example, are familiar with the limits of power on

Professor of history and American studies at Amherst College, Henry Steele Commager is the author of numerous books. In 1967 he testified at the Senate Foreign Relations Committee hearings on the war in Vietnam. An adaptation of his testimony appeared in the Hillman Reprint Series.

homely levels. A marriage in which husband and wife ascertain and use all their lawful powers is headed for the rocks. Parents have great legal and material power over their children, at least until they are 21, but any parent who imposes his will on older children by the overt exercise of power is shortsighted indeed. Boards of regents and trustees may have extensive powers over presidents and faculties of universities, but the quickest way for them to wreck a university is to indulge immoderately in that power. To consider the matter on a somewhat higher level, even the vast power of the United States is not able to enforce decisions of the Supreme Court everywhere in the nation.

What is true on the domestic scene is even more true on the turbulent and inscrutable global scene. Except perhaps in time of war—and even then sensible statesmen impose limits on themselves—nations find almost insuperable difficulties in the application of power. We have for years been alarmed at the power of Soviet Russia, but for all her immense power she cannot impose her will on Yugoslavia. She cannot even impose her will on tiny Albania, which persistently snubs and defies her. We ourselves have almost limitless power, but we cannot impose our will on Cuba. And when we used our power in the Dominican Republic we paid a high price for our self-indulgence.

Of all the limitations on power in foreign relations, the most effective appear to be those rooted in nationalism. All the might of Britain was insufficient to impose British will on Ireland in the 18th and 19th centuries. All the might of Austria could not subdue the states of northern Italy in the 19th century. In our own day, France discovered that she could not have her way with any of her provinces in North Africa, and withdrew from them—without loss of face, I may add. We ourselves have recently found it advisable to come to terms with little Panama.

Our whole history, and our political philosophy, is a monument to the belief that power is limited, and that power *should* be limited. That is, in a sense, what the American Revolution itself was about—a repudiation of the British claim, set forth in the Declaratory Act—that Parliament had the right "to bind colonies and people of America *in all cases whatsoever.*" The American position was, quite simply, that no government had all power. That is part of the meaning of our written constitutions, documents which enumerate with the greatest care the powers which governments may exercise. That is at the heart of our elaborate system of checks and balances—the determination to limit the authority and the power of government. That is what the Bill of Rights, state and Federal, are about—limitations on government. That is what judicial review is about—judicial limitations on the power of the other branches of government.

As Americans have required, and provided, restraints on the domestic scene, so they are pledged to restraint in the international arena. Almost all our traditions emphasize limitations on power. The first major principle of American foreign policy was set forth by none other than George Washington in the Neutrality Proclamation, which announced that we were not required to take sides in European wars nor to enter conflicts not of our own choosing. The second and more fundamental principle was the Monroe Doctrine, which was likewise a policy of restraint: Europe was to stay out of the affairs of these Western continents and we would, in turn, stay out of the "internal affairs" of Europe. Our third major foreign policy, the Open Door, was also designed as a restraint, primarily on European powers looking hungrily at China, but by implication at ourselves as well.

In the great watershed of the eighteen-nineties we found ourselves, somewhat to our own surprise, a world power. We waged a war with Spain that nobody much wanted and, in a fit of absent-mindedness, acquired Cuba, Puerto Rico and the Philippines; we annexed Hawaii. We fought a three-year war against the Filipinos which everyone has pretty well forgotten. But at the same time we repudiated imperialism. We were not ready to govern Cuba and very sensibly gave the island back to the Cubans. We did a good job in the Philippines but were eager to get out, and did so. We incorporated Hawaii into the Union and Puerto Rico into the political system, and we go before the world with clean hands, as it were. We do not have "colonies." The fact is that we are not very good at the "dominion over palm and pine" sort of thing, and avoid it almost by instinct. And a very good instinct it is.

After 1914 we were inextricably involved in the affairs of Europe—and beyond. But it was President Wilson who called for "peace without victory"—something to remember now. Though we had helped win World War I we did not use victory as a basis for acquiring power either in the Old World or in Asia; indeed, we withdrew far too hastily from our obligations and allowed the League of Nations to sicken and decay. Although we used something like total power in World War II, once victory had been achieved we contented ourselves with trying to put the broken fragments of the war-torn world together again. We used aid, we used influence, we used military power; but we did not use the ultimate power of nuclear weapons, nor did we attempt to order the affairs of Asia. It has remained for the statesmen of this decade to insist that we are an Asian power, and have the same kind of responsibility for Asia that we have for Western Europe.

We do not, however, have the material, intellectual or moral resources to be at once an American power, a European power and an Asian power. Justice Holmes used to say that the first lesson a judge had to learn was that he was not God. It is a lesson every man has to learn and a lesson every nation has to learn. For, as the great historian Herbert Butterfield has said, "The hardest strokes of Heaven fall in history upon those who imagine that they can control things in a sovereign manner, as though they were kings of the earth, playing providence not only for themselves but for the far future, reaching out into the future with the wrong kind of far-sightedness."

It is not our duty to keep peace throughout the globe, to put down aggression wherever it starts up, to stop the advance of Communism or other isms which we may not approve of. It is primarily the responsibility of the United Nations to keep the peace, to settle disputes, to discourage aggression, and if that organization is not strong enough to do the job we should bend our major energies to giving her the necessary authority and the tools.

We are still committed to vast but as yet unrealized reforms in Latin America; we are committing ourselves to incomparably larger responsibilities in Asia. We should not be astonished if the rest of the world wonders at our ambition and our temerity, or if it asks why, if we have the power and the resources to carry through these projects, we do not use them to put our own house in order.

Perhaps one-fifth of our population lives in poverty; we do not have the resources to wipe out that poverty. Our cities are decaying; we do not have the resources to restore them. Our educational enterprise is desperately inadequate; we do not have the resources to bring it up to the standards which we ourselves set. Our rivers and streams are polluted and the very air we breathe is poisonous, but we lack the resources to cleanse them. Racial discrimination and injustice flourish in every section of the nation, but we lack the resources to eradicate them from our society or our economy. Crime flaunts itself in the streets of our cities, but we lack the resources to control it. Would it not be wise—many are asking at home and abroad—if we used our immense power and resources to wipe out poverty and injustice and waste at home before launching ourselves upon crusades to wipe out these things in distant continents?

Our problem is not primarily one of material resources or material power. It is possible that if we were to use for peaceful purposes all of the wealth we now use for war, we would indeed have the resources to lift standards of living in Latin America, Asia and Africa as well as at home. What we lack, what every nation lacks, is the political, the intellectual and the moral resources for such global enterprises.

One explanation of our obsession with Communism and, more particularly now, with "Communist aggression" in Asia is to be found in a deep and persistent trait of the American mind: the belief in Old World corruption and New World innocence. The men who won the independence of America from the mother country were convinced that the Old World was abandoned to tyranny, misery, ignorance, injustice and vice, and that the New World was innocent of these sins.

They were not altogether wrong. Thus, in his first inaugural address, Jefferson—for whom this principle was almost an obsession—proclaimed that the United States was "kindly separated by Nature and a wide ocean from the exterminating havoc of one-quarter of the globe" and "too high-minded to endure the degradations of the others." This theme persisted into the 20th century and was one of the many strands in the fabric of isolationism.

The notion of an international Communist conspiracy which a good many Americans still cling to fits neatly into this shibboleth of Old World wickedness and New World virtue. And so, too, does our habit of throwing a mantle of morality over our own wars. We tend, perhaps more than other nations, to transform our wars into crusades. The Mexican War was part of our "manifest destiny."

The Spanish-American War was a crusade to free Cuba from Spanish tyranny. World War I was a crusade to make the world safe for democracy. World War II did indeed have moral purposes, more clearly than almost any other war of modern times.

Our current involvement in Vietnam is cast, increasingly, in a moral mold. It is, quite simply, a war to halt "Communist aggression." By a kind of circular argument, this provides and embraces the "vital interest" which we have in that area, for on closer examination our "vital interest" is precisely the interest in halting Communism.

Closely associated with the notion of New World virtue is the somewhat more activist notion of New World mission. This, too, is a familiar theme: providence, or history, has imposed a special responsibility on the American people to spread the blessings of liberty, democracy and equality to other peoples of the earth. Sometimes, indeed, this mission even included religion. The decisive argument with President McKinley when it came to the annexation of the Philippines was that "there was nothing left for us to do but to . . . educate the Filipinos and uplift and Christianize them." In fact, most of them had been Christians for centuries.

When other nations expanded, they did so on practical and selfish grounds, but when we expanded, our conduct was not only practical but highly moral. The notion of mission has colored our conception of the meaning of the Monroe Doctrine. It has conditioned our relations with Europe and, more recently, with Asia.

Nations that are self-righteous and powerful are almost irresistibly prone to creating, or accepting, a double standard of conduct. Britain was guilty of such conduct during much of the 19th century and it is not surprising that the United States indulges in it today. We think that we are better than other nations and doubtless, in many respects, we have been and are. We have not fought wars for the subjugation of alien peoples, except the Indians. We have not exploited colonies for our benefit. We have been magnanimous toward our foes, except the Mexicans, and generous to most other peoples. We have opened our doors to immigrants. We have never permitted religious tyranny or class warfare. We have, for the most part, kept the military subordinate to civilian authority. Yet even in domestic affairs we have not been beyond criticism; when we speak, as we often do, of Communist slavery we might remember that we retained legal slavery in the United States long after other civilized nations had abandoned it.

It is in the realm of foreign relations, where we instinctively take for granted (as do other nations) the justice of our policies, that we exhibit most markedly the traces of a double standard. The most conspicuous example is the attitude toward expansionism, aggression and imperialism, and here we share a certain parochialism with the whole of Western Europe.

The free nations of the West are greatly and justly disturbed by what appear to be aggressive tendencies on the part of the two great Communist powers, and "Communist aggression" has almost become (like "damn Yankee" of earlier days) a single word. We forget, most of us, that since the Crusades, and certainly since the age of discovery, aggression has been Western and European. It was Europe that expanded and conquered and laid waste, created empires and planted colonies and ruled from afar. Christian Europe divided up Africa and established its rule over much of Asia. It discovered America, wiped out the native civilizations here, planted colonies and ruled them as long as it was able. It was the West—not Communist countries—that invented imperialism and colonialism.

Most of us have been greatly alarmed by the prospect of Soviet expansion and are now no less alarmed by the prospect of Chinese aggression and expansion, and some protagonists of our war in Vietnam defend it chiefly on the ground that it is designed to put a halt to "Chinese aggression." We should remember that in the eyes of the 19th-century world, it was the United States that was pre-eminently an expansionist and aggressive nation. In the first half of the century, this new nation—with an ideology as pernicious in the eyes of legitimist governments as Communism is in our eyes—expanded from the Mississippi to the Pacific. We bought Louisiana, forced Spain out of West Florida and maneuvered her out of East Florida. We annexed Texas and fought a war with Mexico which ended by stripping her of half of her territory—the Southwest and California. We ousted the British from the Pacific Northwest. Thus, in half a century, we trebled our territory at the expense of France, Spain, Mexico and Britain. In the same period, our Presidents announced the Monroe Doctrine and the Polk doctrine, proclaiming, in effect, American hegemony in the Western

Hemisphere. If China today should put on a show of this kind, we might truly be alarmed.

One item in this catalogue of expansion has special relevance to our current concern. I refer to the settlement of boundary disputes. A good many of us have been outraged by Chinese belligerence over her border with India. It is a complex matter about which the experts disagree, but what is most impressive about the dispute is that it has not led to a general war.

In 1846, when the United States had a border dispute with Mexico, we did not settle it amicably or after a few border skirmishes. We made it a *casus belli,* invading Mexico from all sides and taking half her territory. Whatever the rights and wrongs of the Chinese dispute with India—and it is interesting that Indira Gandhi refused to brand China as an "aggressor" and that India voted for China's admission to the United Nations—the conclusion that China is irremediably aggressive because she invaded disputed territory comes with ill grace from Americans.

Other examples of our double standard come readily to mind. We maintain powerful military installations in a great arc around China—from Japan, Okinawa, the Philippines, Taiwan, Guam, to Vietnam and Thailand. But if—this requires some stretch of the imagination—China should set up powerful military installations in British Columbia, Mexico, Cuba, Bermuda, and Newfoundland, we might think poorly of it.

We claim, in all sincerity, a vital interest in Vietnam though we did not tolerate a Soviet claim to a vital interest in Cuba. Nor, for that matter, do we accept the claim of China to a vital interest in South Vietnam, which is rather closer to Peking than Saigon is to Washington. We have long asserted a sphere of influence in the Caribbean, but we are not prepared to concede to China a comparable sphere of influence in Southeast Asia. We consider ourselves justified in intervening in the domestic affairs of Guatemala and the Dominican Republic, but we would be surprised if Cuba intervened in Florida to put down guerrilla organizations, or Mexico plunged into the affairs of Texas.

We look with alarm on the spread of nuclear weapons, as indeed we might, and President Johnson asserted that it was "a dark day" when China detonated a nuclear bomb. But we appear to forget that so far we are the only nation that has used the atomic bomb in anger, though it must not be supposed that the Japanese have forgotten.

In short, we need to cultivate patience, tolerance, the long view and sympathy with the new nations of the globe even if their emergence on the crowded stage of history is turbulent and dangerous. We would do well to recover something of Jefferson's perspective on the French Revolution, which horrified most Western peoples just as Communism does today. It was, he said, "the agonizing spasms of infuriated man, seeking through blood and slaughter his long-lost liberties." To be sure, "long-lost liberties" is not the phrase we instinctively apply to either the Russians or the Chinese, for they did not, alas, enjoy liberty in their historical past. But I think it is beyond dispute that they sought and are seeking to throw off what they assume to be tyranny and exploitation—in the case of the Soviets, a homegrown brand, in the case of China, a foreign variety—and achieve independence and progress, in their way.

Underlying much of the current crisis is our failure, as a people and a Government, to appreciate what is probably the greatest revolution since the discovery of America and the transfer of the center of historical gravity from the Mediterranean to the Atlantic. I refer to the revolt of Asia and Africa against the West and the emergence into modernity of perhaps two-thirds of the peoples of the globe. We are witnessing the upheaval of peoples and civilizations, the throwing off of centuries of misrule and exploitation, the convulsive efforts to catch up in a single generation with progress the West has made with bloodshed and war and revolution over a period of four or five centuries.

Materially, to be sure, we have given aid to this enterprise, particularly to those peoples we sought to win to our side in the struggle against Communism. In other and important ways, however, we have allowed ourselves to be maneuvered into the position of opposing revolution and what some of these peoples think of as progress. We have allowed ourselves to drift into the position that Britain occupied in much of the 19th century and France in part of the 20th—that of the champion of the status quo, the defender of the Western way of life, of Western government and ideology. It is difficult to doubt that most of the world looks upon us today as the leading opponent of revolutionary change.

What is sobering, and even paradoxical, is that the new nations of the globe are trying to carry through their revolution with the tools which we have fashioned. The political instrument is nationalism, the social instrument is equality, the economic instrument is science and technology. All of them are Western inventions. So we must inescapably bear much of the responsibility for what is going on in the underdeveloped nations of the world, even in nations like China.

The United States was the first nation to be founded squarely on the right of revolution—that is, the right to "alter or abolish government and institute new government." As James Madison wrote:

If there be a principle that ought not to be questioned within the United States, it is that every nation has a right to abolish an old government and establish a new one. This principle is not only recorded in every public archive, written in every American heart, and sealed with the blood of a host of American martyrs, but it is the only lawful tenure by which the United States hold their existence as a nation.

Certainly the Declaration of Independence is far more subversive than the Communist Manifesto and those ardent conservatives who fear revolution everywhere might logically start by banning the Declaration from schools and textbooks. Its principles were, and are, explosive: all men are equal; all men have a right to life, liberty and happiness; the purpose of government is to secure these rights; men make government, can unmake it and make it over again.

Nor did our subversive activities come to an end with the winning of independence. We adopted other institutions and practices that were deeply subversive of existing governments and rulers: no kings, no aristocracy, no established church, no military establishment, no colonies to exploit. And the positive features of the new society were just as bad: self-government, limited government, religious freedom, universal education and a classless society.

We showed the world that men could quite deliberately create a new nation and soon the peoples of Spanish America were busy following our example, and eventually scores of other nations throughout the world—some 60 since 1945.

Americans also were the first people who took for granted and exploited fully the potentialities of change. Americans not only believed in orderly progress, they even believed that human nature could be changed. Given a beneficent environment, education, freedom, men could throw off the shackles of the past and lift themselves by their bootstraps. Just give them a chance. Free them from tyranny, free them from superstition, free them from poverty and ignorance, free them from the curse of war, and they would write a new and more glorious chapter in the history of man. Of all peoples, we should be the most ready to sympathize with those who are trying to close the desperate gap between what they are and what they might be.

We were taught to resent the Holy Alliance, but the Holy Alliance, for all its bold declarations, merely huffed and puffed; it never did blow any houses down. What would we think had the Holy Alliance sent a vast army to support the legitimate governments and put down the rebels in Latin-American states? We are taught, some of us, to resent British support for those who would break up the American union in 1861, but Britain did not, in fact, intervene in American affairs. What would we think had Britain intervened to support the Confederacy or recognized an exiled Jefferson Davis as the legitimate head of a Confederacy, as we persist in recognizing Chiang Kai-shek as the legitimate head not only of the Government of Taiwan but of China—17 years after his expulsion?

Americans are on the whole amiable, generous and friendly; they do not bear grudges or nurse animosities. We have made up with Germany and Japan very speedily.

But our previous quarrels with other nations were national. Now—for the first time, really—we are tempted not by national but by ideological animosities. And these have always been deeper, more obsessive and more stubbornly ineradicable, as the prolonged and savage religious wars of 17th-century Europe testify. Perhaps because we have had so little experience with ideological quarrels, we take them harder than we do other kinds. Monstrous as it was, there was no obsession with the Nazi danger comparable to our prolonged obsession with the Communist danger.

Hatred does a great deal of harm and never does any good. It blurs that clarity of vision so necessary for the objective calculations and decisions we must make in the conduct of foreign policy. And it leaves lasting scars.

The British have forgotten their treatment of the Irish in the 18th and 19th centuries, but the Irish have not forgotten. We have forgotten the Mexican War, but the Mexicans have not forgotten. It is a fair observation that the Negro has a longer memory of slavery than has the white. And it is a pretty safe prophecy that the Chinese will not find it as easy to forget our implacable hostility over a period of 17 years, or the Vietnamese our bombing, as we shall.

We of this generation are called upon to learn what no other great nation ever really learned: how to be a world power.

We have resources greater than those ever before commanded by any one nation. Will we use them to strengthen the international community, or to strengthen ourselves?

We have an historical experience which admonishes us to patience, prudence, tolerance and restraint. Will we apply the lessons of our own history to the history of new emerging nations and the lessons of our past to the future, or will we turn away from our history and tradition?

We have the intellectual and the professional skills to bring succor and hope to the hundreds of millions of peoples of three continents who are the victims of age-old exploitation, poverty, disease and war. Our resources are not illimitable. Will we use them for benevolent purposes or for the aggrandizement of our power?